D1537660

Interactive Computing Series

Microsoft® Windows® XP

Introductory Edition

Kenneth C. Laudon • Kenneth Rosenblatt

David Langley

Boston   Burr Ridge, IL   Dubuque, IA   Madison, WI   New York   San Francisco   St. Louis
Bangkok   Bogotá   Caracas   Kuala Lumpur   Lisbon   London   Madrid   Mexico City
Milan   Montreal   New Delhi   Santiago   Seoul   Singapore   Sydney   Taipei   Toronto

McGraw-Hill Higher Education

*A Division of The **McGraw-Hill** Companies*

MICROSOFT WINDOWS XP INTRODUCTORY EDITION
Published by McGraw-Hill/Irwin, an imprint of The McGraw-Hill
Companies, Inc., 1221 Avenue of the Americas, New York, NY 10020.

Copyright 2002, by The McGraw-Hill Companies, Inc. All rights reserved.
No part of this publication may be reproduced or distributed in any form or
by any means, or stored in a database or retrieval system, without the prior
written consent of The McGraw-Hill Companies, Inc., including, but not
limited to, in any network or other electronic storage or transmission, or
broadcast for distance learning.

This book is printed on acid-free paper.

2 3 4 5 6 7 8 9 0 QPD/QPD 0 9 8 7 6 5 4 3

ISBN   0-07-247176-x

Publisher: *George Werthman*
Developmental editor: *Diana Del Castillo*
Senior marketing manager: *Jeff Parr*
Senior project manager: *Pat Frederickson*
Senior production supervisor: *Michael R. McCormick*
Senior designer: *Pam Verros*
Supplement producer: *Mark Mattson*
Cover photograph: *Bill Brooks/© Masterfile*
Interior design: *Asylum Studios*
Cover designer: *JoAnne Schopler*
Compositor: *Azimuth Interactive, Inc.*
Typeface: *10/12 Times*
Printer: *Quebecor Printing Book Group/Dubuque*

Library of Congress Control Number: 2001098770

www.mhhe.com

InformationTechnology

Information Technology at McGraw-Hill/Irwin

At McGraw-Hill Higher Education, we publish instructional materials targeted at the higher education market. In an effort to expand the tools of higher learning, we publish texts, lab manuals, study guides, testing materials, software, and multimedia products.

At McGraw-Hill/Irwin (a division of McGraw-Hill Higher Education), we realize that technology has created and will continue to create new mediums for professors and students to use in managing resources and communicating information with one another. We strive to provide the most flexible and complete teaching and learning tools available as well as offer solutions to the changing world of teaching and learning.

MCGRAW-HILL/IRWIN IS DEDICATED TO PROVIDING THE TOOLS FOR TODAY'S INSTRUCTORS AND STUDENTS TO SUCCESSFULLY NAVIGATE THE WORLD OF INFORMATION TECHNOLOGY.

- **Seminar series**—Technology Connection seminar series offered across the country every year demonstrates the latest technology products and encourages collaboration among teaching professionals.

- **Osborne/McGraw-Hill**—This division of The McGraw-Hill Companies is known for its best-selling Internet titles: Harley Hahn's Internet & Web Yellow Pages, and the Internet Complete Reference. Osborne offers an additional resource for certification and has strategic publishing relationships with corporations such as Corel Corporation and America Online. For more information visit Osborne at www.osborne.com.

- **Digital solutions**—McGraw-Hill/Irwin is committed to publishing digital solutions. Taking your course online does not have to be a solitary venture, nor does it have to be a difficult one. We offer several solutions that will allow you to enjoy all the benefits of having course material online. For more information visit www.mhhe.com/solutions/index.mhtml.

- **Packaging options**—For more about our discount options, contact your local McGraw-Hill/Irwin Sales representative at 1-800-338-3987 or visit our Web site at www.mhhe.com/it.

Interactive Computing Series

GOALS/PHILOSOPHY

The *Interactive Computing Series* provides you with an illustrated interactive environment for learning software skills using Microsoft Office. The text uses both "hands-on" instruction, supplementary text, and independent exercises to enrich the learning experience.

APPROACH

The *Interactive Computing Series* is the visual interactive way to develop and apply software skills. This skills-based approach coupled with its highly visual, two-page spread design allows the student to focus on a single skill without having to turn the page. A Lesson Goal at the beginning of each lesson prepares the student to apply the skills with a real-world focus. The Quiz and Interactivity sections at the end of each lesson measure the student's understanding of the concepts and skills learned in the two-page spreads and reinforce the skills with additional exercises.

ABOUT THE BOOK

The **Interactive Computing Series** offers *two levels* of instruction. Each level builds upon the previous level.

Brief lab manual—covers the basics of the application, contains two to four chapters.

Introductory lab manual—includes the material in the Brief textbook plus two to four additional chapters. The Introductory lab manuals prepare students for the *Microsoft Office User Specialist Proficiency Exam (MOUS Certification)*.

Each lesson is divided into a number of Skills. Each **Skill** is first explained at the top of the page in the Concept. Each **Concept** is a concise description of why the Skill is useful and where it is commonly used. Each **Step (Do It!)** contains the instructions on how to complete the Skill. The appearance of the *MOUS Skill* icon on a Skill page indicates that the Skill contains instruction in at least one of the required MOUS objectives for the relevant exam. Though the icons appear in the Brief manuals as well as the Introductory manuals, only the Introductory manuals may be used in preparation for MOUS Certification.

Figure 1

Skill: Each lesson is divided into a number of specific skills

skill   Finding and Replacing Text

Concept: A concise description of why the skill is useful and when it is commonly used

concept

The Find command enables you to search a document for individual occurrences of any word, phrase, or other unit of text. The Replace command enables you to replace one or all occurrences of a word that you have found. Together, the Find and Replace commands form powerful editing tools for making many document-wide changes in just seconds.

Do It!: Step-by-step directions show you how to use the skill in a real-world scenario

do it !

Use Find and Replace to spell a word consistently throughout a document.

1. Open student file, wddoit12.doc, and save it as Report12.doc.

2. If necessary, place the insertion point at the beginning of the document. Word will search the document from the insertion point forward.

3. Click Edit, and then click Replace. The Find and Replace dialog box appears with the Replace tab in front and the insertion point in the Find What text box.

4. In the Find What box, type the two words per cent. Click in the Replace With box, and type the one word percent (see Figure 3-37).

Hot Tips: Icons introduce helpful hints or trouble-shooting tips

5. Click Replace All to search the document for all instances of per cent and to replace them with percent. A message box appears to display the results. In this case, one replacement was made (see Figure 3-38). In short documents the Find and Replace procedure takes so little time that you usually cannot cancel it before it ends. However, in longer documents you can cancel a search in progress by pressing [Esc].

6. Click OK to close the message box. Click Close to close the Find and Replace dialog box.

7. Save and close the document, Report12.doc, with your change.

More: Provides in-depth information about the skill and related features

more

Clicking the Replace All button in the Find and Replace dialog box replaces every instance of the text you have placed in the Find What box. To examine and replace a word or phrase manually instead of automatically, start by clicking the Find Next button. If you desire to replace that instance, click the Replace button. Continue checking the document like this, clicking the Find Next button and then, if desired, the Replace button. Keep clicking the pairs of buttons until you have run through the entire document. Unless you absolutely must do otherwise, use the method for shorter documents only.

The first button under the Replace With box usually displays the word More. Click this button when you want to display the the Search Options area of the dialog box. With the area displayed, the More button converts to a Less button. Clicking on the Less button will hide the Search Options area. The Search drop-down list under Search Options determines the direction of the search relative to the insertion point. You can search upward or downward through the document or keep the Word default setting of All to check the whole document, including headers, footers, and footnotes. The Format drop-down list enables you to search criteria for fonts, paragraphs, tabs, and similar items. The Special drop-down list enables you to search for paragraph marks, tab characters, column breaks and related special characters. The No Formatting button removes all formatting criteria from searches. For information on the Search Option activated by the check boxes, consult Table 3-3.

The Find tab of the Find and Replace dialog box matches the Replace tab except it lacks the replace function and only searches documents for items that you specify.

In the book, each skill is described in a two-page graphical spread (Figure 1). The left side of the two-page spread describes the skill, the concept, and the steps needed to perform the skill. The right side of the spread uses screen shots to show you how the screen should look at key stages.

Figure 1 (continued)

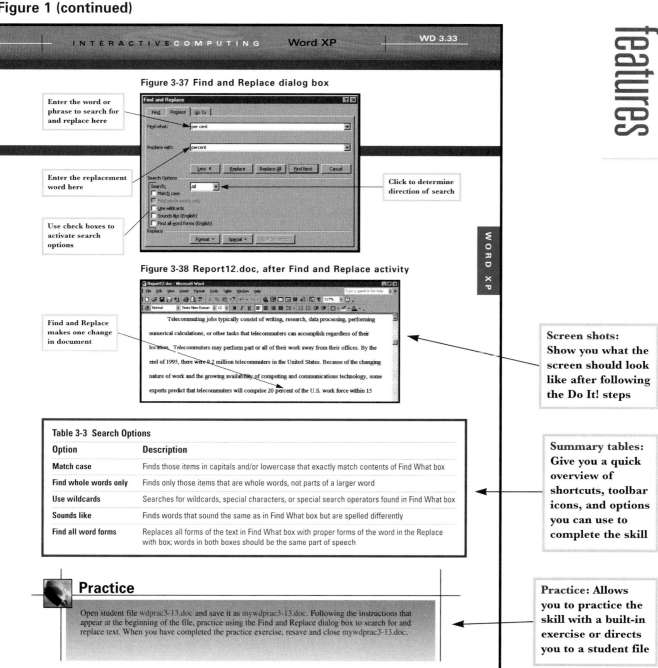

features

WORD XP

INTERACTIVE COMPUTING **Word XP** WD 3.33

Figure 3-37 Find and Replace dialog box

Enter the word or phrase to search for and replace here

Enter the replacement word here

Use check boxes to activate search options

Click to determine direction of search

Figure 3-38 Report12.doc, after Find and Replace activity

Find and Replace makes one change in document

> Telecommuting jobs typically consist of writing, research, data processing, performing numerical calculations, or other tasks that telecommuters can accomplish regardless of their location. Telecommuters may perform part or all of their work away from their offices. By the end of 1995, there were 9.2 million telecommuters in the United States. Because of the changing nature of work and the growing availability of computing and communications technology, some experts predict that telecommuters will comprise 20 percent of the U.S. work force within 15

Screen shots: Show you what the screen should look like after following the Do It! steps

Table 3-3 Search Options

Option	Description
Match case	Finds those items in capitals and/or lowercase that exactly match contents of Find What box
Find whole words only	Finds only those items that are whole words, not parts of a larger word
Use wildcards	Searches for wildcards, special characters, or special search operators found in Find What box
Sounds like	Finds words that sound the same as in Find What box but are spelled differently
Find all word forms	Replaces all forms of the text in Find What box with proper forms of the word in the Replace with box; words in both boxes should be the same part of speech

Summary tables: Give you a quick overview of shortcuts, toolbar icons, and options you can use to complete the skill

Practice

Open student file wdprac3-13.doc and save it as mywdprac3-13.doc. Following the instructions that appear at the beginning of the file, practice using the Find and Replace dialog box to search for and replace text. When you have completed the practice exercise, resave and close mywdprac3-13.doc.

Practice: Allows you to practice the skill with a built-in exercise or directs you to a student file

END-OF-LESSON FEATURES

In the book, the learning in each lesson is reinforced at the end by a Quiz and a skills review called Interactivity, which provides step-by-step exercises and real-world problems for the students to solve independently.

The following is a list of supplemental material available with the Interactive Computing Series:

Skills Assessment

SimNet eXPert (Simulated Network Assessment Product)—SimNet provides a way for you to test students' software skills in a simulated environment. SimNet is available for Microsoft Office 97, Microsoft Office 2000, and Microsoft Office XP. SimNet provides flexibility for you in your course by offering:

- Pre-testing options
- Post-testing options
- Course placement testing
- Diagnostic capabilities to reinforce skills
- Proficiency testing to measure skills
- Web or LAN delivery of tests
- Computer-based training materials (New for Office XP)
- MOUS preparation exams
- Learning verification reports
- Spanish Version

Instructor's Resource Kits

The Instructor's Resource Kit provides professors with all of the ancillary material needed to teach a course. McGraw-Hill/Irwin is dedicated to providing instructors with the most effective instruction resources available. Many of these resources are available at our Information Technology Supersite www.mhhe.com/it. Our Instructor's Kits are available on CD-ROM and contain the following:

Diploma by Brownstone—is the most flexible, powerful, and easy-to-use computerized testing system available in higher education. The diploma system allows professors to create an Exam as a printed version, as a LAN-based Online version, and as an Internet version. Diploma includes grade book features, which automate the entire testing process.

Instructor's Manual—Includes:
–Solutions to all lessons and end-of-unit material
–Teaching Tips
–Teaching Strategies
–Additional exercises

PowerPoint Slides—NEW to the *Interactive Computing Series*, all of the figures from the application textbooks are available in PowerPoint slides for presentation purposes.

Student Data Files—To use the *Interactive Computing Series*, students must have Student Data Files to complete practice and test sessions. The instructor and students using this text in classes are granted the right to post the student files on any network or stand-alone computer, or to distribute the files on individual diskettes. The student files may be downloaded from our IT Supersite at www.mhhe.com/it.

Series Web Site—Available at www.mhhe.com/cit/apps/laudon.

Digital Solutions

Pageout—is our Course Web site Development Center. Pageout offers a Syllabus page, Web site address, Online Learning Center Content, online exercises and quizzes, gradebook, discussion board, an area for students to build their own Web pages, and all the features of Pageout Lite. For more information please visit the Pageout Web site at www.mhla.net/pageout.

Digital Solutions (continued)

OLC/Series Web Sites—Online Learning Centers (OLCs)/Series Sites are accessible through our Supersite at www.mhhe.com/it. Our Online Learning Centers/Series Sites provide pedagogical features and supplements for our titles online. Students can point and click their way to key terms, learning objectives, chapter overviews, PowerPoint slides, exercises, and Web links.

The McGraw-Hill Learning Architecture (MHLA)—is a complete course delivery system. MHLA gives professors ownership in the way digital content is presented to the class through online quizzing, student collaboration, course administration, and content management. For a walk-through of MHLA visit the MHLA Web site at www.mhla.net.

Packaging Options—For more about our discount options, contact your local McGraw-Hill/Irwin Sales representative at 1-800-338-3987 or visit our Web site at www.mhhe.com/it.

Visit www.mhhe.com/it
THE ONLY SITE WITH ALL YOUR CIT AND MIS NEEDS.

teaching resources (continued)

acknowledgments

The *Interactive Computing Series* is a cooperative effort of many individuals, each contributing to an overall team effort. The Interactive Computing team is composed of instructional designers, writers, multimedia designers, graphic artists, and programmers. Our goal is to provide you and your instructor with the most powerful and enjoyable learning environment using both traditional text and new interactive multimedia techniques. Interactive Computing is tested rigorously in both CD-ROM and text formats prior to publication.

Our special thanks to George Werthman, our Publisher; Sarah Wood, our Developmental Editor; and Jeffrey Parr, Marketing Director for Computer Information Systems. They have provided exceptional market awareness and understanding, along with enthusiasm and support for the project, and have inspired us all to work closely together. In addition, Steven Schuetz provided valuable technical review of our interactive versions, and Charles Pelto contributed superb quality assurance.

The Azimuth team members who contributed to the textbooks and CD-ROM multimedia program are:

Ken Rosenblatt (Editorial Director, Writer)
Russell Polo (Technical Director)
Robin Pickering (Developmental Editor, Writer)
David Langley (Writer)
Chris Hahnenberger (Multimedia Designer)

Interactive Computing Series

Microsoft® Windows® XP

Introductory Edition

contents

Windows® XP
Introductory Edition

Windows® XP continued

Windows® XP continued

Windows® XP continued

Introduction to Windows XP

Windows XP is an operating system that controls the basic functions of your computer, such as loading and running programs, saving data, and displaying information on the screen. Operating system software is different from application software, such as a word processor or spreadsheet program, which you apply to letter writing or calculating data. Operating system software provides the user interface—the visual display on the screen that you use to operate the computer by choosing which programs to run and how to organize your work. Windows XP offers a graphical user interface or GUI (pronounced "gooey") that presents you with pictorial representations of computer functions and data.

It is through these pictures, or icons, that you interact with the computer. Data files are represented by icons that look like pieces of paper and can be organized into groups called folders, which look like manila folders. The My Computer icon, represented by a small desktop PC, allows you to organize these files and folders. Other icons allow you to run programs such as a word processor, a Web browser, or Windows' built-in file manager, Windows Explorer.

Windows XP is a powerful operating system that allows you to perform a variety of high-level tasks. Windows XP is actually the successor to the Windows NT 4.0 operating system, but it looks, acts, and responds in much the same manner as Windows 2000. For instance, the GUI is very similar, using many of the same icons as Windows 2000. It also includes integrated Web features. Thus, Windows XP gives you the ease of use of Windows 2000, with the power, stability, and security previously provided by Windows NT. This makes Windows XP an ideal tool for operating a business whether it runs on a laptop computer, a desktop system, or a large business server.

Windows XP is easy to use and can be customized with the preferences and options that you desire. Built-in programs called Accessories can be used to help you with day-to-day tasks. Help and Support feature offers fast tutorial and troubleshooting advice. This book will teach you about the basic elements of Windows XP and how to use them. You will learn file management, advanced Windows functions, Internet skills, and some of the other special features of Windows XP.

skills

- 𝄞 **Creating and Moving the Desktop Icons**
- 𝄞 **Opening, Moving, and Resizing a Window**
- 𝄞 **Using the Start Menu**
- 𝄞 **Using the Taskbar**
- 𝄞 **Using Menus**
- 𝄞 **Using Dialog Boxes**
- 𝄞 **Getting Help**
- 𝄞 **Shutting Down Windows XP**

Lesson Goal:

In this lesson, you will learn to create and move the desktop icons. You will also learn to open, move, and resize a window, and use the Start menu, taskbar, menus, and dialog boxes. Additionally, you will learn to use the Help and Support feature of Windows XP. Finally, you will learn to shut down Windows XP.

skill

Creating and Moving the Desktop Icons

concept

The screen you see when Windows XP completes the StartUp procedure is called the desktop. Do not be surprised if your desktop does not look exactly like the one pictured in Figure 1-1 as computer setups vary from machine to machine. (Throughout this book the appearance of your desktop and windows will depend on the software installed and the configuration of various settings of your computer.) Like the desk at which you are sitting, the Windows desktop is the workspace on which all actions are performed. You can create small pictures called icons, which are pictorial representations of a task, program, folder, or file, on the desktop. Each icon represents an application or utility that you can start. By default, Windows XP displays only the Recycle Bin icon. You use the mouse—a hand-controlled input device that, when connected to the computer and moved along a clean, flat surface, will move the graphical pointer around the screen. Using the mouse you can open an application or a file by double-clicking the icon of application or file. The buttons on the mouse are used to give commands, and there are four basic ways you can use the mouse: pointing, clicking, double-clicking, and dragging.

do it!

Create the My Documents icon on the desktop and use the pointer around the desktop to move the My Documents icon.

1. Right-click on the desktop to open the shortcut menu.

2. Click the Properties command. This will display the Display Properties dialog box.

3. Click the Desktop tab. This will display the options under the Desktop tab (see Figure 1-2).

4. Click [Customize Desktop...]. This will display the Desktop Items dialog box.

5. Select the My Documents check box and click [OK].

6. Click [OK]. This will display the My Documents icon on the desktop. Similarly, create the My Network Places and Internet Explorer icons on the desktop.

7. Using the mouse, move the pointer over various areas of the desktop to get a feel of how the pointer moves in relation to the motion of the mouse. Positioning the pointer over an item is called pointing. ⬤ If your mouse movements are running off the mouse pad, position the mouse pointer in the middle of the screen, and then pick up the mouse and place it in the middle of the mouse pad.

8. Locate the My Documents icon on the desktop. Place the pointer on the icon and click the left mouse button once (throughout this book, the term click will always refer to pressing and releasing the left mouse button once quickly; other types of clicks will be specified as necessary). This will select the icon, indicating that it has been selected. Click a blank area of the screen to undo this selection. Note that primary mouse functions are done using the left button.

(continued on WN 1.4)

Figure 1-1 The Windows desktop

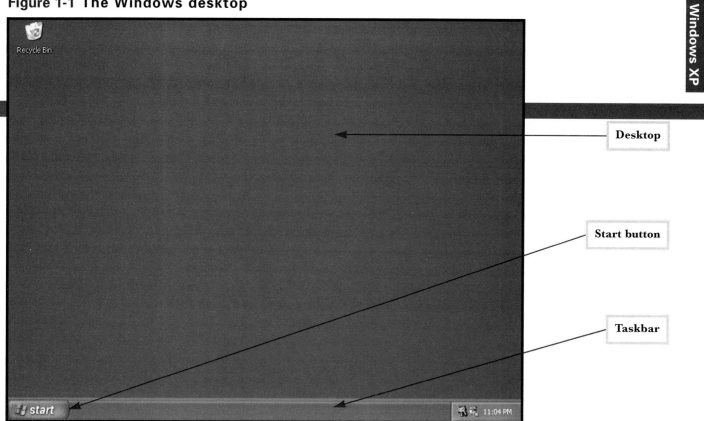

Desktop

Start button

Taskbar

Figure 1-2 Display Properties dialog box

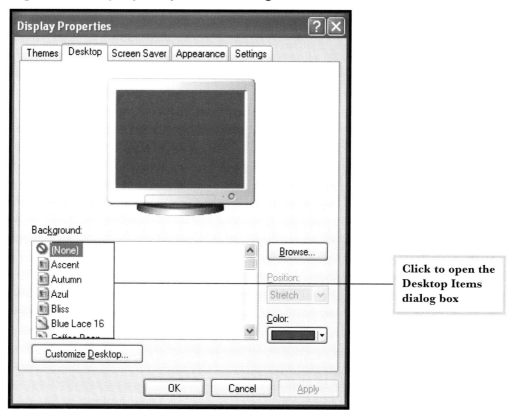

Click to open the
Desktop Items
dialog box

skill Creating and Moving the Desktop Icons (continued)

do it!

9. Double-clicking is done to open a program, file, or window. Open the My Documents window by placing the pointer on the My Documents icon and clicking the left mouse button twice quickly. The My Documents window, shown in Figure 1-3, will appear on the desktop.

10. To close the window you have just opened, position the pointer over the Close button ⊠ in the upper-right corner and click the left mouse button.

11. Icons are not fixed on the desktop and can be moved by dragging. Move the pointer to the My Computer icon, then click and hold down the button. You have grabbed the icon.

12. With the mouse button held down, move the icon by dragging it to the center of your desktop. A faint image of the icon will appear to indicate the current position of the icon on the desktop. Release the mouse button to drop the icon into position. Then return the icon to its original position.

more

Windows XP allows you to change the way you work with icons so that the interface behaves more like a Web page. To make this change, click on the word Tools on the Menu bar in the My Documents window. This will cause a list of commands, called a menu, to appear. Click the Folder Options command on the Tools menu to open the Folder Options dialog box. Whenever you see an ellipsis (...) following a command, it indicates that the command will open a dialog box revealing options for the execution of the command. The dialog box will open to a tab named General. In the bottom section of this dialog box, the default option is Double-click to open an item (single-click to select), which is the traditional way of interacting with Windows icons. If you select the first option in the section, Single-click to open an item (point to select), the operating system will switch to a Web-like environment.

Figure 1-3 My Documents window

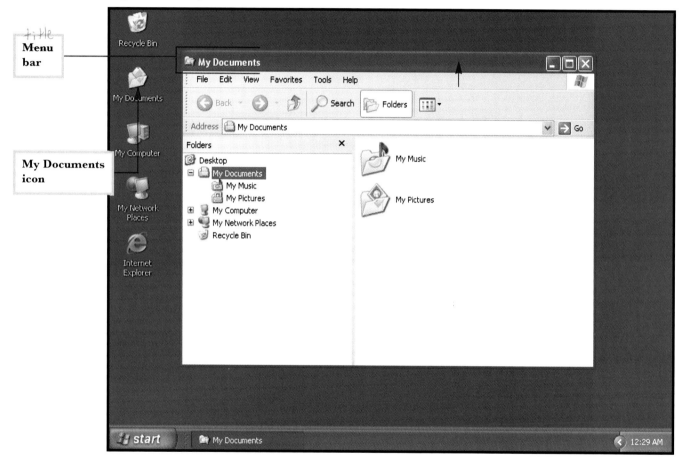

Menu bar

My Documents icon

Practice

Create the My Computer desktop icon and open the My Computer window by double-clicking its icon. Use the Close button to close the window.

skill | Opening, Moving, and Resizing a Window

concept

As you saw in the previous Skill, icons are pictorial representations of different items on your computer, most common of which are folders, files, and applications. When you double-click an icon to open it, its contents are displayed in a window or on-screen frame. It is in this window that you interact with a program or utility. Windows are flexible and can be moved, resized, reshaped, and even hidden.

do it!

Open the My Computer window and resize, move, minimize, and close it.

1. Double-click the My Computer icon. This will display the My Computer window, as shown in Figure 1-4.

2. You cannot resize or move a window that is maximized or fills the entire desktop. Look at the three sizing buttons at the right end of the window's title bar, the band at the top of the window that contains the name of the application. The middle button's appearance will change depending on the window's state. If the Restore button 🗗 is visible, click it so the window will no longer be maximized. Once the window is restored to its previous size, the button will change to the Maximize button 🔲. A summary of the sizing buttons can be found in Table 1-1.

3. Position the mouse pointer on the right edge of the window. This will change the pointer to a double-headed arrow ◄——► that is used to resize an object. In Windows XP, the appearance of the mouse pointer changes to reflect its function during various tasks.

4. Click and hold the left mouse button, drag the edge of the window towards the center of the screen, and then let go of the mouse button to drop the side of the window into place. As you drag the mouse, the border of the window will move with the double-headed arrow, toolbar buttons will disappear behind the border that is being dragged (do not worry; their respective commands can still be accessed through menus), and scroll bars (see More below) may appear. This action may be repeated on any of the window's four sides or at any corner. Resizing from the corner will alter both the height and the width of the window.

5. Windows can be dragged and dropped just as icons can. Move the pointer over the title bar of the My Computer window, and then click and hold the left mouse button to grab the window.

6. With the mouse button depressed, drag the window to another area of the desktop.

(continued on WN 1.8)

Figure 1-4 My Documents window

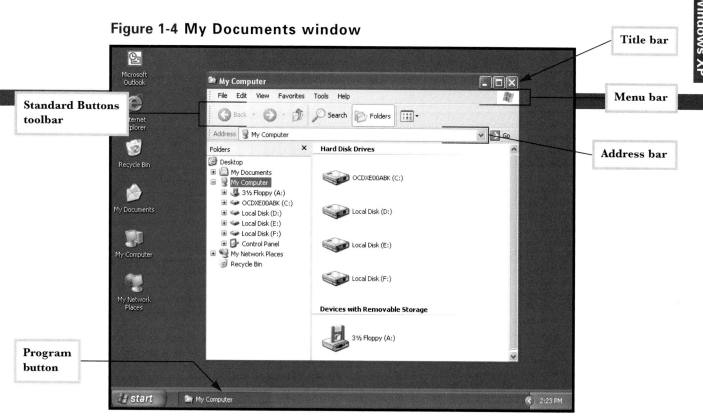

Title bar

Menu bar

Standard Buttons toolbar

Address bar

Program button

Table 1-1 Sizing buttons

Sizing Buttons		Function
Close	✕	Closes a window or program
Maximize	▢	Enlarges the window so that it fills the entire screen, with the taskbar remaining visible
Minimize	▬	Shrinks the window so that it appears only as a program button on the taskbar
Restore	▣	Returns the window to its previous size

skill

Opening, Moving, and Resizing a Window (continued)

do it!

7. Click the Minimize button ▬ . The My Computer window will disappear from the desktop and be reduced to a program button on the taskbar, as shown in Figure 1-5.
   Clicking the Show Desktop button 🄴 on the taskbar minimizes all open windows. Clicking the button again opens all of the previously visible windows. You can display the Show Desktop button 🄴 on the taskbar by selecting the Show Quick Launch check box in the Taskbar and Start Menu Properties dialog box.

8. Click the My Computer program button on the taskbar to restore the window to its previous size.

9. Click File on the Menu bar. The File menu will appear as shown in Figure 1-6.

10. Position the pointer over the last command, Close, to select it, and then click the mouse button. The Close command will be executed, just as it would if you clicked the Close button ✖ , and the window will disappear from the desktop.

more

When a window is too small to display all of its information, scroll bars (Figure 1-7) will appear on the right edge of the window. Scroll bars are context-sensitive objects and appear only when the situation is appropriate. The scroll bars are used to slide information inside the window so that you can see additional contents of the window. If you need to scroll slowly or only a short distance, click a scroll bar arrow located at the end of the scroll bar. The scroll bar box indicates at which section of the window you are looking. Clicking above or below the scroll bar box (in the gray area) moves the display in large increments. Dragging the scroll bar box allows you to control the slide of the window's information precisely.

In the above Skill, you clicked the My Computer program button to unhide the window and make it active. An active window is identified by its dark colored title bar and will be the frontmost window on your desktop if more than one program is running. You can click the program button of a visible window to minimize it. Right-clicking a program button will display a shortcut menu with commands for resizing a window. These commands can also be found by clicking the Control icon, the icon at the left edge of the title bar representing the application, or by right-clicking the title bar. Right-clicking will usually cause a context-sensitive menu to appear; this menu will contain commands that relate to the task you are performing. Double-clicking the title bar will restore or maximize a window.

Figure 1-5 Minimized My Computer window

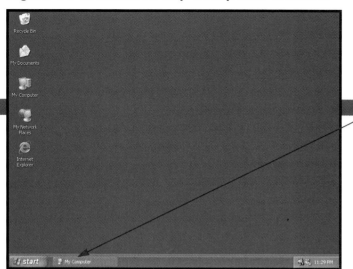

Minimized window

Figure 1-6 Working with the File menu

Control icon

Click File to open
the File menu

Close command selected
on the File menu

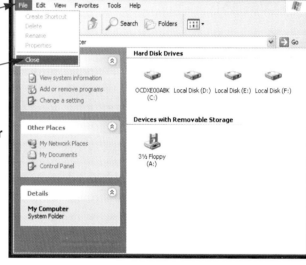

Figure 1-7 My Computer window with scroll bar

Scroll bar box

Scroll bar arrow

Practice

Open and maximize the My Documents window. Then restore the window and drag its right border
outward. Close the window when you are done.

skill | Using the Start Menu

concept

The Start button located on the left side of the taskbar provides a quick and easy way to open and organize the applications on your computer. Clicking the Start button opens a special menu called the Start menu (shown expanded in Figure 1-8) that contains left-to-right lists of program groups. Items with an arrow ▶ next to them contain submenus. Pointing to an item selects it, and a simple click will then open the program you wish to use.

The Start menu in Windows XP displays the name of the user logged on. The programs listed in the Start menu are divided into two categories: Pinned items list, which is present above the separator line, and Most frequently used Programs list, which is present below the separator line. Program items in the pinned item list are always available for use. However, the program items listed in the most frequently used programs list display the programs that have been used recently.

do it!

Use the Start button to access the Start menu and run Windows Explorer, a file management utility that will be discussed in detail in Lesson 2. (If you do not see an item that is named in this Skill, click the double arrow at the bottom of the menu).

1. Click ⊞ start on the taskbar, usually located at the bottom of your desktop. The Start menu will open. Do not be surprised if your Start menu does not match Figure 1-8 exactly. The appearance of your Start menu depends on the software installed and the shortcuts created on your computer.

2. Point to All Programs (notice the arrow) to open the All Programs menu. The All Programs menu contains a list of shortcuts to some of the applications found on your hard drive as well as folders that hold groups of related shortcuts to other frequently used programs and utilities.

3. In the All Programs menu, point to Accessories. The Accessories menu will appear alongside the All Programs menu.

4. In the Accessories menu, click the Windows Explorer command to launch it. Figure 1-9 displays Windows Explorer with the My Documents folder selected. Notice that a program button displaying the name of the folder selected in Windows Explorer has appeared on the taskbar. ◣ You can use the Start button's shortcut menu commands for quickly opening Windows Explorer and the Search feature.

5. Click the Close button ✕ on the title bar to exit Windows Explorer.

more

Items on the Start menu and its submenus are really shortcuts to the actual folders and files that they represent. The My Recent Documents menu contains a list of the files that have been opened most recently. This helps you to access your most recently and most often used data quickly. One of the keys to using a computer is being able to locate the data you need. The Search menu offers you multiple ways in which to find information. You can search for files or folders on your computer, content on the World Wide Web, and the names of the people in locally stored address books and Internet directories.

Figure 1-8 Start menu

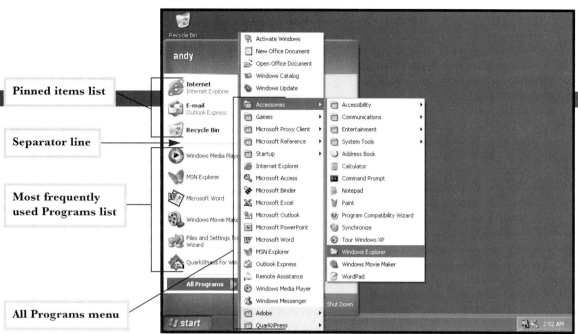

Pinned items list

Separator line

Most frequently used Programs list

All Programs menu

Figure 1-9 Windows Explorer

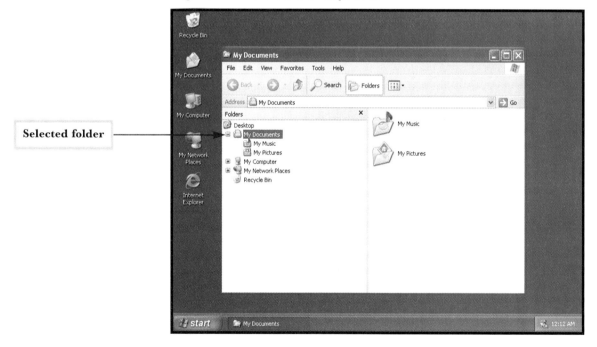

Selected folder

Practice

Use the Start button to open the Control Panel window. Close the Control Panel window from the Title bar.

skill   Using the Taskbar

concept

The taskbar is your guide to the applications running on your system. Each open application creates its own program button on the taskbar, so switching between programs is as simple as the click of a button. While the taskbar is usually found at the bottom of the desktop, it is fixed in neither size nor location.

There might be situations when you are working on a number of applications simultaneously. In such situations, the taskbar gets cluttered with the program buttons of all the applications. Windows XP provides the features of taskbar button grouping. Windows XP displays the taskbar buttons of the documents opened by a program in the same area of the taskbar. If there are a number of documents opened by a program, all the documents are grouped into one taskbar button. The grouped taskbar button is labeled with the name of the program. To access any one of the documents that has been grouped in the taskbar button, click the grouped taskbar button. This will display the names of all the opened documents. Click the name of the document to open it.

do it!

Use the taskbar to open two applications and switch between them. Then, move and resize the taskbar.

1. Click [start] to open the Start menu, point to All Programs, point to Accessories, and then click Windows Explorer. This will display the Windows Explorer window.

2. Again, click [start], point to All Programs, point to Accessories, and then click Calculator. The calculator will open and two windows will be on your desktop with their respective program buttons on the taskbar, as shown in Figure 1-10.

3. Click the Windows Explorer program button, which is labeled My Documents. The Windows Explorer window will become active, moving to the foreground of the desktop. Notice that its title bar is now dark blue, and its program button on the taskbar is depressed.

4. Click the Calculator program button on the taskbar to make the Calculator window active. You can move between open applications by holding [Alt] and then pressing [Tab]. Press [Tab] again to cycle through the list of all running applications. Release the [Alt] key when the correct icon is selected. Right-click the taskbar for more options.

5. Prior to adjusting the height of the taskbar, be sure that it is unlocked. To do this, right-click anywhere on the taskbar (where a program button is not located) and select the Unlock the Taskbar command. Now you can position the mouse pointer on the top edge of the taskbar. The pointer will change to a vertical double-headed arrow $\updownarrow$ when it is in the correct location.

6. Press and hold the mouse button and drag the top of the taskbar up, until it is three times its original height. The taskbar can be enlarged to up to half of your desktop.

7. Click a blank area on the taskbar, and then hold the mouse button down while dragging the taskbar to the right edge of your desktop (Figure 1-11). The taskbar can be placed on the top, bottom, left, or right of the desktop.

8. Drag the taskbar back to its original place on the desktop and then resize it so that it is one program button high.

9. Click each application's Close button ☒ to remove the windows from the desktop.

more

Additional taskbar settings can be found in the Taskbar and Start Menu Properties dialog box, accessed by right-clicking the Start button and then clicking the Properties command. Click the Taskbar tab to view its options. You can lock the taskbar by selecting the Lock the taskbar check box. If the taskbar is locked, you cannot move or resize the taskbar. Selecting the Keep the taskbar on the top of other windows check box prevents any window from obscuring the taskbar. With Auto-hide the taskbar check box selected, the taskbar will not be visible when it is not in use. You will need to move the pointer to the bottom of the desktop to make it reappear. You can turn the taskbar clock on or off with the Show the clock command. You can customize the taskbar to display the program icons by selecting the Show Quick Launch check box.

Figure 1-10 Two open applications

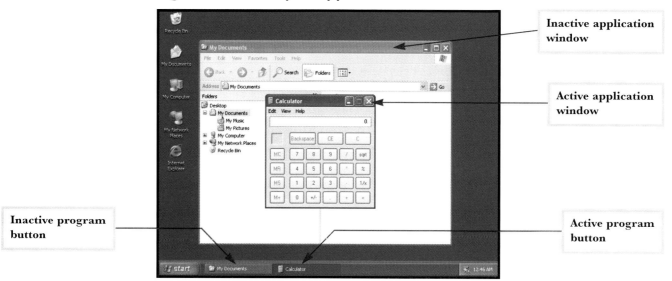

Inactive application window

Active application window

Inactive program button

Active program button

Figure 1-11 Resized and moved taskbar

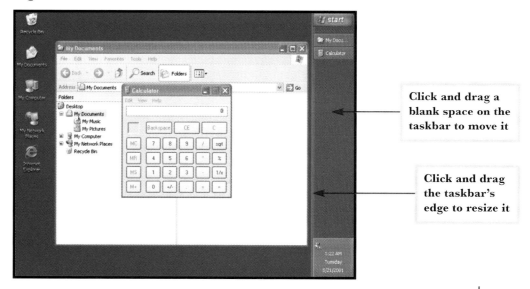

Click and drag a blank space on the taskbar to move it

Click and drag the taskbar's edge to resize it

Practice

Turn on the Auto-hide the taskbar option. Then open Windows Explorer, My Computer, and Calculator. Practice moving among the open windows. If you do not like the Auto hide option, turn it off again.

skill | Using Menus

concept

A menu is a list of related operations, also known as commands, that you use to perform specific tasks. The menus that are available to you in any particular window are listed on the Menu bar, which is situated just below the window's title bar. Each Windows program has its own selection of menus, though many are similar. To access a menu, simply click on its menu item on the Menu bar. Some menu commands have shortcut buttons that allow you to execute them by clicking on a toolbar button. You will also find that many commands have keyboard shortcuts. If you prefer the keyboard to the mouse, Windows also provides a way to open all menus and choose any command without clicking.

do it!

Examine and use a typical menu in the My Computer window.

1. Double-click the My Computer icon on the desktop to open its window.

2. Click View on the Menu bar to open the View menu, shown in Figure 1-12.

3. You will notice that in addition to commands, several symbols appear on the menu. A right-pointing triangle ▶ after a command indicates that the command has a submenu. Point to the Toolbars command to reveal the Toolbars submenu.

4. Move the mouse pointer down to the Status Bar command. The Toolbars submenu closes. The check mark ✔ to the left of the Status Bar command indicates that the feature is currently turned on. A bullet ● next to a command tells you which command in a set is currently active. Only one command in a set such as the Icons view command may be active at a time.

5. Open the Toolbars submenu again. Then click the Standard Buttons command, which is turned on, to turn it off. The menu closes and the Standard Buttons toolbar disappears, as shown in Figure 1-13.

6. You also can use the keyboard to open a menu and execute a command. One letter in each menu title is underlined. Pressing this letter while pressing the [Alt] key will open the corresponding menu. With the My Computer window active, press [Alt], then press [V] to open the View menu.

7. Each command on a menu also has an underlined letter. Pressing this letter on the keyboard initiates the command. Press [T] to open the Toolbars submenu. Then press [S] to execute the Standard Buttons command from the submenu, turning the Standard Buttons toolbar back on. Once a menu has been opened, you can use the arrow keys on the keyboard to move from command to command (up and down arrows) or from menu to menu (left and right arrows). Press [Enter] to execute a selected command.

more

Some commands have keyboard shortcuts that you can use to avoid opening menus altogether. You can learn many of these shortcuts simply by seeing them listed on a menu. For example, if you open the Edit menu in the My Computer window, you will see that the Select All command is followed by [Ctrl]+[A]. This means that you can use the Select All command by holding down the [Ctrl] key and pressing [A].

Windows XP

Figure 1-12 View menu

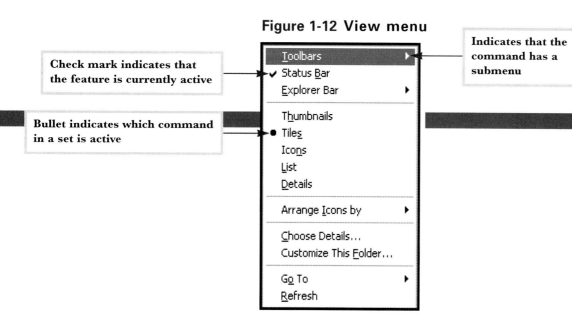

Check mark indicates that the feature is currently active

Bullet indicates which command in a set is active

Indicates that the command has a submenu

Figure 1-13 My Computer window without Standard Buttons toolbar

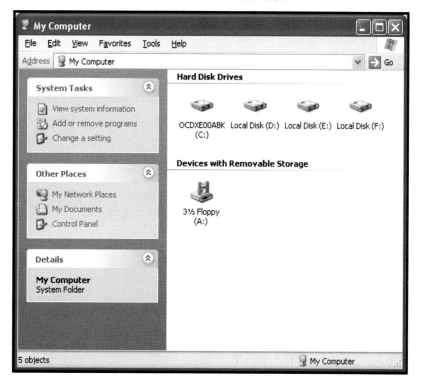

Practice

Open the My Documents window by double-clicking its icon. Then use the Close command on the File menu to close the window.

skill | Using Dialog Boxes

concept

Some commands require additional information before Windows will perform the operations that accompany them. In these cases, a dialog box will appear. Dialog boxes enable you to customize a command's options according to your needs or preferences. Commands that open a dialog box are followed on a menu by three dots (...), called an ellipsis.

do it!

Open the WordPad application and then use the Print command to access and examine the Print dialog box.

1. Click 🔲 start , point to All Programs, point to Accessories, and then click WordPad. This will open the WordPad window. ◥ WordPad is the built-in word processor of Windows XP.

2. To add text to a WordPad document, you can simply begin typing. Type I'm learning to use dialog boxes in Windows XP. Your document should look like Figure 1-14.

3. Open the File menu and click the Print command. The Print dialog box will be displayed, as shown in Figure 1-15. The Print dialog box contains a number of common dialog box features, each connected to a specific printing option.

4. Refer to Figure 1-15 to gain an understanding of how each of these features work.

5. Click [Cancel]. The dialog box closes without executing the Print command. ◥ When a dialog box has more than one option, you can use the [Tab] key to cycle through the options.

6. Close the WordPad window. Windows will ask you if you want to save changes made to the document. Click [No].

more

Dialog boxes contain their own help tool. In the upper-right corner of a dialog box, you will find a button marked with a question mark. If you click on this button, a question mark will be attached to your mouse pointer. When you click on any dialog box feature with this pointer, a ScreenTip (Figure 1-16) will appear that explains the feature. Click the mouse button again to erase the ScreenTip and restore the pointer to its normal state.

Figure 1-14 WordPad document

Click Save button to save a WordPad document

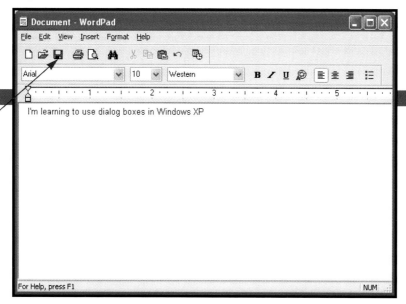

Figure 1-15 Dialog box features

Click to get help on dialog box items

Use text box to enter a value

Select check box to activate associated option

Option buttons allow you to select one option in a set

Click up or down arrow to change value in the spin box

Click to execute a command

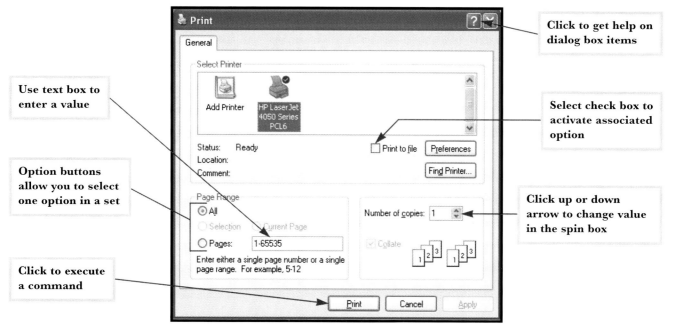

Figure 1-16 Example of a dialog box ScreenTip

If you have selected more than one copy, specifies whether you want the copies to be collated.

Practice

Find three other WordPad commands that use dialog boxes. View the features of each dialog box.

skill | Getting Help

concept

You might find that you need a little assistance along the way as you explore Windows XP. The Help and Support command in the Start menu provides you with an extensive list of topics that provide aid, troubleshooting advice, and tips and tricks. You can use Windows XP help while you work and even print topics when it is inconvenient to use help on the fly.

do it!

Use the Windows XP Help facility to learn about working with programs and word processing.

1. Click **start**, then click Help and Support on the Start menu. This will display the Help and Support Center window, as shown in Figure 1-17.

2. Click inside the Search text box and type WordPad.

3. Click the Start searching button → to start the search. The search results are displayed in the Search Results section of the window (see Figure 1-18). When you move the mouse pointer over the topic, the pointer will change to a hand 🖑, and the topic will be underlined, much like a Web page hyperlink.

4. Click Using WordPad. The topic will be displayed in the right section of the window.

5. Click the Close button ✖ to exit Help.

more

The Help and Support Center window is divided into different sections that provide you information on various topics. For instance, the Pick a Help Topic section of the Help and Support Center window enables you to view information of a specific help topic, such as new features in Windows XP, Windows basics, networking and Web, and Security and Administration. The Ask for assistance section provides you the options of getting help from a computer expert or from a product support expert.

Figure 1-17 Windows Help facility

Search text box

Click to start the search

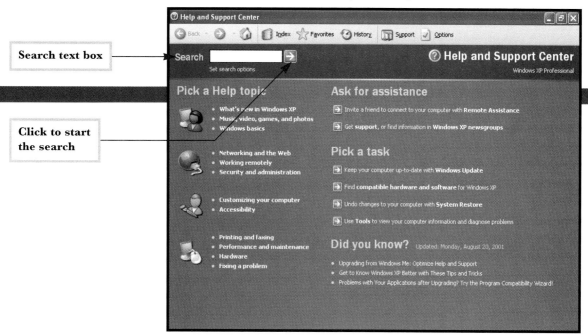

Figure 1-18 Help topics on WordPad

Search results

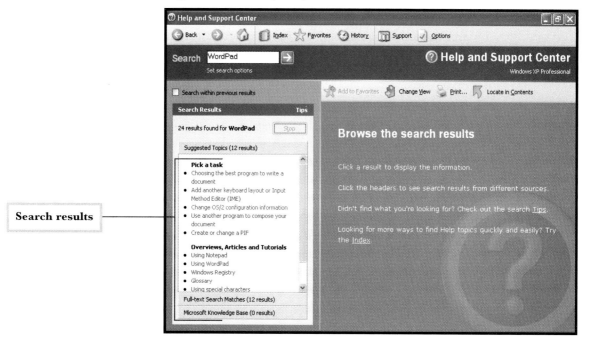

Practice

Get help on printing a document using Windows XP Help and Support Center.

skill | Shutting Down Windows XP

concept

It is important to shut down Windows XP properly. Failure to do so can result in loss of unsaved data. When you go through the shutdown procedure, Windows XP checks all open files to see if any unsaved files exist. If any are found, you will be given the opportunity to save them. It also uses the shutdown procedure to copy to your hard disk the data it has logged while your system was running.

do it!

Shut down your computer to end your Windows XP session.

1. Click [start] to open the Start menu (Figure 1-19).

2. Click [Shut Down]. The Shut Down Windows dialog box (Figure 1-20) will appear on your desktop.

3. A list in the center of the dialog box allows you to choose whether you want to log off the current user, shut down, restart, stand by or hibernate the computer (see Table 1-2). If the list box is set to Shut down, leave it as is. If not, click the list arrow at the right end of the box, and then click Shut Down on the list that appears. You also can access the Log off User and Shut down commands of the Shut Down Windows dialog box by pressing [Ctrl]+[Alt]+[Delete] keys.

4. Click [OK]. Windows will execute its shutdown procedure and your computer will be shut down.

more

Table 1-2 Shutdown options

Shutdown Options	Result
Log off User	Ends the current session, but leaves the computer running so that another user may log on
Shut down	Prepares the computer to be turned off
Restart	Ends the current session, shuts down Windows XP, and then starts Windows again
Stand By	Puts the computer in the sleep mode, where it is on and available for use, but drawing less power
Hibernate	Saves every information to the hard disk and when the computer restarts, restores the desktop settings

Figure 1-19 Shut Down Windows dialog box

Start menu

Figure 1-20 Shut Down Windows dialog box

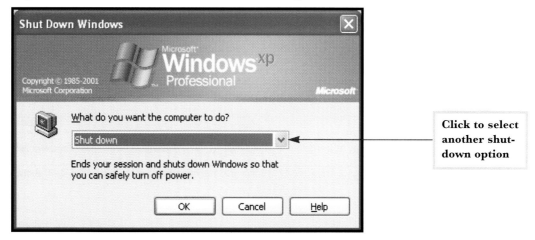

Click to select another shut-down option

Practice

Make sure all files and applications on your computer are closed, and then restart your computer.

shortcuts

Function	Button/Mouse	Menu	Keyboard
Close window	☒	Click Control icon, then click Close or click File, then click Close	[Alt]+[F4]
Maximize window	☐	Click Control icon, then click Maximize	
Minimize window	▬	Click Control icon, then click Minimize	
Restore window	❐ Or click program button on taskbar	Click Control icon, then click Restore	
Change active window	Click the window, if visible, or click program button on taskbar		[Alt]+[Tab]
Get Help on a specific item in a dialog box	?		[F1]

A. Identify Key Features

Name the items indicated by callouts in Figure 1-21.

Figure 1-21 Components of the Windows XP interface

1. _____
2. _____
3. _____
4. _____
5. _____
6. _____
7. _____
8. _____
9. _____

B. Select the Best Answer

10. Traditional way of opening a file, program, or window

11. Returns a maximized window to its previous size

12. Appears when a window is too small to display its information

13. Where you provide additional information before a command is carried out

14. Where program buttons appear

15. Used to manipulate the pointer on the screen

16. Minimizes all open windows

17. Contains a list of related commands

a. Scroll bar

b. Menu

c. Show Desktop button

d. Double-clicking

e. Restore button

f. Taskbar

g. Dialog box

h. Mouse

quiz (continued)

C. Complete the Statement

18. All of the following are basic ways you can use a mouse except:

a. Clicking

b. Dragging

c. Keying

d. Pointing

19. You can move a window:

a. When it is maximized

b. By dragging its title bar

c. When it is minimized

d. By using the double-arrow pointer

20. To open a context-sensitive shortcut menu:

a. Click the mouse

b. Click the Start button

c. Double-click an icon

d. Right-click the mouse

21. To scroll through a window in large increments:

a. Click above or below the scroll bar box

b. Click a scroll bar arrow

c. Click the scroll bar box

d. Right-click the Control icon

22. You can view the information on the new features in Windows XP in the Help and Support Center window using the:

a. Ask for assistance section

b. Pick a Help topic section

c. Search section

d. Pick a task section

23. To reposition the taskbar:

a. Open the Taskbar Properties dialog box

b. Select it and press the arrow keys

c. Drag it to a new location

d. Right-click it and choose the Move command

24. A standard menu contains a list of:

a. Related commands

b. Shutdown options

c. Help topics

d. Icons

25. Windows XP's pictorial representation of a computer's functions and data is called:

a. An IBI or "ibbey" (Icon Based Interface)

b. A LUI or "louie" (Local User Interface)

c. A HUI or "huey" (HTML Unified Interface)

d. A GUI or "gooey" (Graphical User Interface)

26. An ellipsis after a command indicates that:

a. Windows is still working

b. The command is not available

c. The command has a keyboard shortcut

d. The command uses a dialog box

27. To open a menu, click on its title on the:

a. Menu bar

b. View menu

c. Standard Buttons toolbar

d. Keyboard

interactivity

Build Your Skills

1. Create the Internet Explorer icon on the desktop:

   a. Right-click on the desktop.

   b. Click Properties.

   c. Click the Desktop tab.

   d. Click the Customize Desktop button.

   e. Select the Internet Explorer check box.

   f. Click the OK button.

   g. Click the OK button.

2. Work with an open window:

   a. Open the My Computer window.

   b. Move the window so that its title bar touches the top of the screen.

   c. Maximize the window.

   d. Restore the window.

   e. Use the mouse to resize the window until it is shaped like a square.

3. Run multiple programs:

   a. Open Windows Explorer and Calculator from the Start menu.

   b. In turn, make each of the three open windows the active window.

   c. Minimize all open windows.

4. Use the taskbar:

   a. Move the taskbar to the top of the desktop.

   b. Make the taskbar twice its original size.

   c. Return the taskbar to its original location and size.

   d. Close all open windows and applications.

interactivity (continued)

Build Your Skills (continued)

4. Use the Windows XP help facility and then shut down Windows:

a. Open the Help and Support Center window.

b. Use the Pick a Help topic section to read about What's new in Windows XP.

c. Close the Help and Support Center window.

e. Shut down Windows XP properly and turn off your computer.

Problem Solving Exercises

1. Using the skills you learned in Lesson 1 and your knowledge of the Windows XP operating system arrange your desktop so that it resembles the one shown in Figure 1-22. Remember that computers can be configured in a number of different ways, and settings can be changed over time. Therefore, your setup, and the icons made available by it, may prevent you from replicating the figure exactly. Do not delete icons without consulting your instructor first.

Figure 1-22 Example of a Windows XP desktop

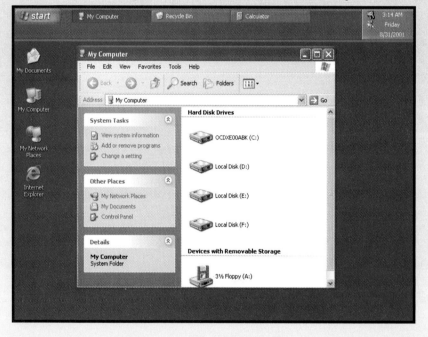

2. You have noticed an item on your Accessories menu named Notepad, but you are not sure what its function is. Use Windows XP's Help and Support Center feature to find out as much as you can about Notepad. Then use the help facility to find out how to store the Notepad help topics.

3. You are working on a project that requires you to use two applications at the same time, Windows Explorer and Notepad. Open each application from the Start menu. Then resize and arrange the two open windows so that you can view them side by side on the desktop.

4. You are new to the Windows XP operating system, but you have used another operating system with a graphical user interface. You have decided to set up your desktop so that it resembles this system. Move all of your desktop icons to the right side of the desktop. Then move the taskbar so that it is anchored to the left side of the screen instead of to the bottom of it.

Managing Files with Windows Explorer

A file is a text document, picture, or any other collection of information that is stored under its own unique name. A folder, much like a paper folder, is a collection of files that also can house other folders. Your computer stores electronic files and folders as you might store paper ones in a filing cabinet. To make searching for files and folders easier, you should group them in an organized and logical manner. The manner in which your files and folders are arranged is called a file hierarchy.

A file hierarchy, as shown in Figure 2-1, is similar to a family tree. The parent, child, and grandchild branches are represented by disk drives and folders. A file hierarchy depicts all the drives, applications, folders, and files on your computer. Placing similar files into well-named folders is the best way to create a meaningful file hierarchy. By viewing the higher levels of your file hierarchy, you will be able to get a sense of where files are stored without having to open each particular folder.

My Computer and Windows Explorer are both file management tools. File management can be complex and even tricky at first. The key to understanding file management is being able to visualize and organize the placement of your files. Having to search through the entire file hierarchy every time you wish to locate an item can become time-consuming and frustrating. Learning how to manage your files effectively, by understanding My Computer and Windows Explorer, will help you to get the most out of your computer. My Computer and Windows Explorer are similar in function and in use. After a brief examination of My Computer, we will concentrate on Windows Explorer, the more versatile file organizer.

skills

※ **Viewing Folders with My Computer**

※ **Using Windows Explorer**

※ **Creating New Folders and Files**

※ **Moving and Copying Files and Folders**

※ **Creating Shortcuts**

※ **Using the Recycle Bin**

※ **Searching for Files or Folders**

Lesson Goal:

In this lesson, you will learn to navigate through files and folders using the My Computer window. You will also learn to use the Windows Explorer and to create new folders and files in Windows XP. Additionally, you will learn to move and copy files and folders, create shortcuts, use the Recycle Bin, and the Search feature of Windows XP.

skill | Viewing Folders with My Computer

concept

My Computer is a tool that shows you the organization of the drives and configuration of folders on your computer. You can use My Computer to navigate through the files of your system. Opening an icon in the My Computer window, usually of a drive or a folder, will show you that particular icon's contents. My Computer allows you to view the contents of your computer in five different ways: by Tiles, by Small Icons, in List form, with Details, and as Thumbnails.

do it!

To get a better understanding of file management, explore your C: drive by viewing its contents with the different View options.

1. Click **start** to open the Start menu.

2. Click the My Computer command on the Start menu; this will display the My Computer window, as shown in Figure 2-2. Double-click the C: drive icon to view its contents. You can also double-click the My Computer icon on the desktop to open the My Computer window.

3. To toggle between views, you need to make sure the Standard Buttons toolbar is visible. Click View on the Menu bar to open the View menu and then point to Toolbar. If there is no check mark beside the Standard Buttons command, point to it and click the left mouse button.

4. The My Computer window displays icons that represent your computer's disk drives and system control folders. Double-click the C: drive icons to view the folders and files on your hard drive (your C: drive may have a different label than the one shown here).

5. To view the items as Tiles, click the Views button on the right end of the Standard Buttons toolbar. A menu will appear, shown in Figure 2-3, allowing you to select your choice of views. The bullet marks the current view, Icons.

6. Click Tiles on the Views button menu. The icons will become larger, and they will be arranged alphabetically, as shown in Figure 2-4.

(continued on WN 2.4)

Figure 2-1 Sample file hierarchy

Figure 2-2 My Computer window

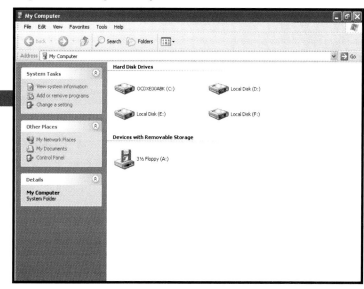

Figure 2-3 Views button menu

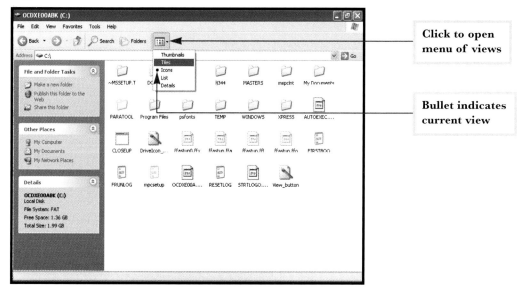

Click to open menu of views

Bullet indicates current view

Figure 2-4 C: drive window in Tiles view

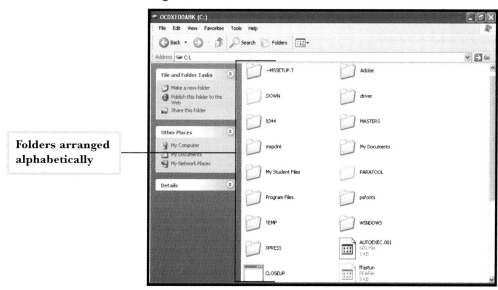

Folders arranged alphabetically

skill Viewing Folders with My Computer (continued)

do it!

7. Click Views button 🖽▾ again, then click List. This will list all the files and folders in the form of a list along with small icons, as shown in Figure 2-5.

8. Click Views button 🖽▾ again, then click Details. Figure 2-6 shows Details view, which will tell you the name of an item, its size if it is a file rather than folder, its type, and even the last time you modified it.

9. To return to the top level of the hierarchy, click the Up button 🗂 on the Standard Buttons toolbar. The Up button steps you up one level in the file structure, while the Back button ⬅ Back ▾ returns you to the last file or folder you viewed regardless of its place in the hierarchy.

10. Right-click the title bar of the C: drive window, then select Close from the shortcut menu that appears to remove the window from the desktop.

more

Using the Thumbnails view, you can generate a preview, a small image of the file, called a thumbnail, as shown in Figure 2-7. Thumbnails view allows you to preview all the image files in a folder rather than file icons of the image files. Audio and video previews will contain controls for playing the particular file from the window without having to open another application.

The columns that are shown in Details view for a particular folder are determined by the options you select in the Choose Details dialog box, which can be accessed by clicking the Choose Details command from the View menu. The dialog box provides a list of column headings that are available for viewing in the Details view. Check boxes next to each heading allow you to activate and deactivate the headings according to your needs and preferences. You can also alter the order in which the column headings appear and specify their individual widths.

You can customize the appearance of a folder by clicking the Customize This Folder command in the View menu. The command displays the Properties dialog box for the selected folder. Using the Folder pictures section of the Properties dialog box, you can put an image associated with the selected folder on the folder to remind you of the contents of the folder in the Thumbnails view. To recognize the folder contents in the views other than the Thumbnail view, you can change the icon of the folder.

The number and type of drives installed in a computer can vary greatly. The drive designated with the letter A is almost always a $3\frac{1}{2}$-inch floppy disk drive. The drive designated with the letter C is generally the computer's main hard drive. The D designation is usually assigned to the computer's CD-ROM drive. Traditionally, the letter B is reserved for a second floppy drive. If your hard disk is divided into a number of drives, the last letter is designated to the CD-ROM drive.

Figure 2-5 C: drive window in List view

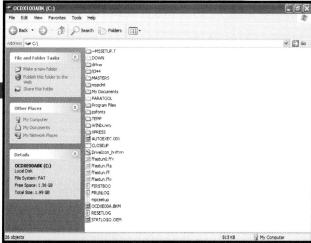

Figure 2-6 C: drive window in Details view

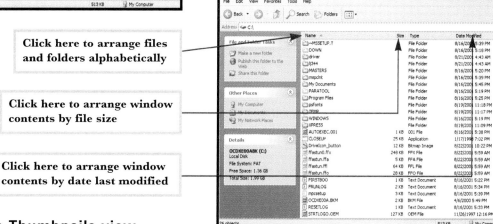

Click here to arrange files and folders alphabetically

Click here to arrange window contents by file size

Click here to arrange window contents by date last modified

Figure 2-7 A file in Thumbnails view

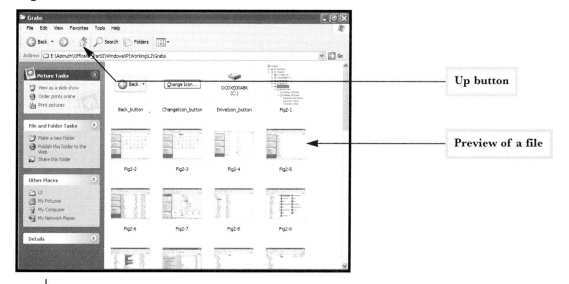

Up button

Preview of a file

Practice

Open the Control Panel window and use the Views button to display the items in each of the available views. Leave the window in the view you like best. Close the window when you are finished.

skill | Using Windows Explorer

concept

Windows Explorer, found on the Accessories menu in Windows XP, is similar to My Computer. Both are file management tools that allow you to view the contents of your computer. But Windows Explorer is more powerful and provides you with more options than My Computer. Windows Explorer displays itself as the two-paneled window you see in Figure 2-8, allowing you to work with more than one drive, folder, or file at a time. The left panel, which usually consists of the Folders Explorer bar, shows all the folders and disk drives on your computer. The right panel, the contents panel, is a display of the items located within the folder or drive that is selected in the Folders Explorer bar. This two-paneled window creates a more detailed view of a specific folder and makes for easier file manipulation, especially copying and moving.

do it!

Use Windows Explorer to examine folders on your computer.

1. Click ⊞ start , point to All Programs, point to Accessories, and then click the Windows Explorer command. This will open the Windows Explorer window. If you do not see the Folders Explorer bar on the left, click 🗀 Folders on the Standard Buttons toolbar.

2. Click the plus symbol ⊞ next to My Computer in the Folders Explorer bar (left panel). The plus symbol ⊞ next to an item in this panel indicates that the item can be expanded to reveal its contents. You should now see the same drives and folders in the right panel, which you saw previously in the My Computer window listed below My Computer in the left panel. Notice that the plus symbol ⊞ you clicked has now changed to a minus symbol ⊟ . This symbol indicates that a drive or folder is already expanded. Clicking the minus symbol ⊟ collapses a drive or folder's content back into the parent drive or folder. 🌑 If a folder contains files but no subfolders, a plus sign will not appear next to it.

3. Click plus symbol ⊞ next to your C: drive in the Folders Explorer bar to expand the drive, revealing its top-level contents. The list of items you see in the left panel will differ from computer to computer depending on the files that have been installed and the way they have been configured.

4. Click the Windows (or WINNT) folder in the left panel. Now that the folder is selected, its contents, including subfolders and files, are displayed in the right panel.

5. Double-click the Media folder in the right panel to open the folder. You also could have expanded the Windows folder in the left panel and then clicked the Media folder there to display its contents in the right panel. Notice that the Windows folder is now expanded in the Explorer bar and the Media folder is shown with an open folder icon. The files inside the Media folder are sound files that were installed automatically with Windows XP.

6. Press [Ctrl]+[A]. All of the items in the right panel will be selected, as shown in Figure 2-9. Pressing [Ctrl]+[A] is the keyboard shortcut for the Select All command on the Edit menu.

7. Switch to the Icons view and then press [End] on the keyboard. The last file in the Windows folder will be selected. Press [Home] to select the first item listed in the Media folder.

(continued on WN 2.8)

Figure 2-8 Selecting all the items of a folder

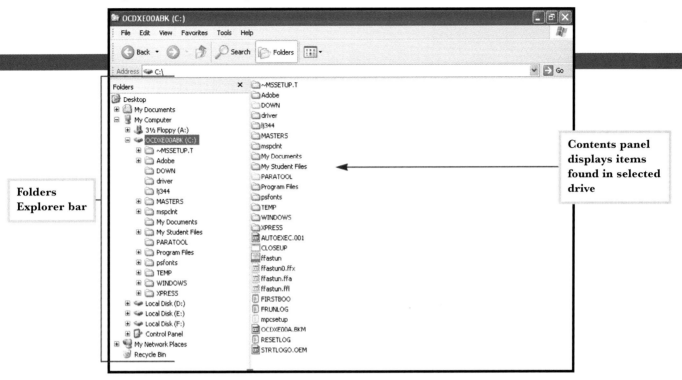

Folders Explorer bar

Contents panel displays items found in selected drive

Figure 2-9 Search Explorer Bar

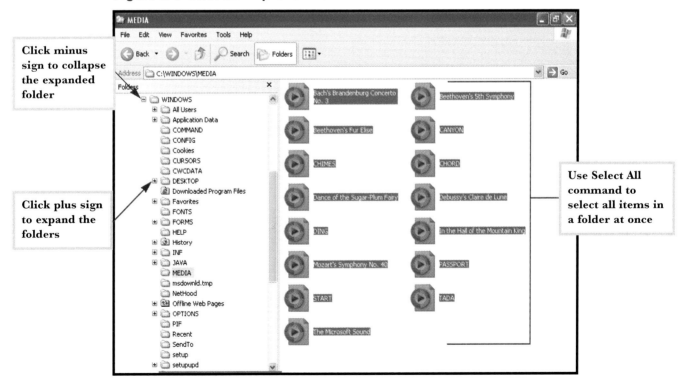

Click minus sign to collapse the expanded folder

Click plus sign to expand the folders

Use Select All command to select all items in a folder at once

skill | Using Windows Explorer (continued)

do it!

8. Press [D] to select the first item in the folder that begins with the letter D. This is useful if you know the name of a file or folder and want to jump to it quickly.

9. Press [D] again to move to the next item in the list that begins with the letter D. Continuing to press [D] will cycle you through all the items in the folder that begin with D. Stop when you return to the first D item in the list. Holding the [Ctrl] key down while you click allows you to select multiple, nonconsecutive files or folders.

10. Click the file named Beethoven's 5th Symphony to select it and simultaneously cancel the selection of the chord file.

11. Hold [Shift], then click the file PASSPORT. All of the files between the two files you clicked will be selected, as shown in Figure 2-10. Holding the [Shift] key while you click allows you to select all of the items between the first and the last items selected.

12. Click a blank area to the right of the file names in the right panel to deselect all of the currently selected items. Leave Windows Explorer open for use in the next Skill.

more

Windows Explorer is a unique tool. As you saw in the Skill above, its two-paneled structure allows you to view all the folders on a specified drive while working within a particular folder. One of the more powerful features of Windows Explorer is the left panel. The left panel, called the Folders Explorer bar, can be used to view the contents of any folder. By default, Windows Explorer opens in Folders view, which allows you to view any folders, files, or utilities found on your computer or your network. You can resize the panels of Windows Explorer. To do this, place the pointer on the bar that divides the window (it will change to ↔), then drag to the left or right to resize the bar.

In Windows XP, you can view different Explorer bars, such as Search, Favorites, and History. You can view these Explorer bars by selecting the required Explorer bar from the Explorer Bar submenu of the View menu. If you select the Search command from the Explorer Bar submenu, Windows XP displays the Search Companion (see Figure 2-11) for searching files and information on a machine. If you would like to see a list of the locations you have visited recently, including local and network drives and Web sites, select the History Explorer bar. Clicking the address or name of the place you want to view will load the site into the contents panel. You can choose to view items in the History Explorer bar by date, site name, frequency of visits, or sequence visited today. The Favorites Explorer bar allows you to store the places you visit most frequently so you can access them with a simple click. This feature is especially helpful with Web sites, which often have long, cumbersome addresses that are difficult to remember.

Figure 2-10 A range of files selected

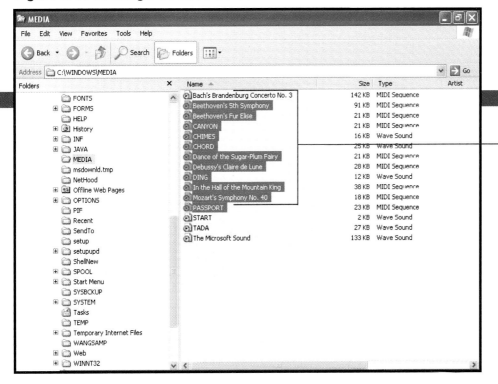

Hold down the [Shift] key while clicking, to select a range of folders or files

Figure 2-11 Windows XP Search Companion

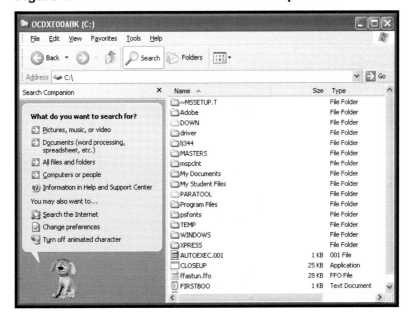

Practice

Expand the Windows folder and select the Fonts folder in the Folders Explorer bar. The files for all of the fonts installed on your computer will appear in the contents panel. Use the keyboard to select the font called Verdana.

skill Creating New Folders and Files

concept

Creating folders is necessary when you want to store files related to one project in a single location on a drive. Creating, naming, and placing folders properly in your hierarchy makes your work easier and more efficient. While most files are created in the program with which they will be used, you also can make new, blank files right in the folder where they will be stored.

do it!

Create a new folder on your C: drive, and then create another folder within that folder. Finally, create two files in the folder that you made.

1. In Windows Explorer, expand the C: drive, and then click its icon in the left panel of Windows Explorer to view the items of the hard drive in the contents panel.

2. Click File on the Menu bar. The File menu will open.

3. Point to New, then click Folder on the submenu that appears. A folder with the default name New Folder will appear in the contents panel with its name selected, ready to be changed.

4. Type My Student Files, then press [Enter] to give the folder a unique name so you can find it again. Notice that the new folder also appears in the left panel.

5. Click the icon of the new folder in the left panel of Windows Explorer to select it and reveal its contents. The right panel should be blank since this folder is empty.

6. Click File, point to New, then select Folder to create a new folder within your My Student Files folder.

7. Type Alice, then press [Enter] to name the new folder. The folder will be in the contents panel and a plus will appear next to My Student Files (Figure 2-12) in the left panel to indicate that at least one folder is located within the parent folder.

8. Click the plus symbol ⊞ next to the My Student Files folder in the Folders Explorer bar to expand the folder and reveal the Alice folder located inside.

9. Click File, select New, and then click Wordpad Document on the menu that appears. A new file with the default name New WordPad Document will be created with the name of the file selected.

10. Type Letter to rename the new file. Press [Enter] to confirm the file name.

11. Repeat the above step to create a WordPad document named To Do List. Your window should look similar to the one shown in Figure 2-13.

(continued on WN 2.12)

Figure 2-12 Creating a new folder

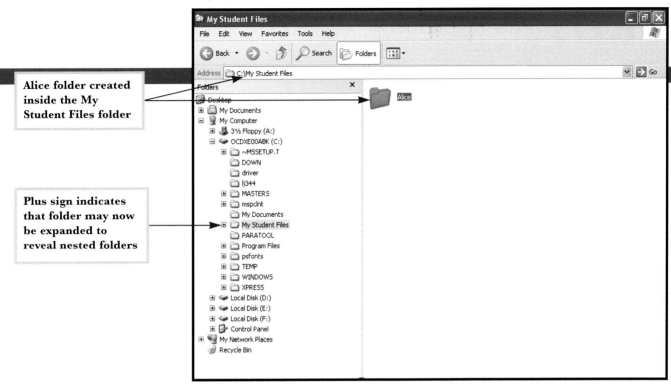

Alice folder created inside the My Student Files folder

Plus sign indicates that folder may now be expanded to reveal nested folders

Figure 2-13 File hierarchy including new folder and files

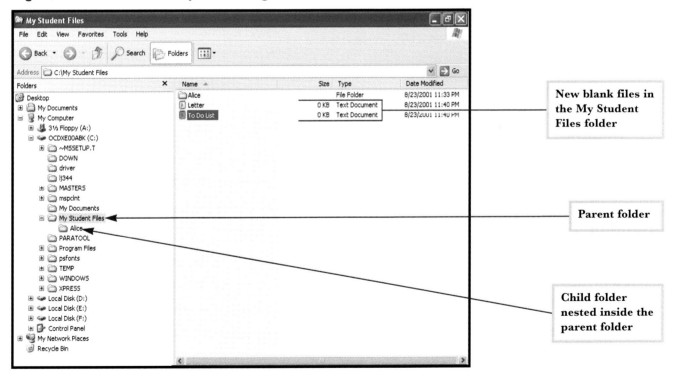

New blank files in the My Student Files folder

Parent folder

Child folder nested inside the parent folder

skill Creating New Folders and Files (continued)

more

After creating a new folder, you can right-click the folder to access commands, such as Delete, Rename, Cut, Copy, Sharing and Security, Open, and Search (see Figure 2-14), in the shortcut menu.

If you right-click a file, a shortcut menu is displayed. The commands displayed in the shortcut menu of a file are different from the commands displayed in the shortcut menu of a folder. Figure 2-15 shows the menu that appears when you right-click a file. The Open command opens the file with the application associated with the file's extension (such as .txt for a text file or .wav for a sound file). The Open With command allows you to select a different application with which to open the file. The Print command lets you create a hard copy of the file without having to open the application with which it was created first. You also can use commands on the shortcut menu to cut, copy, delete, or create a shortcut to the file or folder you right-clicked. The Rename command allows you to change the name of the file or folder. Selecting a file or folder, pausing, and then clicking it again will also let you rename an item, as will selecting it and pressing [F2].

The shortcut menu that appears when you right-click a folder differs slightly from the File menu. It includes commands for opening the folder in Windows Explorer and setting network sharing options.

You can set options for each folder on your computer that control the way the folders appear and the way in which you interact with them. To do this, select a folder, click the Tools menu on the Menu bar, and then click the Folder Options command. The Folder Options dialog box is displayed. By default, options under the General tab are displayed, as shown in Figure 2-16. On the General tab, the Tasks section lets you determine if the folder contents should look and work like Web pages or if there should be hyperlinks to common folder tasks. The Browse folders section is responsible for whether each folder you open appears in the same window or in a separate window. Finally, you can use the Click items as follows section to set your preferences for selecting and opening icons.

The View tab in the Folder Options dialog box contains Advanced Settings sections. This section enables you to set options for files and folders, such as the option to display entire file paths in the Address bar and the option to hide file extensions for known file types. The File Types tab is where associations between file types (extensions) and applications are set. The Offline Files tab allows you to make network files accessible when you are not connected to your network.

Figure 2-14 Shortcut menu for a folder

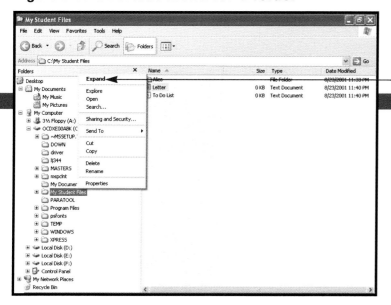

Click to view contents of
the folder in contents panel

Figure 2-15 Shortcut menu for a file

Select Delete to send the
file to the Recycle Bin

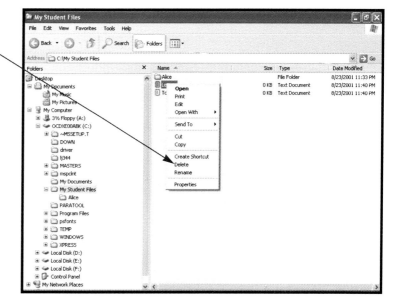

Figure 2-16 Folder Options dialog box

Click to restore the
default settings of
Windows XP

Practice

Create a folder inside the My Documents folder called Practice. Then create a new WordPad file
called wnprac2-3.txt inside this folder.

skill | Moving and Copying Files and Folders

concept

There are times when you will want to move or copy folders or files. Moving an item to group it with other files or folders that contain similar data can increase the overall efficiency of your work. Moving a folder changes its location and alters your file hierarchy accordingly. Copying a file or folder can be done to create a duplicate in another location on your system.

do it!

Move the Letter.txt and To Do List.txt files into the Alice folder, and then make a copy of the Alice folder inside the My Student Files folder.

1. Open Windows Explorer using the Start menu if it is not already open.

2. Click the My Student Files folder in the left panel to select it (expand My Computer and the C: drive if necessary). The contents of the My Student Files folder—the Alice folder, Letter.txt, and To Do List.txt—will appear in the contents panel.

3. Click the plus symbol ⊞ next to the My Student Files folder so you can see the Alice folder in the left panel of Windows Explorer.

4. Hold down the [Ctrl] key, while you click Letter and To Do List to select both files.

5. Drag the selected files from the right panel to the Alice folder in the left panel to move them. When you begin to drag, a faint outline of the files will follow the pointer. In certain areas, the pointer may become a circle with a line through it ⊘, indicating that you cannot drop your files at that particular location. You will know that the files are in the correct position when the Alice folder is selected, as shown in Figure 2-17. As soon as this occurs, release the mouse button to drop the files into the folder.

6. Click the Alice folder in the right panel to select it.

7. Click Edit on the Menu bar to open the Edit menu, then click the Copy command to place a copy of the Alice folder on the Clipboard. The Clipboard is a temporary storage area in your computer's memory that holds copied or cut items until they are replaced on the Clipboard by another item or the computer is shut down. You can relocate a file using the Cut command of the Edit menu.

8. Click Edit, then select Paste from the menu. A copy of the Alice folder will appear in the My Student Files folder as shown in Figure 2-18.

more

There are many ways to move and copy items in Windows XP. Dragging and dropping files and folders from panel to panel in the Windows Explorer is one of the easiest ways to manage the information stored on your computer. Moving and copying also can be accomplished by dragging almost any item from your desktop to another system window or vice versa. You also can move and copy with toolbar buttons: first, select the item you wish to move or copy; then, click either Move To Folder command or Copy To Folder command in the Edit menu. When you click the Move to Folder command, the Move Items dialog box is displayed and when you click the Copy to Folder command, the Copy Items dialog box is displayed. Using the Move Items and Copy Items dialog boxes you can select a destination for the item to be moved or copied. Moving or cutting an item removes it from its original location. Copying leaves the original item in its original location.

Figure 2-17 Moving files

Selected files being moved

Alice folder selected, ready to receive files

Outline of the files being moved, attached to the mouse pointer

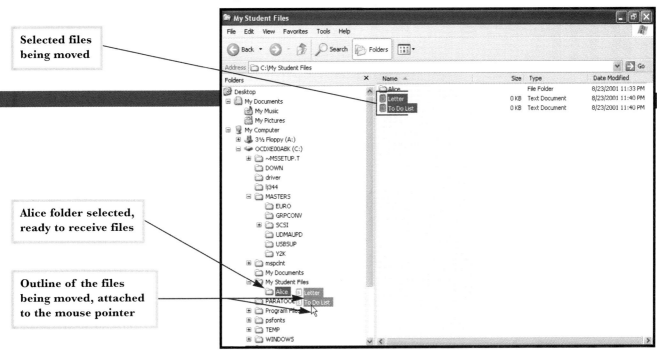

Figure 2-18 Copying a folder

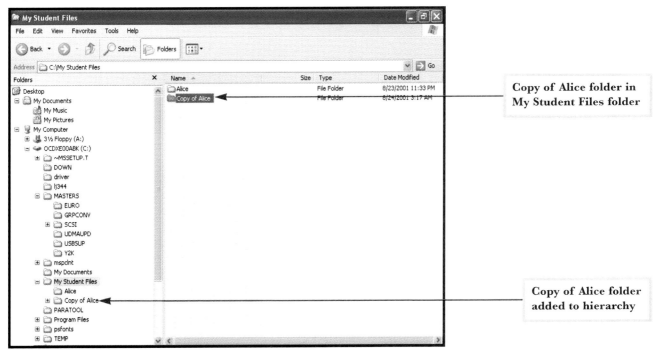

Copy of Alice folder in My Student Files folder

Copy of Alice folder added to hierarchy

Practice

Make a copy of wnprac2-3.txt in the My Documents folder. Rename the copied file to wnprac2-4.txt. Then move wnprac2-4.txt back to the Practice folder using the Cut command.

skill | Creating Shortcuts

concept

Shortcuts are icons that give you direct access to frequently used items so that you do not have to open applications or folders in order to work with them. Shortcuts can be created for programs, folders, files, Internet addresses, or even devices like printers. You can place shortcuts directly on the desktop or Start menu, or anywhere else you find convenient.

do it!

Create a shortcut to the My Student Files folder on the desktop, rename it, and then change its icon.

1. Open Windows Explorer if it is not already open on your desktop.

2. If the Windows Explorer window is maximized, click the Restore button 🗗 so you can scc a few inches of the desktop. You may have to resize the window so that more of the desktop is visible.

3. Expand the appropriate icons so that the My Student Files folder is visible in the Folders Explorer bar (left panel) of Windows Explorer. Place the mouse pointer over the folder's icon.

4. While holding down the right mouse button, drag the My Student Files folder to a blank space on your desktop. As the folder is dragged, a dimmed representation of it will move with the pointer. When you release the mouse button, you will see the shortcut menu shown in Figure 2-19.

5. Click Create Shortcuts Here. A new folder named Shortcut to My Student Files will be created. The small arrow 🡕 in the corner of the icon denotes that the folder is a shortcut, allowing you to access the My Student Files folder from the desktop without actually storing the folder on the desktop.

6. Right-click the Shortcut to My Student Files folder. A shortcut menu with commands relating to the folder will appear.

7. Click Rename. The name of the folder will be selected so you can edit it.

8. Type To Be Deleted, then press [Enter] to rename the folder. Figure 2-20 displays the shortcut with its new name.

9. Right-click the To Be Deleted folder, then select Properties from the shortcut menu. The To Be Deleted Properties dialog box will be displayed (Figure 2-21). By default, the Shortcut tab is displayed. This tab contains the data related to the shortcut properties of the selected folder.

(continued on WN 2.18)

Figure 2-19 Creating a shortcut

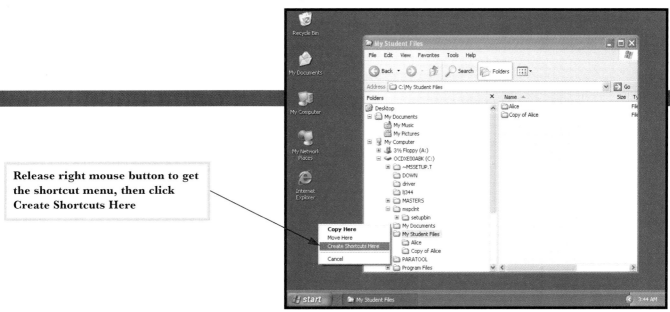

Release right mouse button to get
the shortcut menu, then click
Create Shortcuts Here

Figure 2-20 Renamed shortcut folder on desktop

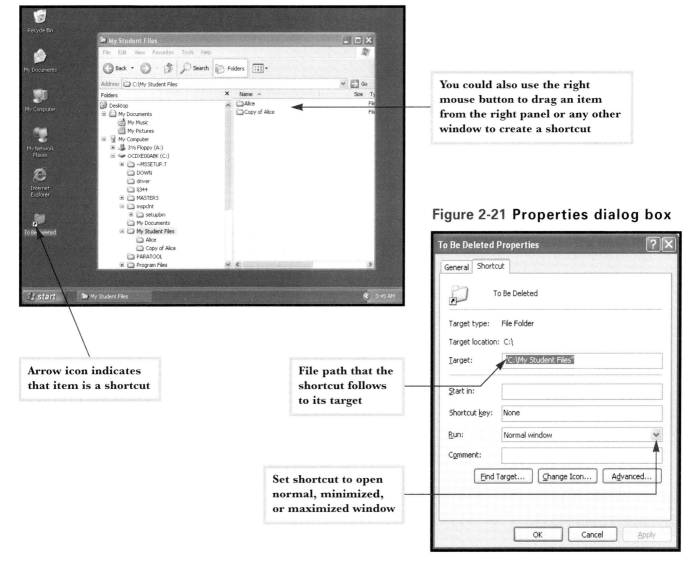

You could also use the right
mouse button to drag an item
from the right panel or any other
window to create a shortcut

Arrow icon indicates
that item is a shortcut

Figure 2-21 Properties dialog box

File path that the
shortcut follows
to its target

Set shortcut to open
normal, minimized,
or maximized window

skill Creating Shortcuts (continued)

do it!

10. Click Change Icon... . This will display the Change Icon dialog box (Figure 2-22).

11. Drag the horizontal scroll bar box to the right until the tree icon is visible. Click the tree icon to select it.

12. Click OK . The Change Icon dialog box will close, returning you to the To Be Deleted Properties dialog box. The preview icon in the upper-left corner of the Shortcut tab will change to reflect your selection.

13. Click OK . The To Be Deleted Properties dialog box will close and the folder icon will be replaced with the tree icon, as shown in Figure 2-23.

more

Shortcuts can be made for many items stored on your computer, including files, folders, and drives that you access over a network. For example, you can make a shortcut to a frequently used folder that you access over a network for quick access to its files. Shortcuts do not have to be placed only on the desktop. You can create a folder of shortcuts to your favorite programs and place it on your C: drive, or even the Start menu.

As you have seen, many tasks can be accomplished using drag-and-drop techniques. One of the more powerful Windows XP features allows you to drag files to program icons. Doing so will open the file with the program whose icon you drop it on, provided the file and application are compatible. For example, you can create a shortcut to your word processing program and place it on the desktop. Then you can drag word processing files to that shortcut to open them. This also works with printers.

In the above exercise, you changed the name and icon for the shortcut you created without altering the folder to which the shortcut points. While a shortcut points to a specific item, that object can be renamed without affecting the shortcut. However, target objects that are moved to another folder or drive will cause the shortcut to malfunction. If a target item is moved, Windows XP has the ability to find it, or you can specify the new path manually. Since shortcuts are icons that point to the actual file, folder, or program that they represent, deleting a shortcut will not affect the target item.

You also can create a shortcut by right-clicking an item and then choosing Create Shortcut from the shortcut menu that appears. The shortcut will be created in the same folder as the original item. You can then move the shortcut to the desired location. If you drag a shortcut to the Start button, the Start menu will open. You can drop the shortcut on the Start menu or any of its submenus.

Figure 2-22 Change Icon dialog box

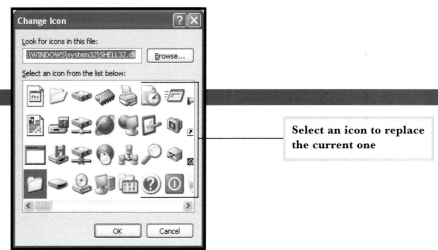

Select an icon to replace the current one

Figure 2-23 Desktop shortcut with new icon

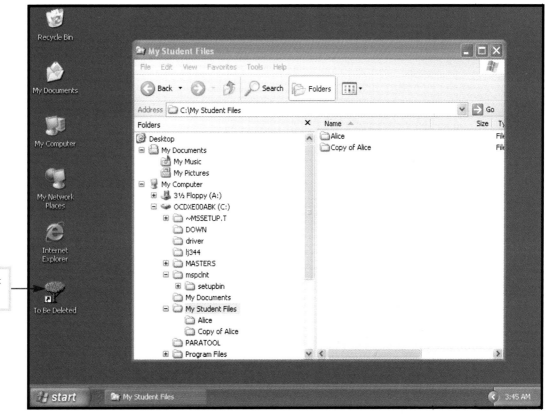

Renamed shortcut with tree icon

Practice

Place a shortcut to the Practice folder on your desktop.

skill Using the Recycle Bin

concept

The Recycle Bin is a storage place for files that have been deleted. Files that you no longer need should be deleted in order to save disk space and maximize the efficiency of your computer. If you decide that you need a file again, or have accidentally deleted a file, you can rescue it from the Recycle Bin. If you know you will never need a file again, you can delete the file permanently.

do it!

Send the Copy of Alice and To Be Deleted folders to the Recycle Bin. Then restore To Be Deleted from the Recycle Bin. Finally, delete both items from your hard drive permanently.

1. Open Windows Explorer from the Start menu.

2. Expand the necessary icons, and then click the My Student Files folder in the left panel to select it.

3. Click the Copy of Alice folder in the right panel.

4. Click File on the Menu bar and click the Delete command. This will display the Confirm Folder Delete dialog box (Figure 2-24) asking if you are sure you want to move the folder to the Recycle Bin.

5. Click [Yes]. The dialog box will close and the folder will be moved to the Recycle Bin.

6. Click the Close button ⊠ to exit Windows Explorer.

7. Click and drag the To Be Deleted shortcut from the desktop to the Recycle Bin. When the Recycle Bin becomes selected (indicated by modified shading of the icon), release the mouse button. The shortcut is now moved to the Recycle Bin.

8. Double-click the Recycle Bin icon. The Recycle Bin window will open. Figure 2-25 shows the contents of the Recycle Bin displaying all the files and folders you have sent there.

9. Drag the To Be Deleted shortcut from the Recycle Bin window to an empty space on the desktop. The shortcut appears on the desktop and is now an accessible item that can be used. Items still in the Recycle Bin cannot be opened.

10. Right-click the To Be Deleted shortcut and choose the Delete command from the shortcut menu to send the folder back into the Recycle Bin.

11. Click [Yes] to confirm the operation.

12. Click the Recycle Bin button on the taskbar. Click File on the Menu bar and then click Empty Recycle Bin. The Confirm Multiple File Delete dialog box will appear.

13. Click [Yes] to delete the folders from your hard drive permanently.

14. Click the Close button ⊠ to close the Recycle Bin window. ◣ You also can empty the Recycle Bin by right-clicking it and then choosing the Empty Recycle Bin command.

more

Table 2-1 Ways to delete and restore a selected file

To Delete	To Restore
Right-click and select Delete from the shortcut menu	Right-click the file in the Recycle Bin and select Restore
Drag the file to the Recycle Bin	Drag the file from the Recycle Bin to any other location
Press the [Delete] key or click the Delete button ✕ on the Standard Buttons toolbar	Go to the File menu in the Recycle Bin and select Restore

Figure 2-24 Confirm Folder Delete dialog box

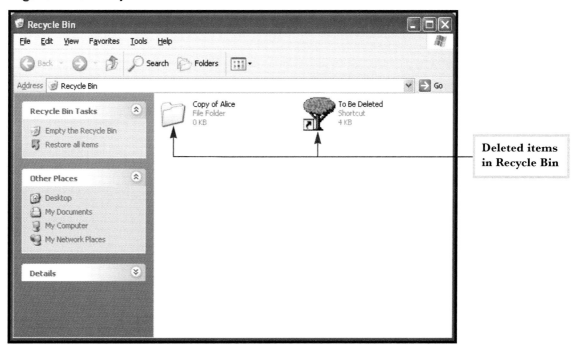

Click to close dialog box and to move indicated folder to Recycle Bin

Click No to cancel move to Recycle Bin

Figure 2-25 Recycle Bin window

Deleted items in Recycle Bin

Practice

Move the Practice shortcut you created in the last skill to the Recycle Bin. Then move the shortcut out of the Recycle Bin and back to the desktop. Delete the shortcut a second time using a different technique. Finally, delete the shortcut permanently.

skill | Searching for Files or Folders

concept

Managing your files effectively includes knowing how to locate an item when you need it. The Search command on the Start menu is a tool that allows you to search your computer for files and folders when you do not know exactly where they are stored. You can also access the Search facility when working in Windows Explorer or My Computer by clicking the Search button [Search] on the Standard toolbar to activate the Search Explorer Bar.

do it!

Use the Search command to locate the Discover folder.

1. Click [start] , then click Search. This will display the Search Results window (see Figure 2-26). The left panel of the Search Results windows displays the Search Companion section.

2. In the Search Companion section, click All files and folders.

3. In the All or part of the file name text box, type discover.

4. The Look in box should show your main hard drive. If not, click the arrow at the right edge of the box and select your main hard drive from the list.

5. Click [Search] . Windows will begin to search the hard drive of your computer for any files or folders named discover. When the search is complete, the results will be displayed in the right panel of the Search Result window (Figure 2-27). When your search is successful, you can open or run the item you have found by double-clicking it directly in the Search Results window. In this particular case, the item you have found is actually a folder.

6. Close the Search Results window.

more

When you do not know the exact name of the file or folder you are looking for, you can use the wildcard character * in your search request. For example, if you search for all files or folders named J*, the search will return all files and folders whose names begin with the letter J. When you search for a file or folder, you can specify the date of modification and size of the file or folder using the options When was it modified and What size is it, respectively, of the Search Companion section. You can also search the system folders, hidden files and folders, and subfolders using the More advanced options section of Search Companion.

Figure 2-26 Search Companion

Figure 2-27 Result of the search for the discover folder

Practice

Use the Search command to locate your computer's Desktop folders.

shortcuts

Function	Button/Mouse	Menu	Keyboard
Tiles view		Click View, then click Tiles	[Alt]+[V], [S]
Icons		Click View, then click Icons	[Alt]+[V], [N]
List view		Click View, then click List	[Alt]+[V], [L]
Details view		Click View, then click Details	[Alt]+[V], [D]
Thumbnails view		Click View, then click Thumbnails	[Alt]+[V], [H]
Move up one level in file hierarchy		Click View, then click Go To, then click Up One Level	[Alt]+[G], [U]
Back	Back	Click View, then click Go To then click Back	[Alt]+[Left Arrow]

A. Identify Key Features

Name the items indicated by callouts in Figure 2-28.

Figure 2-28 Standard Buttons toolbar

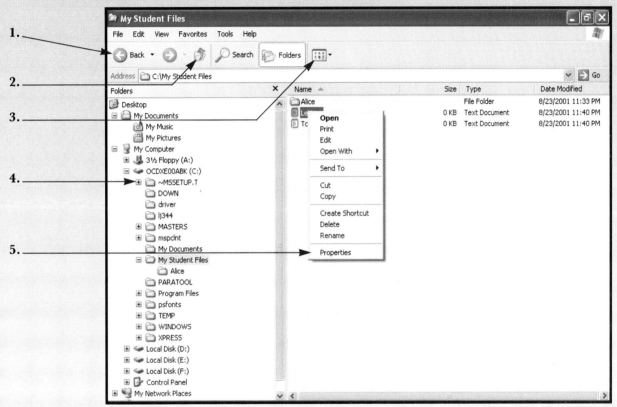

B. Select the Best Answer

6. Right side of the Windows Explorer window

7. One of the Explorer bars

8. Allows you to relocate a selected file or folder

9. Storage place for deleted items

10. Its keyboard shortcut is [Ctrl]+[A]

11. An icon that gives you direct access to a frequently used item

12. Tool that allows you to view and organize the contents of your hard drive

a. My Computer

b. Shortcut

c. Contents panel

d. Select All command

e. Folders

f. Cut command

g. Recycle Bin

quiz (continued)

C. Complete the Statement

13. A small arrow attached to the bottom-left corner of an icon signifies:

a. A selected icon

b. An expanded folder

c. A shortcut

d. A restored file

14. The temporary storage device that holds cut and copied items is called the:

a. Recycle Bin

b. Explorer window

c. My Computer window

d. Clipboard

15. Clicking the Views button:

a. Automatically puts the icons in List view

b. Automatically puts the icons in Details view

c. Opens the Views list menu

d. Cycles to the next view on the Views menu

16. To preview all the image files in a folder, put the icons in:

a. Details view

b. List view

c. Tiles view

d. Thumbnail view

17. A plus sign next to a folder or drive in the Folders Explorer Bar indicates that it can be:

a. Collapsed

b. Expanded

c. Moved

d. Deleted

18. A file in the Recycle Bin:

a. Has been deleted permanently

b. Can be opened by double-clicking it

c. Can be restored by dragging it to a new location

d. Must be copied and pasted to be restored

19. You can search a file or folder in Windows XP using:

a. Search Companion

b. Search Master

c. Find Folder window

d. Find Files window

20. The powerful two-paneled tool that allows you to work with more than one drive, file, or folder is:

a. My Computer

b. Windows Explorer

c. The Recycle Bin

d. The Create Shortcut dialog box

interactivity

Build Your Skills

1. View the folders and files on your hard drive:

   a. Use My Computer to display the contents of your hard drive (C:).

   b. Put the contents of your hard drive in the Thumbnails view.

   c. Change to the List view using the Menu bar.

   d. Return to the top level of the file hierarchy.

   e. Close the My Computer window using the Close button.

2. Use Windows Explorer to view and select items on your hard drive:

   a. Open Windows Explorer.

   b. Expand My Computer, your C: drive, and then the Program Files folder.

   c. Select the Internet Explorer folder so that its contents are displayed in the contents panel.

   d. Select all of the items in the contents panel.

   e. Select the PLUGINS folder in the contents panel.

   f. Select every other item in the contents panel.

   g. Select the last four items in the contents panel.

3. Create a new folder and a new file, then copy the file to another folder:

   a. Create a new folder on your C: drive (not in the Internet Explorer folder) called WN.

   b. Make a copy of the folder.

   c. Create a new WordPad document called wnskills1-1.txt in the original WN folder.

   d. Place a copy of the wnskills1-1 WordPad document in the My Documents folder.

4. Create a shortcut and practice using the Recycle Bin:

   a. Place a shortcut to the original WN folder on your desktop.

   b. Send the copy of WN folder to the Recycle Bin without dragging the folder.

   c. Drag the copy of wnskills1-1 WordPad document that you placed in the My Documents folder to the Recycle Bin.

   d. Empty the Recycle Bin.

interactivity (continued)

Build Your Skills (continued)

5. Create a new shortcut and then use the Search Companion to locate it on your hard drive:

   a. Place a shortcut to your C: drive on the desktop.

   b. Practice using the Search Companion by locating the shortcut you just created.

   c. Access the shortcut from the Search Results window.

   d. Close all windows and delete the shortcut you created in step a.

Problem Solving Exercises

1. You have been running a successful guitar instruction business for several years now. Since your business continues to grow, you have decided to start managing it with a computer running Windows XP. The first step of this project is to set up your hard drive with a system of useful folders. Start with a main folder called Business. Within the Business folder you should place a folder for each day of the week that you teach, Monday through Friday. Eventually, each of these folders will contain a folder for each student who has a lesson on that day. For now, each day-of-the-week folder should hold a new WordPad document called [Insert day] Schedule. Back inside the Business folder, create one WordPad document with the name Student List and another called Master Schedule. Finally, place a shortcut to Master Schedule inside each day-of-the-week folder.

2. Your supervisor has asked you to be in charge of the New Media department's new multimedia software and documentation. Create a folder on your C: drive named New Media. Create two folders inside the New Media folder named Programs and Documentation. Open the Documentation folder and place a new WordPad document named Tech Support inside the folder. Copy the document to your My Documents folder. Then rename the Programs folder you created to Software.

3. Before you install Windows XP throughout your office, you want to review the software's end user license agreement, but you are not sure where to find it. Use Windows XP's Search Companion to look for a file named eula on your local hard disk. If you find it successfully, double-click the file in the Search Results window to open it. Then close the file and create a shortcut to it on your desktop.

Working with Internet Explorer

Microsoft Internet Explorer is a software application that gives you the tools you need to take full advantage of the World Wide Web. Its integration with the Windows XP operating system makes it easy to browse the Web whether you want to find a local take-out restaurant, e-mail your sister to tell her about your new job, or find a message board relating to mandolins.

One of the most used facets of the Internet is the World Wide Web. It has increasingly become a key element of business, culture, community, and politics. You have already seen the browser window, as it is the same one used for My Computer and the Windows Explorer. The function of a browser is just that: it lets you browse or surf, and view the pages that make up the Web. The World Wide Web is like a long hypertext document consisting of millions of pages that contain text, pictures, movies, and sounds. Among these pages you can find everything from information on NASA's latest launch to samples from your favorite musical artist's new CD.

- ⚡ **Introduction to the Internet**

- ⚡ **Opening Internet Explorer**

- ⚡ **Navigating the Web**

- ⚡ **Searching the Internet**

- ⚡ **Creating Favorites**

- ⚡ **Managing Favorites**

- ⚡ **Printing a Web Page**

When using Internet Explorer, most Web browsing can be done through a series of mouse clicks. Web pages are made up of hypermedia, which are words and pictures that are linked to other places on the Web and will transport you there when they are clicked. Internet Explorer also has toolbars that contain buttons to help you move through all the interesting material you will encounter on your journey across the Web.

As you wander around the Web, you will encounter pages that you will want to return to later. To go to any page, all you need to do is remember the address (each Web page has its own), and then enter it into the text box provided on Internet Explorer's Address Bar. If you want to visit a page often, there is even a way to create direct links, or shortcuts, to your favorite Web sites. This is a good idea if a site's content changes frequently, such as that of a news service. The nature of the Web allows for frequent updating of a page's data. As you go through this lesson, keep in mind that a page's look or contents may have changed since the authors visited it. Some references may no longer be accurate when compared with what you view on your computer.

Lesson Goal:

In this lesson, you will learn the basics of the Internet, such as opening Internet Explorer, navigating the Web, and searching the Internet. Additionally, you will learn to create and manage favorites and print a Web page.

skill | Introduction to the Internet

concept

The Internet is an extended worldwide computer network that is composed of numerous smaller networks. In the late 1960s, the U.S. Defense Department's Advanced Research Projects Agency (ARPA) created a network of computers designed to withstand severe localized damage, such as that of a nuclear attack. Each computer on the ARPA network was connected to every other machine in such a way as to form a web. Each chunk of data sent from one machine to another was formatted as a packet, which also contained the address of where the packet originated and where it was headed. The web configuration and packet format enabled data to be rerouted if a node along its path in the network should be rendered inoperable. The packet-switching technology developed for ARPAnet became the foundation of today's Internet.

In the early 1980s, the National Science Foundation founded NSFnet, five supercomputing centers connected together on a network. Soon, other government agencies and educational institutions connected to NSFnet as well, adding information and infrastructure upon which an ever-larger network began to grow.

As more scientists, students, and computer enthusiasts became familiar with the Internet, more people began to log on from a variety of locations. Figure 3-1 illustrates the phenomenal growth of Internet use. Soon, new software was developed to facilitate access to the Internet. Along with e-mail and newsgroups, two major uses of the Internet, the World Wide Web began to rise in popularity in the first half of the 1990s.

The WWW is made possible by hypermedia and hypertext, objects such as pictures or lines of text that, when clicked, instruct the browser to go to another location on the Web. These objects allow for a nonlinear presentation of information, making the WWW, in effect, one huge hypermedia document made up of millions of individual files, each with its own address on the Web. The address at which a document is located on the Internet is called a Uniform Resource Locator or URL. A URL consists of three parts: the protocol (such as http or ftp), the location of the server on the Internet (domain), and sometimes the path to the requested data on the server's drive.

The Web works on a client-server model (Figure 3-2). The server, which is the computer containing the requested data, sends information to the client, the computer that receives it. The transfer of data between server and client follows a standardized protocol or information exchange process. The Web standard is HTTP (HyperText Transfer Protocol), which allows all kinds of computers to understand and reliably translate hypertext Web files. Internet Explorer is a Web browser, which, like all Web software, conforms to HTTP standards. Web browsers are programs that allow a computer to translate the hypertext and display it. All Web browsers can read the text of all Web pages because these pages are written with a platform-independent language called hypertext markup language, or HTML. HTML documents consist of the text that will appear on the page, formatting instructions, and references to other files such as graphics that will be displayed on the page. The World Wide Web has become the most popular feature of the Internet, providing access to an almost unimaginable diversity of information.

Figure 3-1 The growth of the Internet

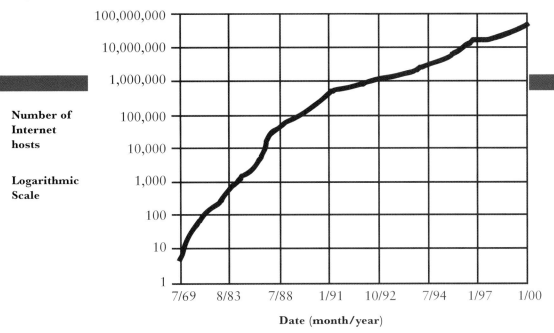

Number of
Internet
hosts

Logarithmic
Scale

Date (month/year)

Figure 3-2 Clients and servers on the World Wide Web

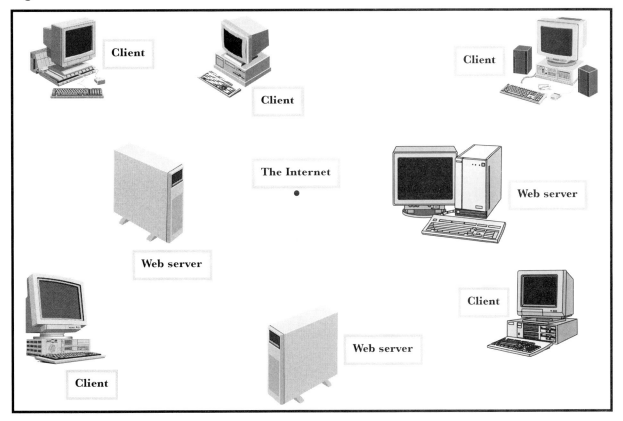

skill | Opening Internet Explorer

concept

Before you can begin surfing the Web with Internet Explorer (IE), you must open the application. You can accomplish this task in a variety of ways, including using the Start menu, the Quick Launch toolbar, or a desktop icon. Internet Explorer 6.0 is installed by default with Windows XP.

do it!

Open Internet Explorer and view its interface.

1. Click ⟨start⟩ to open the Start menu.

2. Click Internet on the Start menu. This will open the Internet Explorer. A page will appear in the browser window, which is shown maximized in Figure 3-3. This is called the home page of the browser and refers to the document that loads automatically when the application is launched. The default home page of Internet Explorer is the Microsoft Network (MSN) home page, http://www.msn.com. (In this instance, the term home page refers to the main page of Microsoft's Web site.) ⬤ Since Windows allows for customization, your browser window may be different than the ones shown, and your startup procedure may vary slightly from the one specified here. For example, you may have to go through a dial-up procedure if you are connecting to the Internet with a modem.

3. Internet Explorer's browser window resembles the standard Windows XP system window with which you are already familiar. You will notice changes in the Standard Buttons toolbar. Table 3-1 explains some of the features of this toolbar and how they allow you to use Internet Explorer most effectively.

more

Changing the home page of your browser is a relatively simple procedure. Open the Tools menu from Internet Explorer's Menu bar and click the Internet Options command. The Internet Options dialog box will open to the General tab. The top section of the General tab is titled Home page, and it contains a text entry box that holds the Web address for the current home page of the browser. This address will be selected automatically when the dialog box opens. You can type any Web address to replace the one that is already there. Then click ⟨ OK ⟩ to confirm the adjustment and close the dialog box. The next time you open your browser or click on the Home button 🏠 on the Standard Buttons toolbar, the Web page whose address you provided will appear in your browser window.

If you have difficulty remembering the functions of the different toolbar buttons, you can customize the Standard Buttons toolbar so that it displays text labels for all buttons. To do this, right-click the Standard Buttons toolbar and then click the Customize command on the menu that appears. Near the bottom of the Customize Toolbar dialog box is a list labeled Text options that provides the options text labels for all buttons, selected buttons, or no text labels. The main part of this dialog box permits you to change which buttons actually appear on the toolbar. ⬤ To restore the original home page setting of your browser, open the Internet Options dialog box from the View menu, then click ⟨ Use Default ⟩ in the Home page section of the General tab.

Figure 3-3 Internet Explorer opened to MSN home page

Address (URL) of
current Web
page displayed
in Address bar

Table 3-1 Internet Explorer's Standard Buttons toolbar's functions

Button	Function
	Stops the loading of a page into the browser window
	Reloads the current page; especially useful for pages that update frequently
Search Favorites	Activates the corresponding explorer bar in the browser window
	Loads the browser's home page into the browser window
	Opens a menu of commands related to working with e-mail
	Instructs a printer properly connected to your computer to print a copy of the current page
	Opens the History explorer bar

Practice

Change the home page of your browser to the following address: http://www.canoe.ca.

skill | Navigating the Web

concept

Since information on the Web is not presented in a strictly linear fashion, it is possible to follow links in any order you like, examining whatever you wish in more detail. This often is referred to as browsing or surfing. Most Web browsing with Internet Explorer is done using a few basic actions and controls.

do it!

Practice moving around the Web using hyperlinks, navigation buttons, and the Address bar.

1. From the MSN home page, you can gain access to news, free e-mail, reference materials, online shopping, and much more. Clickable words and images on the page are called hyperlinks. Position the mouse pointer over the Hotmail link. The pointer will appear as a hand with a pointing finger 🖑 when over the link, indicating that it is an active link. The underlined text also may change color to red.

2. Click the Hotmail link. The Microsoft Windows icon [🪟] at the right end of the Menu bar will animate to indicate that the page you have requested is loading. The page should appear in the browser window momentarily, as shown in Figure 3-4.

3. Locate and click the TERMS OF USE link at the bottom of the Web page. You will be transported to a page that explains the terms of use for Hotmail®, Microsoft's free Web-based e-mail service. Notice that since you started following links, the Back button on the Standard Buttons toolbar has become active. Use the scroll bar to read text that is not visible.

4. Click 〔◉ Back ▾〕 to go back to the previously viewed page, the main Hotmail page.

5. Click the Forward button 〔◉▾〕. The TERMS OF USE page reappears in the window. 〔⬤〕 The Forward button only becomes active once the Back button has been clicked, and reverses the Back command.

6. Position the mouse pointer in the Address bar text box, and then click once. The URL (Uniform Resource Locator) of the current page will be selected.

7. Type http://www.altavista.com to enter this address manually, then press [Enter]. The home page of the altavista search engine, shown in Figure 3-5, will appear.

8. Click the Home button 🏠 to go back to the home page of your browser.

more

The Forward and Back buttons both have small list arrows ⁞ on their right edges. When clicked, these arrows display a list of recently visited pages. The list appears below the button with the most recently visited page at the top. The list of recently visited pages allows you to quickly go back to a previously visited page without having to click the Back button, repeatedly. In the same way, the Forward button list shows sites that can be visited by clicking the Forward button. 〔⬤〕 Right-clicking the Back or Forward button also will bring up these lists.

Figure 3-4 Microsoft's Hotmail® page

Back button now available

Spinning icon indicates that the page is being loaded

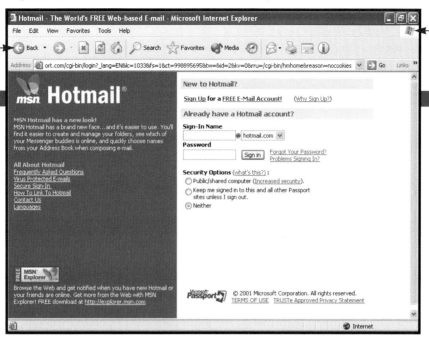

Figure 3-5 Using the Address bar to enter a URL

Click the current address to select it, then type address of page you want to visit

Click Address list arrow to see the URLs entered recently

Press the [Enter] key or click the Go button to go to the address displayed in the Address bar

Practice

Visit the Web page found at http://www.usps.gov. Then use the Standard Buttons toolbar to return to the home page of your browser.

skill | Searching the Internet

concept

There is an inordinate amount of information on the Internet. Being able to find what you want will help make your experience surfing the Web more productive and enjoyable. With the Search Explorer bar of Internet Explorer, you can retrieve and display a list of Web sites related to your topic of interest and then load the actual Web pages into the same window.

do it!

Use the Search Companion to find a Web site that offers used car listings.

1. Click [Search] on the Standards Buttons toolbar of the Internet Explorer window. The Search Companion will be displayed in the left panel of the browser window (Figure 3-6).

2. In the text box displayed in the left section of the browser window, type "used cars" (include the quotes). Enclosing the phrase in quotation marks instructs the search engine to treat the words you enter as a single unit and only search for pages that contain used and cars next to each other in that order. If the keywords are not enclosed in quotation marks, the search will return any pages that simply contain either word.

3. Click [Search] in the Search Companion. The MSN search engine lists links to the Web pages that will most likely satisfy your needs, determined by factors such as proximity of the words to each other and to the top of the page.

4. Click the link Used Car Research from the list of results to visit that page. The site will load in the right panel, as shown in Figure 3-7.

5. To view the page in the entire window, click [Search] on the Standard Buttons toolbar. This will hide the Search Companion.

more

Once you click a link in Internet Explorer, the link will change color so that you know you have already visited it. This is very helpful when you are working with a list of links such as that in the Search Explorer bar. Most searches will return more than 10 results. If the first 10 do not satisfy your needs, you will find a link below them that allows you to view the next set of links that match your search criteria. Most search engines are only case-sensitive with uppercase letters. For example, a search for Bugs Bunny will return sites relating to the cartoon character, while a search on bugs bunny will result in a list of sites on insects and rabbits as well.

Windows XP

Figure 3-6 Internet Explorer's Search Companion

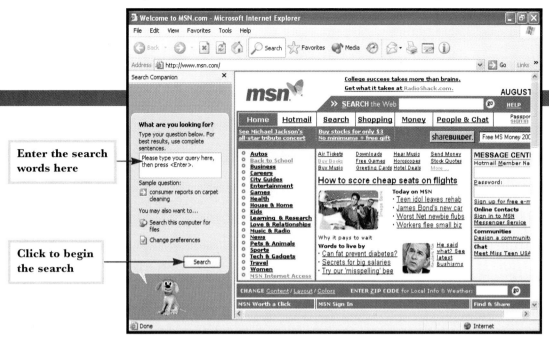

Enter the search words here

Click to begin the search

Figure 3-7 Using search results

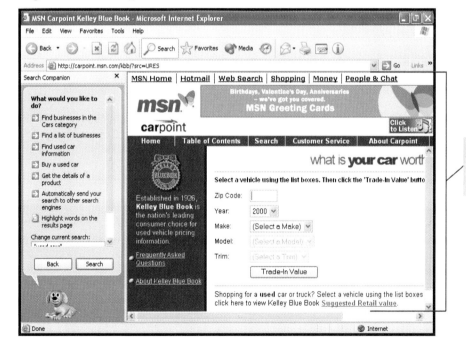

Right panel displays selected Web page

Practice

Use the Search Explorer bar to find Web pages that will allow you to consult airline flight schedules. Then follow one of the links produced by your search.

skill | Creating Favorites

concept

Internet Explorer allows you to make direct links or shortcuts to your favorite Internet sites so that you may revisit them easily without having to remember long URLs. This also is known as bookmarking. The Favorites menu offers several options for adding, organizing, and managing your favorite sites. Shortcuts to frequently visited sites also may be placed on the Links toolbar, on the desktop, or in a folder on your hard drive.

do it!

Create a Favorite for a search engine, search for a site that contains a local weather forecast, and then place a shortcut on the Links toolbar.

1. Click inside the Address text box to select its contents.

2. Type www.excite.com to replace the current URL. Then press [Enter]. Internet Explorer automatically adds the protocol http://, and the Excite search engine/Web guide loads into the browser window.

3. Click Favorites on the Menu bar, then click Add to Favorites. The Add Favorite dialog box will appear, as shown in Figure 3-8.

4. Click [OK] to create the favorite with the default settings and close the dialog box. The shortcut to the Excite page will be added to your Favorites list.

5. Open the Favorites menu to see that your shortcut is there. Then click the Favorites menu title again to close the menu.

6. Click in Excite's search text box to place an insertion point there.

7. Type +weather +[the name of your city]. This instructs the search engine to look for sites that contain both of the words. If the plus signs had been omitted, sites containing either of the words, but not necessarily both, would be found.

8. Click [Search] to initiate the search.

9. Look through the list of matches, using the vertical scroll bar to advance the page as you go. Visit the sites that appear relevant to the original search objective by clicking their hyperlinks. Look for a site with a good local forecast. Click [Back] on the Standard Buttons toolbar to return to the search results page to view additional found sites. When you find a site you like, stay there.

10. If your Links toolbar is just visible at the right end of the Address bar, drag the Links toolbar straight down so that it occupies its own row.

11. Click the Internet Explorer page icon 🔲 in the Address text box and then drag it down to the Links toolbar. As you drag, the pointer will appear as an arrow with the shortcut arrow icon 🔲 attached. An I-beam pointer | will appear in the Links toolbar indicating the place where the new favorite will be created (only when you are between buttons or at the ends of the toolbar). When you release the mouse button, a button for the current site will appear on the Links toolbar (Figure 3-9). A favorite also will be added to the Links folder on the Favorites menu. You can drag any link on a page to create a shortcut just as you would to create it with the Internet Explorer page icon. Dragging a link to the Links toolbar, for example, will create a shortcut for that link rather than the currently displayed Web page.

more

The favorites that you create will appear not only on the Favorites menu in the Internet Explorer window, but also everywhere the Favorites folder is accessible, such as from the Favorites menu on the My Computer and My Documents windows. This can include the Start menu and the Favorites menu in any system window. The favorites that you create also will be added to the Favorites Explorer Bar, which can be left open while you browse the Web for quick access to your shortcuts.

Figure 3-8 Add Favorites dialog box

Default favorite name taken from the page title

Click to create favorite on different level of Favorites hierarchy

Figure 3-9 Adding a favorite to the Links toolbar

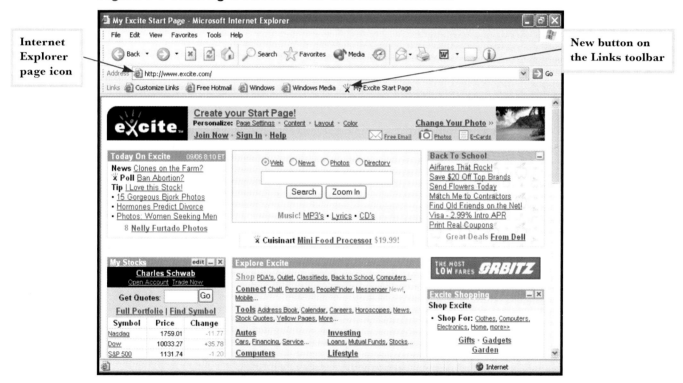

Internet Explorer page icon

New button on the Links toolbar

Practice

Add www.amazon.com to your Favorites folder. Then add the link www.usps.gov to your Links toolbar.

skill | Managing Favorites

concept

Without sufficient attention to organization, a long list of favorites can be difficult to manage. By editing and grouping favorites, you can make them much easier to use. Internet Explorer allows you to create or delete folders on the Favorites menu, redistribute favorites among the folders, and rename favorites and the folders that hold them.

do it!

Create a new folder that will store your personal favorites, move a favorite into that folder, and then rename the favorite.

1. Click Favorites on the Menu bar, then click the Organize Favorites command. The Organize Favorites dialog box will open, as shown in Figure 3-10.

2. Click [Create Folder]. A new folder will be created in the Organize Favorites dialog box with its default name selected, ready to be changed.

3. Type Search Engines, then press [Enter]. The name of the folder will change, and the folder will remain selected.

4. Click the favorite you created for the Excite page in the last skill to select it. Notice that its properties are displayed at the bottom of the dialog box.

5. Click [Move to Folder...]. The Browse for Folder dialog box will be displayed.

6. Click the Search Engines folder you created to select it as the destination folder to which you will move the Excite favorite. When you select the folder, it will be selected and appear as an open folder, as shown in Figure 3-11.

7. Click [OK]. This will close the Browse for Folder dialog box and move the selected favorite. ⬥ You can use the drag-and-drop technique to move favorites from folder to folder inside the Organize Favorites dialog box.

8. Click the Search Engine folder to show its contents in the dialog box.

9. Click the Excite favorite to select it.

10. Click [Rename]. The name of the favorite will be selected.

11. Type Excite.com, then press [Enter] to rename the favorite, as shown in Figure 3-12. ⬥ You can also right-click an item to rename it.

12. Click [Close] to close the Organize Favorites dialog box.

more

The Favorites folder is the default location for creating shortcuts. If you click the Create in button, the Add Favorite dialog box will expand, showing you a pane that displays the current Favorites hierarchy. This pane is similar to the Browse for Folder dialog box, as shown in Figure 3-11. From the pane where the Favorites hierarchy is displayed, you can select the folder in which you wish to create the new favorite, thereby eliminating the process of moving it later.

Figure 3-10 Organize Favorites dialog box

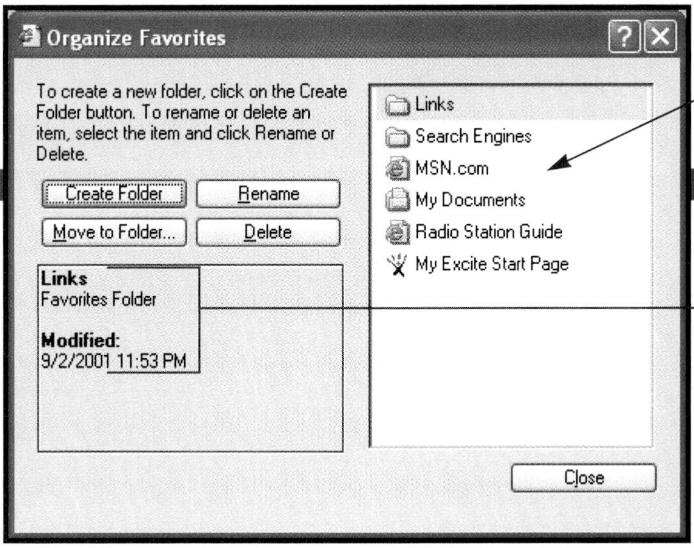

Items on the top level of Favorites hierarchy

Properties of the selected folder appear here

Figure 3-11 Moving a favorite

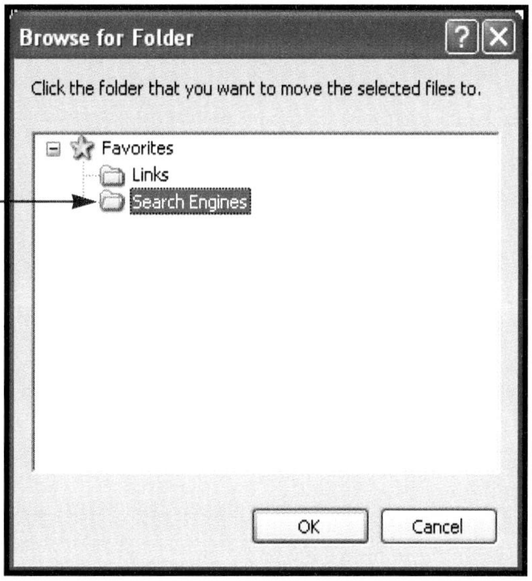

Destination folder selected

Figure 3-12 Renaming a favorite

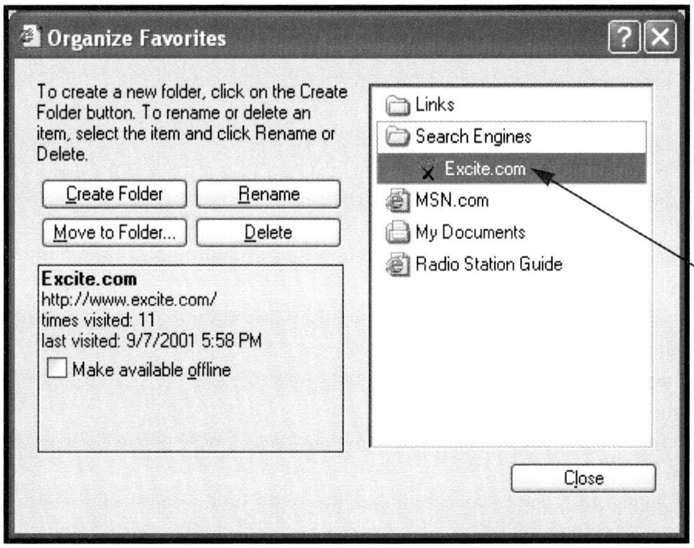

Relocated and renamed favorite

Practice

Create a new Favorites folder called Online Shopping. Then move the Amazon.com favorite into this new folder.

skill | Printing a Web Page

concept

In general, Web pages are designed primarily for on-screen viewing. However, there may be occasions when you want to print a paper copy of a particular page. In fact, most online shopping sites suggest that you print your transaction page when you have completed a purchase so you can keep it for your records. Additionally, many software and hardware manufacturers provide installation instructions online that you can print and then follow as you install new software.

do it!

Use Internet Explorer's Print command to print a paper copy of a Web page.

1. Use the favorite you created earlier to go to www.excite.com.

2. Click File on the Menu bar to open the File menu, and then click the Print command. The Print dialog box, shown in Figure 3-13, appears with the General tab in front.

3. If your computer is connected to more than one printer, you can select the icon for the printer you wish to use in the Select Printer section of the dialog box.

4. When the correct printer is selected, click ⬚ Print ⬚ to print the Web page with the default settings. Your printer should print one copy of the page, but it might require more than one piece of paper to do so since Web pages are not necessarily designed to fit on standard paper sizes.

more

Even though Web pages are designed for the screen rather than paper, you do have some control over how a page will appear when you print it. Before you print, open the File menu and choose the Page Setup command. The Page Setup dialog box will open, as shown in Figure 3-14. In the Paper section of the dialog box, you can select the size of the paper you are printing on and how it is being fed into the machine. In the Headers and Footers section, you can specify text that will appear at the top and bottom of the printed page. The Orientation section determines whether the page will be printed like a traditional document (Portrait), or so that the left-to-right length of the document is greater than its top-to-bottom length (Landscape).

Some Web pages are divided into separate components known as frames. When you print a page that uses frames, the Print frames section on the Options tab of the Print dialog box will be active. From here, you can choose to print the page exactly as it appears on your screen or print a single frame that you select. Just below the Print frames section are two check boxes. The first instructs your printer to print all documents that are linked to the one you are currently printing while the second simply adds a table of these links to the end of the printout. These items are also available on the Print dialog box's Options tab.

You can bypass the Print dialog box by clicking on the Print button 🖨 on the Standard Buttons toolbar. Your document will be printed using the current print settings. The Print dialog box's Collate option allows you to print complete sets of a document in page order when you are printing more than one copy of a multiple-page document.

Figure 3-13 Print dialog box

Double-click icon to set up another printer on your system

Use this section to specify which pages of document to print

Click arrows to change number of copies to be printed

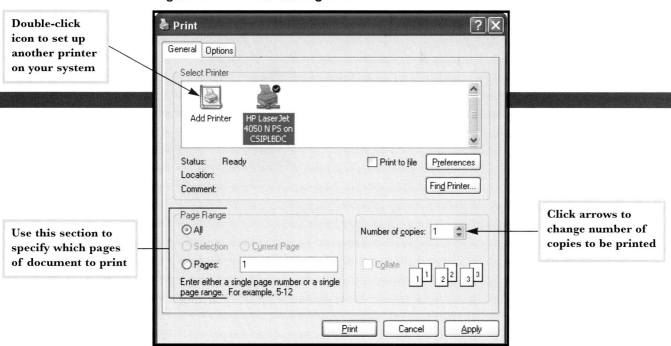

Figure 3-14 Page Setup dialog box

Document preview reflects current dialog box settings

Set page orientation here

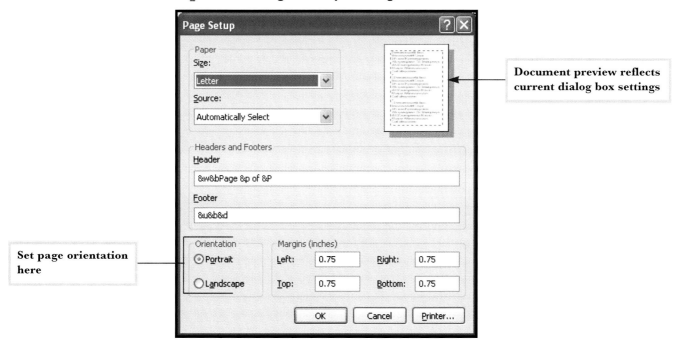

Practice

Print a copy of your browser's home page with the Orientation set to Landscape.

shortcuts

Function	Button/Mouse	Menu	Keyboard
Stop loading page		Click View, then click Stop	[Esc]
Refresh page		Click View, then click Refresh	[F5]
Go to browser's home page		Click View, then point to Go To, then click Home Page	[Alt]+[Home]
Access mail from IE		Click Tools, then point to Mail and News	[Alt]+[T], [M]
Print current page		Click File, then click Print	[Ctrl]+[P]
Browse back	Back	Click View, then point to Go To, then click Back	[Alt]+[Left arrow]
Browse forward		Click View, then point to Go To, then click Forward	[Alt]+[Right arrow]

A. Identify Key Features

Name the items indicated by callouts in Figure 3-15.

Figure 3-15 Internet Explorer's Standard Buttons toolbar

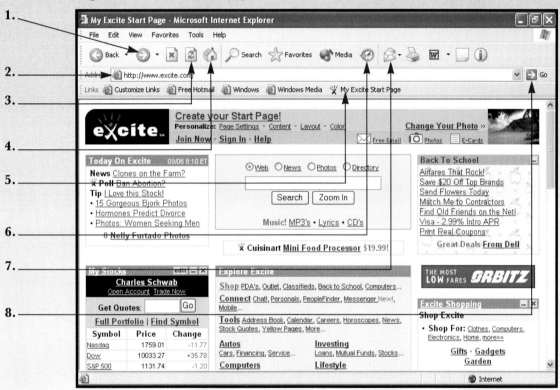

1.
2.
3.
4.
5.
6.
7.
8.

B. Select the Best Answer

9. Click this to go to your browser's home page

10. Dialog box that allows you to create shortcuts to pages you visit frequently

11. Language used to write Web pages

12. Protocol used to transfer data over the Web

13. Dialog box that allows you to relocate a favorite

14. An individual component of a Web page that can be printed independently

15. A Page Setup option

16. Reloads the current page in the browser window

17. Allows you to create buttons for your favorites

a. Refresh button

b. Home button

c. Links toolbar

d. Orientation

e. HTTP

f. Browse for Folder

g. HTML

h. Add Favorite dialog box

i. Frame

quiz (continued)

C. Complete the Statement

18. A document's address on the Web is also known as its:

a. EARL

b. IRL

c. URL

d. HTTP

19. To help you find documents on the Web, you should use:

a. Internet Explorer's Search Companion

b. Windows XP Help facility

c. Outlook Express

d. Internet Explorer's Favorites Explorer Bar

20. All of the following are popular search engines except:

a. AltaVista

b. MSN Search

c. Outlook

d. Excite

21. The Web runs on a:

a. Linear platform

b. Decreasing number of hosts

c. Government regulated network

d. Client-server model

22. You can create a favorite for the current page by dragging and dropping the:

a. Favorites button

b. Internet Explorer page icon

c. Favorites Explorer bar

d. Current URL

23. Clicking on the Print button causes your document to be printed without:

a. Margins

b. Headers and Footers

c. The appearance of the Print dialog box

d. Frames

24. To change your browser's home page, choose the Internet Options command from the:

a. Tools menu

b. File menu

c. Home Page dialog box

d. Favorites menu

25. The mouse pointer changes to a hand with a pointing finger to indicate that:

a. The page you requested has finished loading

b. The link you are pointing to is a favorite

c. You must wait until the page finishes loading

d. You are pointing to an active link

interactivity

Build Your Skills

1. Open Internet Explorer and practice navigating the Web:

   a. Launch Internet Explorer.

   b. If your browser is not set to open to www.msn.com, go to the Web site now.

   c. Look for a link to microsoft.com and click it to go to Microsoft's home page.

   d. Click the Privacy Policy link near the bottom of the page.

   e. Go back to Microsoft's home page.

   f. Return to the Privacy Policy page.

2. Visit a Web page whose address you have entered manually:

   a. Use the Address bar to visit http://www.cnn.com.

   b. Stop the page before it finishes loading.

   c. Refresh the page.

3. Use the Search Explorer bar to find Web sites about your home town and store them as favorites:

   a. Activate the Search Explorer bar.

   b. Conduct a search for Web pages that relate to your home town.

   c. Follow the links generated by the search until you have found two or three that you like.

   d. Add these sites to your Favorites list.

4. Create a new Favorites folder and move existing favorites into it:

   a. Open the Organize Favorites dialog box.

   b. Create a new folder named [Your Hometown] Links.

   c. Move the favorites you created in the previous question into the new folder.

   d. Rename the new folder so that its name is just that of your hometown and does not include the word Links.

interactivity (continued)

Build Your Skills (continued)

5. Print a Web page with Landscape orientation:

   a. Direct your Web browser to one of the home town favorites you created above.

   b. Open the Page Setup dialog box from the File menu.

   c. Change the page orientation from Portrait to Landscape, then click OK.

   d. Open the Print dialog box.

   e. Print two copies of the current page.

Problem Solving Exercises

1. Search the Web for information on guitars and guitar instruction. When you find helpful sites, be sure to bookmark them in appropriately named folders. Create at least four different folders to house favorites for the sites you find. Some categories you might use are Guitar Sales, Online Instruction, and Chords and Tablature.

2. As a sales representative, you fit the title of business traveler perfectly. Fortunately, the World Wide Web can do wonders for your travel expenses. Various Web sites can now assist you in finding the cheapest air fares and hotel rooms available. Use the skills you have learned in this lesson to find at least three such sites on the Web. Add each site to your Favorites list, create a new Favorites folder named Travel Savings, and then move the favorites you have added into the new folder.

3. As the Director of Human Resources at a large accounting firm, it is important for you to stay on top of the issues that affect the workforce. Chief among these is health insurance. Your approach to this topic is twofold. You like to keep one eye on what the insurance companies are saying about themselves and the other on what the watchdogs are saying about the insurance companies. Use your Web skills to find the Web sites of major health care providers. Store the home pages of these sites in a Favorites folder named Health Care Providers. Then focus your Web search on pages that provide reviews of, or news about, particular health care companies. Organize these pages in a Favorites folder named Health Care Reviews. Print the page that offers the best summary of current health insurance issues.

4. Your department is in the market for a new color laser printer. You have been chosen to research the purchase, and recommend a printer to your boss. Use your Web skills to find out as much as you can about four top-of-the-line color laser printers. You should search for the Web sites of companies that actually manufacture and sell the printers as well as independent reviews of printers. When you find a page on a manufacturer's site, save it as a favorite in a folder named Printers. When you find a page that reviews the performance of a particular printer or printers, save it as a favorite in a folder named Printer Reviews. After studying the four candidates you have found, select the printer that you think will best suit your department's needs (a high output rate, low maintenance, network ready, reliable service program). Create a button on the Links toolbar for the Web page of the printer you have chosen.

Using E-mail and News with Outlook Express

One of the most popular services made available by the Internet is electronic mail, or e-mail. Electronic mail allows you to send messages from your computer to another computer just as you would send a letter from your mailbox to someone else's mailbox. Windows XP comes with its own e-mail program, called Outlook Express, that gives you the ability to write, receive, and store messages. Imagine how much time would be required for you to complete an exchange of correspondences by regular mail. It might take more than a week for your letter to reach its recipient and the reply to find its way back to you. With Outlook Express, you can complete this exchange in a matter of minutes.

Outlook Express is not just a carrier for your messages. You can also use it to create an address book and organize your messages. Convenient features allow you to reply directly to a specific message, or forward a message you have received to additional parties. More often than not, an e-mail message consists solely of text. However, it is also possible to attach entire files to a message and embed objects such as pictures and hyperlinks in the body of a message. Since Outlook Express is capable of reading HTML documents, you can compose a message that functions like a Web page.

Outlook Express also serves as a gateway to one of the Internet's other widely used areas: newsgroups. A newsgroup is an electronic bulletin board where users from all over the world post messages on a particular subject. Thousands of newsgroups covering a wide range of subjects exist on a variety of news servers. You can use Outlook Express to read and participate in newsgroups. You will find that many of them provide lively and informative discussions.

Lesson Goal:

In this lesson, you will learn how to start Outlook Express, send e-mails, receive and respond to e-mails, and organize e-mails. You will also be able to create an address book, subscribe to a newsgroup, and post articles to a newsgroup.

skill | Starting Outlook Express

concept

Starting the Outlook Express (OE) program is just like starting any other program. You can launch Outlook Express from the Start menu, the Quick Launch toolbar, a desktop icon, or from a window that contains the executable file of Outlook Express. In order for Outlook Express to function properly, however, you must have both a valid Internet connection and a valid e-mail account. You can set these up by running the Internet Connection Wizard of Windows XP, which you may have already done. More than likely, your instructor or system administrator has done this for you and can provide you with your user name and password. This skill assumes that your e-mail account is in order and your computer is connected to the Internet properly.

do it !

Start Outlook Express and explore the Outlook Express settings.

1. Click █ start , and then click E-Mail on the Start menu. The Outlook Express window is displayed.

2. Click the Maximize button ▣ , if necessary, to maximize the window. The window should now resemble Figure 4-1.

3. Click Tools on the Menu bar, then click the Options command. The Options dialog box is displayed to the General tab. This dialog box provides you with added information on the Outlook Express settings.

4. Click ▭ OK ▭ . The dialog box will close.

more

Like many applications, Outlook Express has its own Menu bar and toolbar. The toolbar will change depending on which area of the program you are using. The lower part of the window is divided into two panels. The left panel lists subfolders of the Outlook Express message folder. See Table 4-1 for descriptions of the subfolders' functions. ◣◆◢ If you click on Go to msn on the top right corner of the right pane of Outlook Express's main page, your Web browser will launch and open to the home page of msn.com.

When you click a mailto: link on a Web page, Outlook Express will launch automatically. It will also launch if you click your browser's Mail button ▨▾ on the Standard Buttons toolbar.

Figure 4-1 Outlook Express window

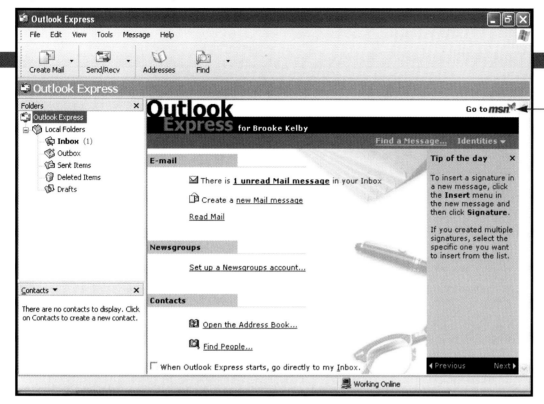

Click to launch Internet Explorer and open the msn Home page

Table 4-1 Outlook Express subfolders

Folder	Function
Inbox	Holds the messages you have received
Outbox	Holds the completed messages you intend to send
Sent Items	Stores a copy of each message you send
Deleted Items	Stores the deleted messages
Drafts	Stores messages you have composed and saved but are not ready to send

skill | Sending an E-mail

concept

For many businesses, government agencies, and academic institutions, e-mail has become the preferred tool for important communications. Its speed and ease of use and organization gives it a distinct advantage over alternative forms of communication. The first step in sending an e-mail message is composition. Outlook Express provides a specialized and user-friendly window from which you can address, compose, and send your messages.

do it!

Open a new message window, address and compose a message, and then send the message.

1. Click [Create Mail] on the Toolbar. The New Message window will appear, as shown in Figure 4-2, with a blinking insertion point in the To field. You will be sending this first message to your own e-mail address so that you familiarize yourself with sending and receiving e-mail. To enhance the appearance of your messages, you can apply graphical Stationery templates to them. When creating a new message, click the arrow on the right edge of [Create Mail] and select a Stationery template from the menu.

2. Type your e-mail address into the To field, for instance Bkelby@azimuth-interactive.com. If you do not have a mail account, ask your instructor or system administrator for it.

3. The next line of the addressing section can be used to send courtesy copies and blind courtesy copies of your message to other recipients. This line is not necessary for this Skill. Click the Subject text box. The text in this field acts as a label describing the purpose or contents of the message, and will be one of the first things the message's recipient sees.

4. Type Testing 1-2-3 as the subject of your message. Notice that the window's title bar now contains the subject you typed.

5. Press [Tab]. The insertion point will move to the composition section of the window. This is where you type the actual text of your message.

6. Type If I am reading this, I have sent e-mail successfully!. Your message window should now resemble the one in Figure 4-3 (the window in the figure is maximized).

7. Click [Send] to send the message and close the message window. The message has been sent to the mail server, which will send it to the chosen address, (yours in this case) effectively rerouting it to your e-mail account.

(continued on WN 4.6)

Figure 4-2 New Message window

Enter e-mail
address of the
recipient here

Specify subject of
the message here

Enter the message
text here

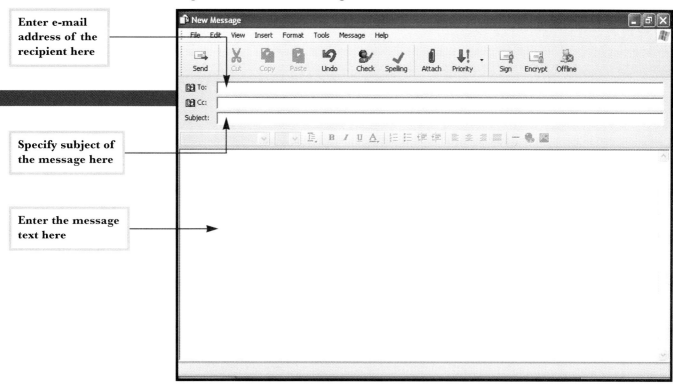

Figure 4-3 Completed message

Click Send
to transmit
the message

Message text

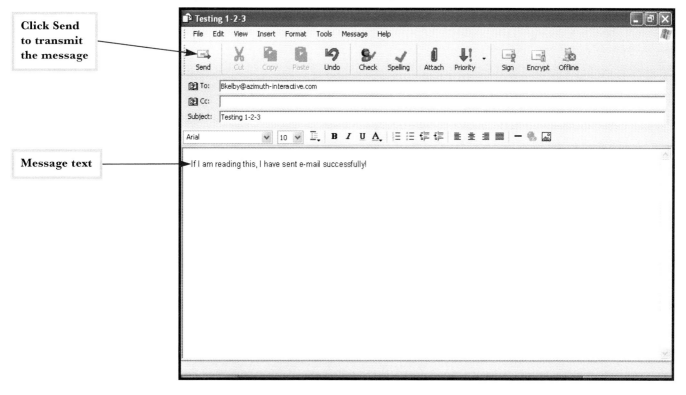

skill Sending an E-mail (continued)

more Outlook Express is an HTML enabled e-mail client. This means that the messages you create are translated into HTML (hypertext markup language), the language used to write Web pages. HTML enabled mail programs allow you to add formatting to your correspondences. You may have noticed that as soon as you clicked in the message composition area of the New Message window, the Formatting toolbar above it became active. For descriptions of some of the features offered on the Formatting toolbar see Figure 4-4. Using this toolbar, or the Format menu, you can change the font, size, and color of your text, create bulleted and numbered lists, italicize, bold, and underline words for emphasis, and even insert a picture to create your own stationery.

You can send entire files by attaching them to an e-mail message. This is a convenient way to share data with friends or co-workers in remote locations. To include a file in a message, maximize the window and click 📎 on the message window's toolbar. Navigate to the location where the file you want to attach is stored, as shown in Figure 4-5. Then select the file in the contents window. Finally, click [Attach] to close the dialog box. Any files you attach will be displayed in the Attach box, as shown in Figure 4-6. When you e-mail a file to someone, it is common courtesy to include details about the file such as its size and type in the text of your message. A paper clip icon 📎 preceding the message, also indicates that a message you have received contains an attachment.

Outlook Express can use the spelling check feature to check your e-mail messages for spelling errors. To perform a spelling check on your e-mail before you send it, open the Tools menu in the message window and then click the Spelling command. If your message has any word that does not appear in the dictionary, the Spelling dialog box will be displayed. This dialog box will provide you with suggestions as an alternative to the word. You also can activate the spelling check by pressing the [F7] key on the keyboard.

Numbering
and Bullets
buttons

Align Left, Center,
Align Right, and
Justify buttons

Font
box

Figure 4-4 Formatting toolbar

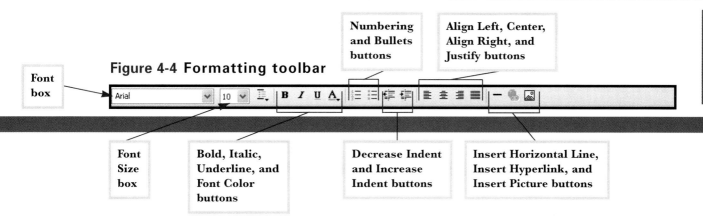

Font
Size
box

Bold, Italic,
Underline, and
Font Color
buttons

Decrease Indent
and Increase
Indent buttons

Insert Horizontal Line,
Insert Hyperlink, and
Insert Picture buttons

Figure 4-5 Insert Attachment dialog box

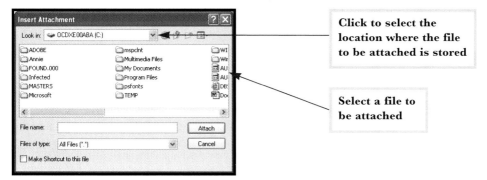

Click to select the
location where the file
to be attached is stored

Select a file to
be attached

Figure 4-6 File attached to the message

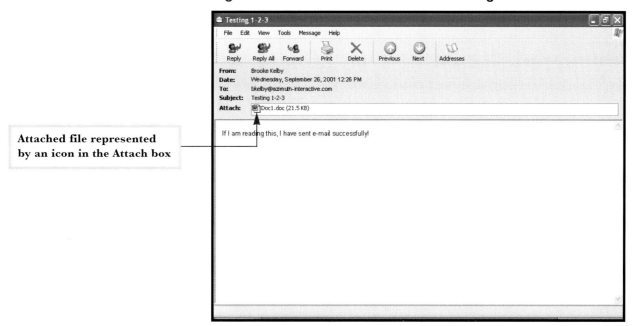

Attached file represented
by an icon in the Attach box

Practice

Compose a new message and send it to a friend.

skill | Receiving and Responding to an E-mail

concept

E-mail that is sent to you is stored on your mail server until you retrieve your messages. When you download your messages, they are transferred from the server to your Inbox so that you can read them. Once you receive a message, you can leave it in your Inbox, move it to another folder, delete it, reply to it, or forward it.

do it!

Retrieve the message you sent to yourself from your mail server, reply to it, and then forward it to another address.

1. Click ☒ on the Toolbar. Outlook Express empties your Outbox if there are any messages waiting in it, and retrieves any messages that are waiting for you on your mail server. The number of new messages you have or the number of unread messages is displayed next to the Inbox in the Folders List on the left side of the window, shown in Figure 4-7. Whenever a folder contains unread messages, the folder name will appear in bold type. E-mail is very fast, but not necessarily instantaneous. If the message you sent in the previous skill has not arrived yet, wait a few minutes and click ☒ again.

2. Click Inbox in the Folders List to display the contents of your Inbox in the right panel of the Outlook Express window. ◖●▶ You could also click the Read Mail or the 2 unread Mail links in the right pane to open the Inbox.

3. When the Inbox is displayed, it is divided into 2 panes (see Figure 4-8). The upper pane displays the message list. This message list contains the summary information or headers, for all of the messages in the Inbox. Headers for unread messages will be listed in bold type. The Preview Pane displays the actual message text for the header that is selected in the message list. Your Inbox may contain more than one message. If the message you sent yourself does not appear in the Preview Pane, click on its header in the message list to display it there.

4. Often, when you receive a message, you will want to reply directly to the sender regarding the same subject. To send such a response, double-click the message you received and click ☒ on the Toolbar in the message window that opens. A customized message window like the one shown in Figure 4-9 will open. The To text box is already filled in with the name or address of the person to whom you are replying (in this case it is your own because you are replying to yourself). The Subject line has already been completed as well with the subject of the message you received preceded by the abbreviation Re. You may edit text, but that often defeats the purpose of using the Reply command. The insertion point appears at the top of the message composition area so that you can compose your reply. Notice also that the original message is quoted at the bottom of the composition area as a reference.

(continued on WN 4.10)

Figure 4-7 Receiving mail

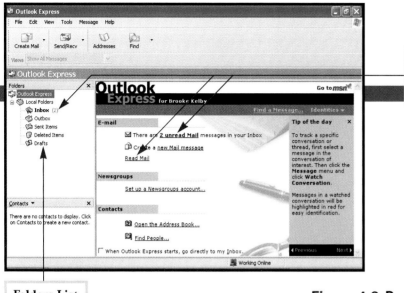

Click any of the three locations to display the contents of your Inbox

Folders List

Figure 4-8 Previewing messages in the Inbox

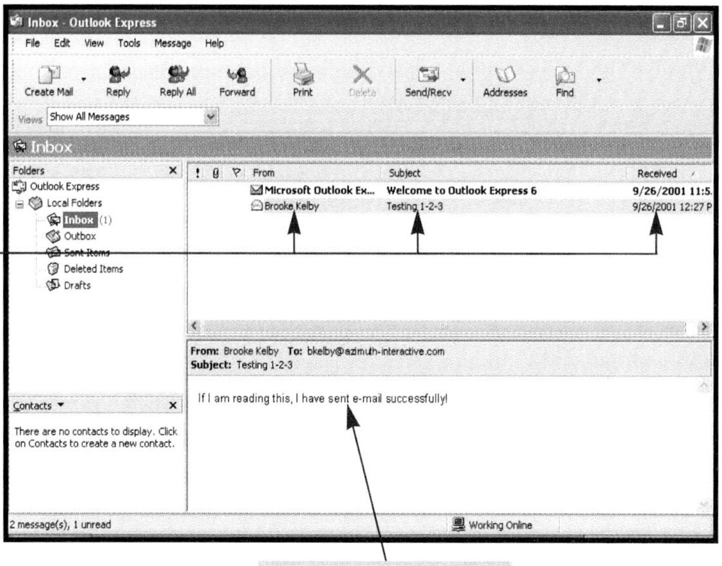

Header information includes message sender's name, message subject and the date on which the message is received

Selected message in the Preview Pane

Figure 4-9 Composing a reply in a message window

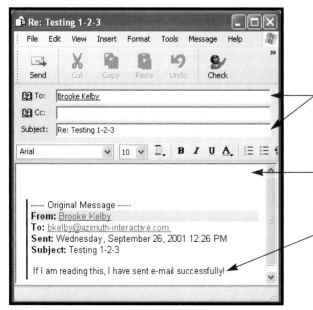

To and Subject text boxes are completed automatically

Add the reply text here

Original message quoted at bottom of the reply mail

skill Receiving and Responding to an E-mail (continued)

do it!

5. Type I have just learned how to reply to an e-mail message!

6. Click [Send]. The window closes and your reply is sent. The message to which you replied should still be selected in the Inbox.

7. Another useful Outlook Express feature is the Forward command, which enables you to pass a message you have received to another address without having to retype or even copy the message. Select the message you want to forward and click [Forward] on the Toolbar. A message window will appear, this time with the Subject line and the message composition area already filled in. The insertion point will be on the To line. You must enter the e-mail address to which you are forwarding the message.

8. Obtain the e-mail address of a friend or co-worker and type it on the To line.

9. When you forward a message, you can add your own text to the existing message. Click above the original message in the composition area to place the insertion point there. Then type I am forwarding this message to you to practice my e-mail skills. The new message window should resemble Figure 4-10.

10. Click [Send] to send the message.

more

It is not uncommon to receive a message that has been sent to several people in addition to you. In this instance, you may want to send a reply to everyone involved in the correspondence, not just the author of the original message. To do this, click [Reply All] instead of [Reply] on the Toolbar. When the message window appears, the To line will be filled in with the addresses of every recipient of the original message in addition to the address of the message's author. This will allow you to communicate with a number of people without having to compose multiple messages.

Figure 4-10 Forwarding a message

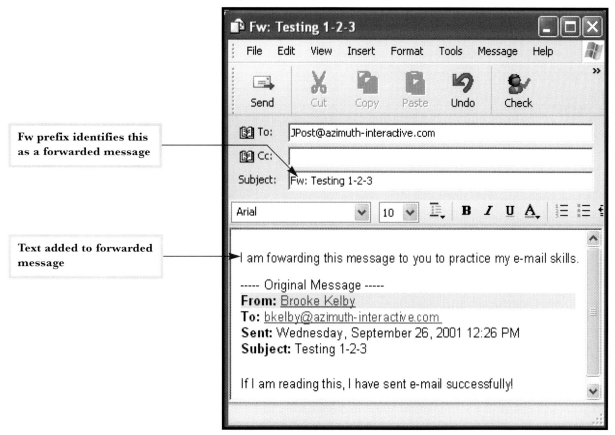

Fw prefix identifies this as a forwarded message

Text added to forwarded message

Practice

Retrieve the reply message, Re: Testing 1-2-3 you sent to yourself and then forward this message to any of your friends.

skill | Organizing E-mails

concept

As you receive more e-mails, your Inbox may begin to become overcrowded. To prevent you from having to browse through header after header or having to delete messages, Outlook Express allows you to create folders in which you can file your messages. That way, those you wish to save can be found quickly. You may create as many of these folders as you wish, and you can transfer messages from one folder to another easily.

do it!

Create a folder in which you can store e-mail messages that you send to yourself, and then move a message into the new folder.

1. Click File on the Menu bar. Point to Folder, and then select the New command from the submenu that appears. The Create Folder dialog box opens with the insertion point in the Folder name text box.

2. Type From Me as the name of the new folder, as shown in Figure 4-11.

3. Click Local Folders in the folder list panel of the Create Folder dialog box to select it as the folder in which the new folder will be created.

4. Click OK. A new folder will appear in the Folders List, as shown in Figure 4-12.

5. Right-click the header of the first message you sent to yourself, Testing 1-2-3 and then click the Move to Folder command from the shortcut menu. The Move dialog box is displayed.

6. The new folder, From Me, is selected by default as the destination folder for the selected message, (see Figure 4-13). Click OK.

7. Click the From Me folder in the Folders List to display its contents in the right pane. Confirm that the message has been moved.

more

You can create subfolders within folders to organize your messages more thoroughly. To do so, in the Create Folder dialog box simply select the folder in which you wish to create a new subfolder, and click OK. To remove a folder that you no longer need, select it in the Folders List and press [Delete], or click the Delete button on the Toolbar—you cannot delete default folders such as Inbox. It will be moved into the Deleted Items folder, where it will be stored until this folder is emptied. You can empty the Deleted Items folder by right-clicking it, and then clicking the Empty 'Deleted Items' Folder command on the shortcut menu that appears.

It is also possible to organize the messages within a folder, sorting them by any criterion in their headers. For example, if you wish to sort the messages in your Inbox alphabetically by sender rather than by date, click the From column header button. Clicking it again will reverse the order of the sorting. To find a misplaced message, point to Find in the Edit menu and click Message in the submenu. In the Find Message dialog box, you can enter important data such as the sender, receiver, subject, or body text of the missing message, and then search individual folders for it.

Figure 4-11 Create Folder dialog box

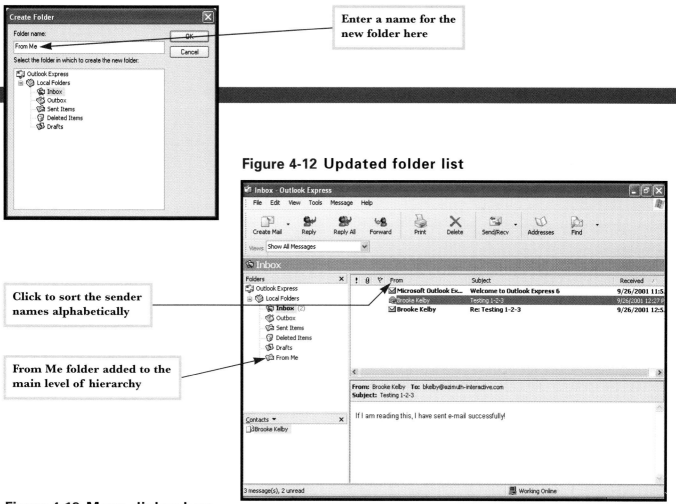

Enter a name for the new folder here

Figure 4-12 Updated folder list

Click to sort the sender names alphabetically

From Me folder added to the main level of hierarchy

Figure 4-13 Move dialog box

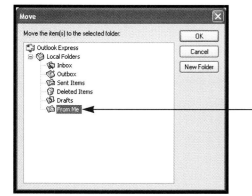

From Me selected as the destination folder for the message being moved

Practice

Create a new folder under Inbox called WinPrac. Then move the reply message that you have sent to yourself, Re: Testing 1-2-3, into the new folder.

skill | Creating an Address Book

concept

In addition to serving as your message composing, retrieving, and organizing tool, Outlook Express gives the ability to create an electronic Address Book for all of your business and personal contacts. Your Address Book contact cards can hold a wealth of information including home and business addresses, phone numbers, e-mail addresses, job titles, and relevant URLs. The Outlook Express Address Book is not just a useful reference tool. It is linked to the application, allowing you to address your e-mail messages and include important contact information in them with just a few quick clicks.

do it!

Open your Address Book, add a new contact, and then use the Address Book to address a new message.

1. Click Outlook Express in the Folders List to display the Outlook Express main page.

2. Click ⌨ on the Toolbar. The Address Book window is displayed.

3. Click 🖾 on the Address Book toolbar and then click the New Contact command on the submenu. The Properties dialog box, shown in Figure 4-14, is displayed with the Name tab activated. The insertion point is placed automatically in the First text box of the Name tab.

4. Type Brooke as the first name. Then press [Tab] twice to move the insertion point to the Last text box. Type Kelby as the last name. Notice that the dialog box's title bar has changed to take into account the information you have entered. Click in the Nickname text box and then type Brooke again.

5. Press [Tab] to move the insertion point to E-Mail Addresses text box. Then type BKelby@azimuth-interactive.com.

6. Click ⌷ Add ⌷ to make this the default e-mail address for Brooke. The e-mail address will appear in the text box below the E-Mail Addresses text box.

7. Click the Home tab and add the following contact information, pressing [Tab] to move from field to field: Street Address: 23 N. Division St.; City: Peekskill; State/Province: NY; Zip Code: 10566; Country/Region: U.S.A, Phone: (914) 555-1212. Leave the other fields blank.

8. Click ⌷ OK ⌷. The dialog box closes and the contact is added to your Address Book, as shown in Figure 4-15.

(continued on WN 4.16)

Figure 4-14 Creating a new contact in the Properties dialog box

Each tab holds a different type of contact information

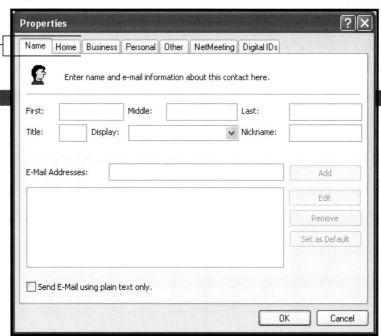

Figure 4-15 Contact added to the Address Book

Click to search your Address Book for a contact

Click the column header buttons to sort contacts by a particular category

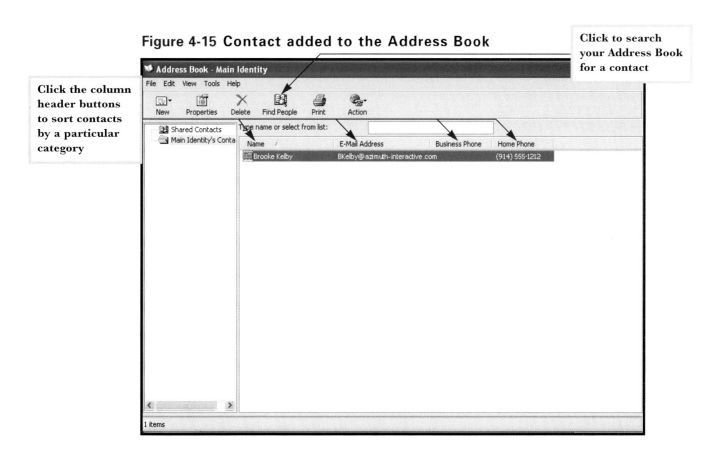

---

skill | Creating an Address Book (continued)

do it!

9. Next, you will use the Address Book to address a new e-mail message. If your Address Book has more than one contact entered, make sure the contact you just created is selected. When you select a contact, a ScreenTip box that contains all of the data you have entered for the contact will appear briefly.

10. Click ![Action] in the Address Book—Main Identity dialog box and select Send Mail from the submenu. The New Message window, addressed to the contact you selected, will open. Do not be concerned that the To line contains Brooke's name rather than her e-mail address. Outlook Express links the name to the appropriate address based on the data you provided in the Properties dialog box.

11. Click the Close button ![X] to close the New Message window without sending the message.

12. Click the Close button to close the Address Book.

more

You can create a mailing list, or group, out of selected contacts using ![New] in the Address Book—Main Identity dialog box. A group may consist of existing contacts or contacts you add as you are creating the group. This feature is especially helpful if you frequently e-mail the same set of contacts the same messages. Instead of selecting each contact from the Address Book separately, you can just select the group name. ![arrow] To view the Properties dialog box for one of your contacts, double-click the contact in the Address Book window.

If you have already opened a new message window, but still want to use your Address Book, click ![To:] in the New Message window. This will open the Select Recipients dialog box, shown in Figure 4-16. From here you can select which of your contacts will receive the message and whether they will be direct recipients, carbon copied, or blind carbon copied. The difference between the carbon copy and the blind carbon copy is that in the carbon copy, the recipient can see the e-mail addresses of all the people to whom you have copied the mail. Whereas, in the blind carbon copy the recipient cannot see the e-mail addresses of the people to whom you have copied the mail.

Figure 4-16 Select Recipients dialog box

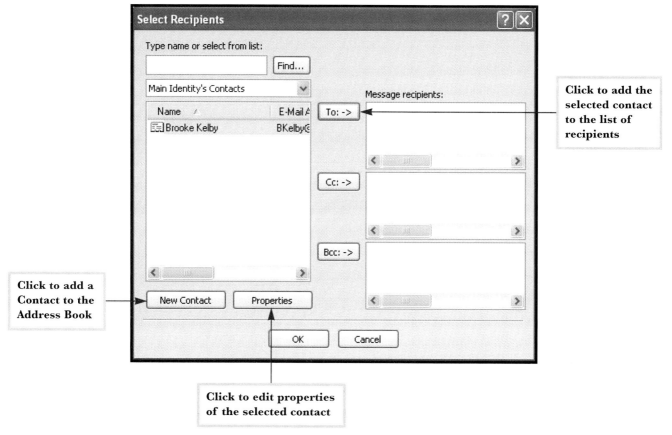

Click to add the
selected contact
to the list of
recipients

Click to add a
Contact to the
Address Book

Click to edit properties
of the selected contact

Practice

Create contacts for yourself and two friends in your Address Book. Complete as many data fields on the different tabs as you can. Select a friend from the Address Book and send an e-mail to him or her.

skill | Subscribing to a Newsgroup

concept

The User Network, or Usenet, is a network of servers connected to the Internet that holds thousands of newsgroups. A newsgroup is like an electronic bulletin board where people with similar interests can post their comments, opinions, and questions that relate to the newsgroup's subject. Newsgroup messages are similar to e-mail messages in a way that you can forward them, reply to them, and copy them to your own Outlook Express folders. Often, lengthy discussions, known as threads, develop as people respond to each other's opinions on a specific topic. You can find a newsgroup that discusses almost any subject. Some serve educational purposes while others exist solely for entertainment. Before you can access newsgroups, you must obtain a news server. In order to obtain a news server, you need to pay a certain amount to the newsgroup service providers. However, there are some news servers, which are free of cost. You can obtain the name of a free and valid news server from your instructor or network administrator and ask him/her to configure the news server. More than likely, your network administrator may have already done it for you. When your news server has been configured correctly, it will appear in the Folders List on the left side of the Outlook Express window. Then you can begin the process of searching for newsgroups that interest you.

do it!

Use Outlook Express to view articles from the newsgroup and then subscribe to the newsgroup.

1. Click the Read News hyperlink on the Outlook Express main screen to start subscribing to a newsgroup. You may receive a warning box asking if you want to make Outlook Express your default news client. If so, click [Yes].

2. A dialog box will appear prompting you to view a list of newsgroups since you are not currently subscribed to any. Click [Yes]. Outlook Express will begin downloading newsgroups from your news server. This process may take several minutes. When all newsgroups are downloaded, the Newsgroup Subscription dialog box is displayed, as shown in Figure 4-17. All of the newsgroups made available by your news server are displayed in the list box in the middle of the dialog box.

3. Type jobs in the Display newsgroups which contain text box at the top of the dialog box. Outlook Express searches through all of the newsgroups you downloaded, and displays only those that contain the word jobs in their names (see Figure 4-18).

4. Scroll down the list of newsgroups and click misc.jobs.misc to select it. If your news server does not offer this group, select a similar newsgroup.

5. Click [Go to]. The Newsgroup Subscriptions dialog box closes, and the newsgroup you selected is added below your news server in the Folders List. Additionally, the headers for the articles contained in the newsgroup are loaded in the message list.

(continued on WN 4.20)

Figure 4-17 Newsgroup Subscriptions dialog box

Enter keywords here to search the newsgroups for specific topics

Newsgroups available on your news server are listed here.

Click to view the selected newsgroup without subscribing

Click to subscribe to the selected newsgroup

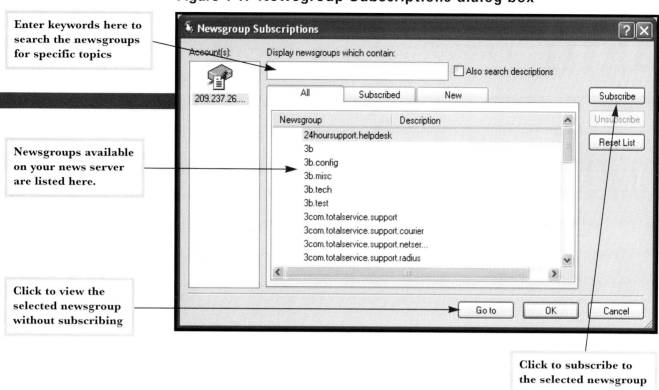

Figure 4-18 Searching for a newsgroup

Newsgroups listed here match the keyword entered in the text box above; click a newsgroup name to select it

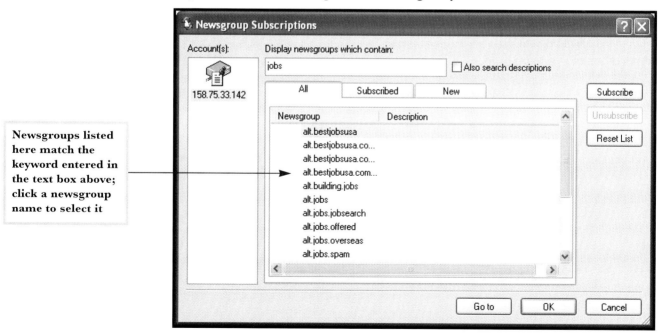

skill | Subscribing to a Newsgroup (continued)

do it!

6. Click the first header in the message list to select it. The article, which is also known as a message or post, will be displayed in the Preview Pane so you can read it, as shown in Figure 4-19. Use the vertical scroll bar to view the entire message if necessary.

7. Click another header of the newsgroups and read the accompanying message. Notice that the headers for messages you have not read are bold, while those you have read are plain text.

8. At this point, you are simply viewing a newsgroup. If you closed Outlook Express now, the newsgroup you selected would not appear on the Folders List the next time you opened the program. In order to keep it there, you must subscribe to the group. Click ⌐ on the Toolbar and then click Newsgroups from the submenu.

9. Since you already know the name of the group to which you want to subscribe, type misc.jobs.misc (or the name of the group you selected earlier) to select the group.

10. Click ⌐ Subscribe ⌐. An icon similar to 🐦 will appear preceding the newsgroup name in the Newsgroup Subscriptions dialog box, to indicate that you have subscribed to the group (Figure 4-20).

11. Click ⌐ OK ⌐ to close the dialog box and confirm your subscription. The newsgroup will now be a permanent part of your Folders List until you unsubscribe from it. The number of unread messages in the group appears in parentheses next to the group name.

more

A newsgroup's name is composed of a series of characters separated by dots. For instance, the newsgroup comp.lang.c++ contains messages relating to the computer language C++. There are several major categories into which most newsgroups fall. One of the largest and most controversial newsgroup categories is the alt (alternative) group. The alt newsgroups contain articles on an incredibly wide variety of topics such as astrology and sports. Articles in the comp (computers) discussion groups, such as comp.lang.javascript, deal with computer-related issues. Articles on Usenet itself can be found in news discussion groups such as news.newusers. The rec (recreation) groups deal with recreation, sports, and the arts. Other large categories include sci (science) for scientific and technical articles, soc (social) for articles on social and politically significant issues, and misc (miscellaneous) for articles that do not fit comfortably in the other categories.

Figure 4-19 Reading a newsgroup message

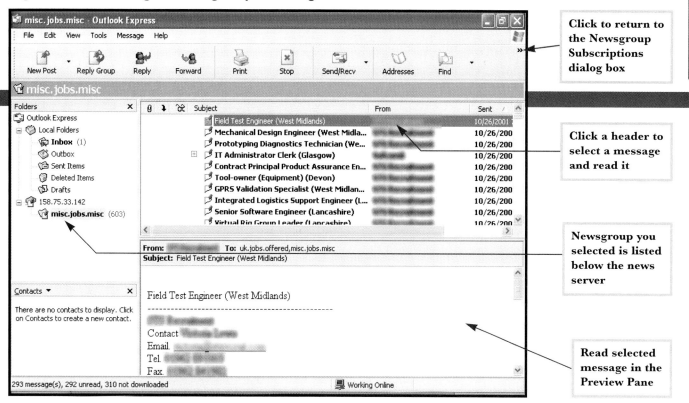

Click to return to the Newsgroup Subscriptions dialog box

Click a header to select a message and read it

Newsgroup you selected is listed below the news server

Read selected message in the Preview Pane

Figure 4-20 Subscribing to a newsgroup

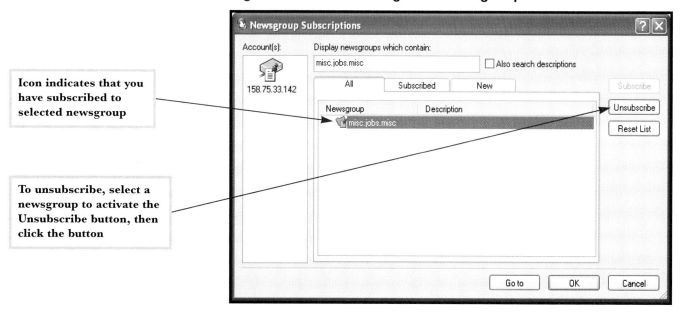

Icon indicates that you have subscribed to selected newsgroup

To unsubscribe, select a newsgroup to activate the Unsubscribe button, then click the button

Practice

Subscribe to the newsgroup alt.test.

skill | Posting to a Newsgroup

concept

Reading messages is only one part of using newsgroups. While some people choose only to read what others post, a practice known as lurking, others participate actively in their favorite newsgroups. Active participants post messages to the newsgroup. Sending a message to a newsgroup is much like sending e-mail. The greatest difference is that your messages appear in a public forum, accessible by millions, rather than in a private Inbox. Before posting to a group that interests you, it is a good idea to post a test message to make sure your copy of Outlook Express is configured correctly for newsgroups.

do it!

Post a test message to the newsgroup alt.test.

1. Subscribe to the newsgroup alt.test, if necessary.

2. Select alt.test in the Outlook Express Folders List. Do not be concerned if the newsgroup does not appear to contain any messages.

3. Click [New Post]. A message window will appear, already addressed to the newsgroup. The insertion point will be in the Subject text box.

4. Type test as the subject of the message. Then press the [Tab] key to move the insertion point to the composition area.

5. Type Testing newsgroups with Outlook Express as the body of the message. Your message should resemble the one shown in Figure 4-21.

6. Click [Send]. A dialog box may appear informing you that your message has been sent to the news server. The dialog box may not appear immediately. Press [Enter] to close the dialog box and the message window.

7. After waiting a short while, check to see that your test message has been posted on the newsgroup by selecting alt.test in your Folders List (see Figure 4-22). If you have trouble locating your post, click the From column header button to sort the messages alphabetically by sender.

more

It is usually wise to lurk on a newsgroup for a few days before you post. That way you can get a feel of what kinds of posts are welcome in that particular group. A newsgroup can have thousands of messages posted to it, but Outlook Express displays 300 messages in the Preview Pane, when you subscribe to a newsgroup. To view the remaining messages, click the related newsgroup in the Folders List. Then click Tools on the Menu bar and click Get Next 300 Headers till the time all the messages of the corresponding newsgroup are downloaded.

Figure 4-21 Composing a newsgroup message

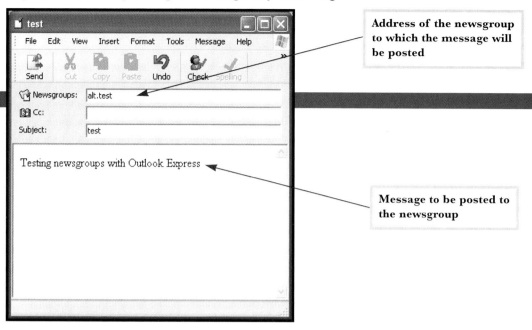

Address of the newsgroup
to which the message will
be posted

Message to be posted to
the newsgroup

Figure 4-22 Reading your test message sent to the newsgroup

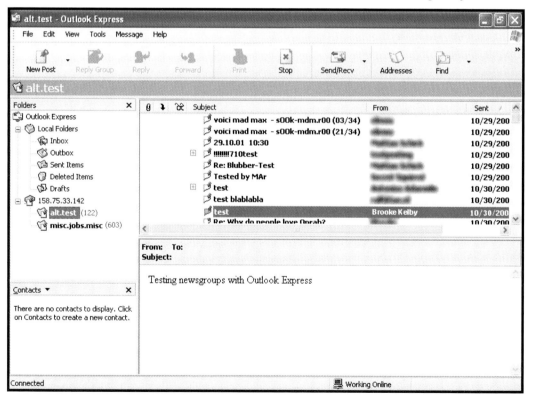

Practice

Find a newsgroup that interests you and post an appropriate message to the newsgroup.

shortcuts

Function	Button/Mouse	Menu	Keyboard
Compose a new e-mail message	Create Mail	Click File, point to New and then click New Message	[Ctrl]+[N]
Send an e-mail message	Send	Click File, then click Send Message	[Alt]+[S]
Open Inbox		Click View, click Go to Folder, then click Inbox	[Ctrl]+[Shift]+[I]
Reply to author	Reply	Click Message, then click Reply to Sender	[Ctrl]+[R]
Reply to author and all recipients	Reply All	Click Message, then click Reply to All	[Ctrl]+[Shift]+[R]
Forward message	Forward	Click Message, then click Forward	[Ctrl]+[F]
Delete the selected message	Delete	Click Edit, then click Delete	[Ctrl]+[D]
Open the Address Book	Addresses	Click Tools, then click Address Book	[Ctrl]+[Shift]+[B]
Create a new contact in the Address Book	New	Click File, then click New Contact	[Ctrl]+[N]
Create a new group in the Address Book	New	Click File, then click New Group	[Ctrl]+[G]
Compose new newsgroup message	New Post	Click File, point to New, then click News Message	[Ctrl]+[N]
Post message to newsgroup	Send	Click File, then click Send Message	[Alt]+[S]

A. Identify Key Features

Name the items indicated by callouts in Figure 4-23.

Figure 4-23 Features of a message window

1. _____

2. _____

3. _____

4. _____

5. _____

6. _____

7. _____

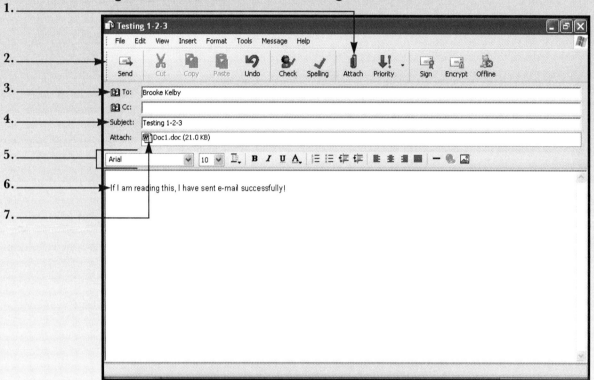

B. Select the Best Answer

8. Click this button to respond directly to a message you have received

9. Stores a copy of each message you send

10. Allows you to send a message you have received to another recipient

11. Allows you to clear your Outbox and retrieve new messages at the same time

12. Contains summary information for a particular message

13. Stores all your contact information

14. Click to access your newsgroups

15. An electronic bulletin board, or discussion group

a. Address Book

b. Forward command

c. Header

d. Newsgroup

e. Read News hyperlink

f. Reply

g. Send and Receive button

h. Sent Items folder

quiz (continued)

C. Complete the Statement

16. To send a response to a message that will be received by the author and all original recipients, click the:

a. Reply button

b. Forward button

c. Reply to All button

d. Send and Receive button

17. You can enhance your text and insert images in your messages by using the message window's:

a. Upper pane

b. Subject: line

c. Attach File button

d. Formatting Toolbar

18. A folder name displayed in bold in the Folders List indicates that the folder:

a. Has been deleted

b. Contains new or unread messages

c. Is the default folder

d. Is empty

19. New e-mail messages are transferred from the:

a. Mail server to your Inbox

b. Mail server to your Outbox

c. Inbox to the last folder you created

d. Mail server to the Move dialog box

20. When you a see a paper clip icon preceding a mail header, it means that the mail:

a. Is a reply to the mail that you had sent earlier

b. Contains no message and is a blank mail

c. Has some attachment

d. Is a forwarded mail

21. To begin adding a new contact in your address book, you need to access the:

a. Name tab

b. Business tab

c. Personal tab

d. Home tab

22. All of the following are examples of newsgroup categories with the exception of:

a. com

b. alt

c. rec

d. comp

23. The network of servers that holds newsgroups over the Internet is called:

a. The Internet Connection

b. Usenet

c. Outlook Express

d. The User Web

24. To view a newsgroup you have just selected without subscribing to it, click the:

a. Unsubscribe button

b. Properties button

c. Go to button

d. News server that contains it

interactivity

Build Your Skills

1. Launch Outlook Express and compose a new message.

   a. Start Outlook Express.

   b. Open the New Message window.

   c. Address the message to yourself using the subject TYS. The text of the message should summarize what you have learned in this lesson.

   d. Send the message.

2. Receive, reply, and forward a message.

   a. Click the Send and Receive button to retrieve the message you sent to yourself.

   b. Read the message, and then compose a reply acknowledging you received it.

   c. Forward the original TYS message to a friend, classmate, or your instructor. Add text to the original message that states why you are forwarding it.

3. Organize your messages.

   a. Create a new folder on the main level of the Outlook Express folder hierarchy called TYS.

   b. Move the TYS message you received in your Inbox to the new folder.

   c. Move the TYS folder into the Deleted Items folder.

4. Add to your Address Book.

   a. Open your Address Book.

   b. Create a new contact using the following information: First: Thomas, Middle: J., Last: Sutton, e-mail: sutton@domain.com, Company: Domain, Inc., Business Address: 1117 W. 57th Street, New York, NY 10001, Job Title: Director of Sales, Business Phone: (212) 555-1212.

   c. Compose an e-mail message to Mr. Sutton asking if his department has any job openings. Do not send the message.

5. Use Outlook Express to access newsgroups:

   a. Open the Newsgroup Subscriptions dialog box.

   b. Subscribe to two newsgroups that interest you.

   c. Read a reasonable number of articles from the newsgroups.

   d. Post an appropriate message on one of the newsgroups to which you subscribed.

interactivity (continued)

Problem Solving Exercises

1. You work for a small publishing company that recently upgraded to Windows XP. Your boss has asked you to be in charge of interoffice communications. Use Outlook Express to create a mailing list consisting of your co-workers' names and e-mail addresses so that it will be easier to send e-mail to the entire office. Name the mailing list Co-workers, and select 4 or 5 classmates to include in the group (if you are taking this course as part of your company's training program, you may use actual e-mail IDs of your co-workers). Write a generic e-mail asking the members of your office to send you more information about themselves such as home address, phone number, fax number, etc. Then update your address book as you receive the new information.

2. You will receive several pieces of e-mail as a result of the exercises carried out in this lesson. In order to keep your Inbox organized, you should have a folder in which you can store the replies. Create a subfolder in your Inbox named Office Mail. As you receive mail from your co-workers, move the messages into the new folder.

3. Subscribe to a newsgroup that discusses cartoons. Read several messages to get a feel of the group. Then, participate in a discussion by replying to a post.

Customizing Windows XP

Windows XP allows you to customize your environment to suit your personal needs and preferences. You can adjust the settings that affect the function and appearance of the Windows operating system, as well as settings that affect the input and output devices such as the mouse and printers.

skills

* Customizing the Mouse Settings
* Setting the Date and Time
* Applying a Screen Saver
* Changing the System Appearance and Display Settings
* Adding Wallpaper to the Desktop
* Working with Themes
* Changing the Size of Objects and Text
* Adding Programs to the Start Menu
* Creating and Using Taskbar Toolbars
* Adding Web Content to the Desktop

Most Windows features can be adjusted using the Control Panel. The Control Panel window contains a number of options that represent various components of the Windows XP operating system. The Printers and Other Hardware option in the Control Panel window permits you to change the settings of the printer or printers connected to your computer. By adding a Web page to the desktop, you can take full advantage of Windows XP's Web capabilities as it allows you to integrate live Web content into your desktop.

Learning how to manage the features available in Windows XP can ensure that you spend your time in front of the computer working comfortably and efficiently.

Lesson Goal:

In this lesson, you will learn to customize mouse settings, date and time settings, system appearance, and add screen saver and wallpaper to your desktop. Additionally, you will learn to create a theme, change the size of Windows objects and text, add programs to the Start menu, create taskbar toolbars, and to add Web content to the desktop.

skill | Customizing the Mouse Settings

concept

You use the mouse to interact with the items on the computer screen. There are some specific properties of the mouse, such as the primary and secondary buttons, speed of the mouse pointer, and time between the mouse click. You can change these mouse properties via Control Panel. From the Control Panel window you can navigate to the Mouse Properties dialog box, which contains five tabs—Buttons, Pointers, Pointer Options, Wheel and Hardware—each relating to a different mouse function.

do it !

Modify your mouse controls by changing the primary button from the left button to the right, increasing the time allowed between clicks when double-clicking, adjusting the speed at which the pointer moves across the desktop, and adding pointer trails.

1. Click **start**, and then click the Control Panel command. This displays the Control Panel window. Click the Printers and Other Hardware link. This will display the Printers and Other Hardware window.

2. In the Printers and Other Hardware window, click the Mouse link. This will display the Mouse Properties dialog box (see Figure 5-1) with the Buttons tab in front.

3. Using the Buttons tab you can change the button configuration and the double-click speed of your mouse. In the Button Configuration section, select the Switch primary and secondary buttons check box to make the right mouse button the primary function button.

4. In the Double-click speed section, the slider controls the time allowed between clicks when double-clicking. Drag the slider to the left—now using the right mouse button instead of the left—to allow a larger amount of time between clicks.

5. Click the Pointer Options tab. The controls for pointer speed and pointer trails are found on this tab, as shown in Figure 5-2.

6. In the Motion section, drag the slider for the pointer speed to the left. This will adjust the speed at which the pointer moves across the screen in relation to the speed at which you move the mouse across your desk.

7. In the Visibility section, select the check box next to Display pointer trails. The shadows the pointer now leaves behind make it easier to spot the pointer on the screen. You can display the mouse pointer while typing by clearing the Hide pointer while typing check box.

8. Click **Apply** to save these settings changes.

9. Click **OK** to close the Mouse Properties dialog box.

more

In addition to Buttons and Pointer Options tabs, the Mouse Properties dialog box contains three other tabs: Pointers, Wheel and Hardware. The Pointers tab provides a list of predefined mouse pointers. You can select any of the mouse pointers from the list. The Wheel tab enables you to specify the range by which a page should scroll when the mouse wheel is rolled once. The Hardware tab displays the details of the mouse attached to your machine.

Figure 5-1 Mouse Properties dialog box

Check box used to set the primary mouse button

Secondary mouse button

Primary mouse button

Drag the slider to alter the double-click speed

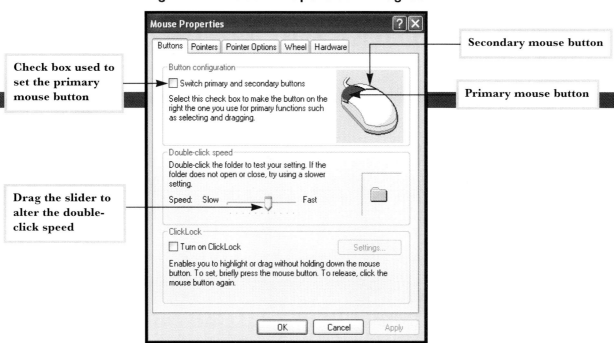

Figure 5-2 Options under the Pointer Options tab

Drag the slider to adjust the pointer speed

Drag the slider to adjust the length of pointer trails

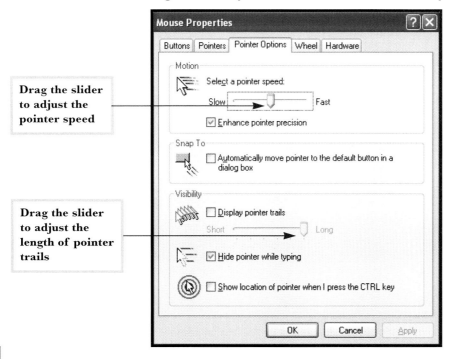

Practice

Restore your mouse properties to their previous settings.

skill | Setting the Date and Time

concept

The time of day is displayed on the right side of the taskbar in an area called the system tray. If you place the mouse pointer on the clock, the day, month, date, and year will be displayed in a small tip box. The option for the time and date adjustment controls is found in the Control Panel.

do it !

Set the date and time displayed on the taskbar to February 9, 2003, 11:30.

1. Open the Control Panel and click the Date, Time, Language, and Regional Options option. This will display the Date, Time, Language, and Regional Options window.

2. In the Date, Time, Language, and Regional Options window, click the Date and Time link. This will display the Date and Time Properties dialog box. You can also double-click the time on the taskbar to display the Date and Time Properties dialog box.

3. In the Date section, click the month list box above the calendar to display all twelve months. Select February by moving the pointer to the second month on the list and clicking once. The calendar will change to reflect the number of days in February.

4. Click 9 on the calendar to set the date.

5. To change the year, click the up arrow button in the spin box, next to the current year list box until the display reads 2003.

6. The Time section is divided into three parts: hours, minutes, and seconds. Move the pointer over the time text box; it will change to an I-beam pointer]. With the I-beam, click the digit representing the hour to get a blinking cursor. Move the pointer to the arrows and click until the hour reads 11. Repeat this procedure for the hours, minutes, and seconds until 11:30:00 is displayed (see Figure 5-3). You can also select the numbers and use the keyboard to type a new time.

7. Click Apply to change the time and date to the settings you just entered.

8. Click OK to close the Date and Time Properties dialog box.

9. Then re-adjust the time and date to reflect the correct settings for the present.

more

The second tab in the Date and Time Properties dialog box (see Figure 5-4), Time Zone, allows you to set the time zone for your computer. If your time zone adjusts for daylight savings time, you can set your computer to automatically make the change by clicking the Automatically adjust clock for daylight savings changes check box. The Internet Time tab of the Date and Time dialog box enables you to synchronize your computer clock with an Internet time server.

Figure 5-3 Date and Time Properties dialog box

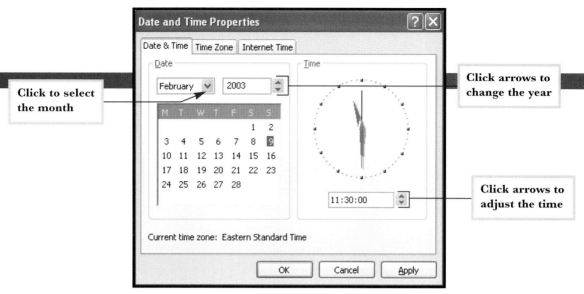

Click to select the month

Click arrows to change the year

Click arrows to adjust the time

Figure 5-4 Time Zone tab

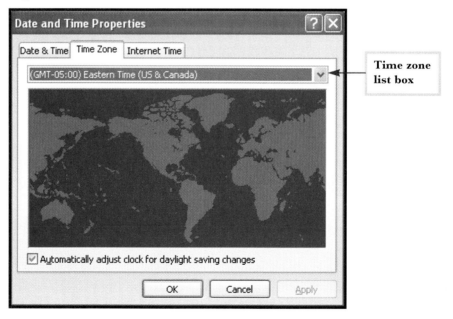

Time zone list box

Practice

Set the time and date of your computer to April 9, 2003, 10:45:20 AM. Then restore the date and time to the correct settings.

skill | Applying a Screen Saver

concept

A screen saver is an image or picture that moves and changes to prevent fixed images from becoming permanently embedded into your display. It also serves to cover your work while you are away from your computer. ◄◙► Do not move the mouse or hit any keys, as this interrupts the screen saver and displays the window of the application on which you were working. You may also apply a screen saver with a password, in which case moving the mouse or pressing a key will display a password-protect box to prevent unauthorized use.

do it !

Apply a screen saver to your computer's display.

1. In the Control Panel window, click the Appearance and Themes link. The Appearance and Themes window will be displayed.

2. Click the Choose a screen saver link in the Appearance and Themes window. The Display Properties dialog box will be displayed with the options for setting the screen saver (see Figure 5-5).

3. Click the list box in the Screen saver section to display a list of available screen savers.

4. Click Starfield to select this screen saver. A preview of the Starfield screen saver will be shown in the monitor at the top of the dialog box. ◄◙► You can use any bitmap image to customize screen savers, such as 3D Flying Objects, 3D FlowerBox, and 3D Pipes.

5. Click [Settings]. The Starfield Simulation Setup dialog box will be displayed, as shown in Figure 5-6.

6. In the Warp Speed section, drag the slider ▥ towards the extreme left.

7. Click [OK]. The dialog box will close and the preview on the monitor will change accordingly.

8. Click [Preview] to view the screen saver in action.

9. Move the mouse to exit the screen saver, then click [OK] to exit the Display Properties dialog box.

more

The Wait spin box on the Screen Saver tab of the Display Properties dialog box determines how many idle minutes your computer will wait before activating your screen saver. If you tend to pause often while using your computer, it is a good idea to make the wait time at least five minutes. Otherwise your screen saver will initiate at times when you do not really require it.

Figure 5-5 Screen Saver tab

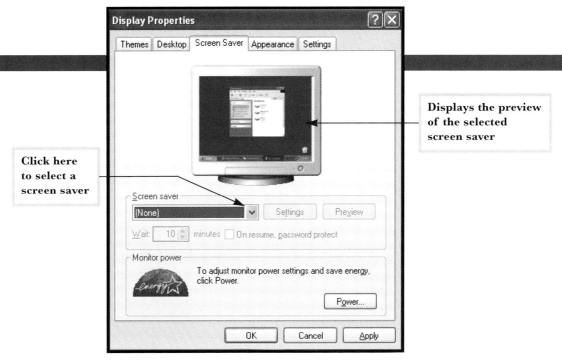

Click here
to select a
screen saver

Displays the preview
of the selected
screen saver

Figure 5-6 Configuring the screen saver settings

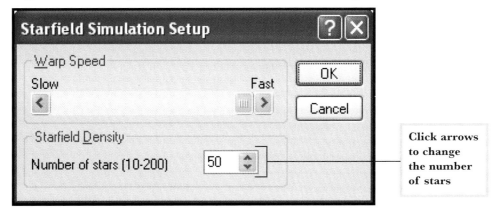

Click arrows
to change
the number
of stars

Practice

Choose a screen saver and set it to activate after a one minute wait period. Allow the screen saver to turn on, then interrupt it and adjust the screen saver settings according to your preferences.

skill

Changing the System Appearance and Display Settings

concept

Windows XP allows you to change the look of the desktop and system features to suit your personal taste. Using the Appearance tab in the Display Properties dialog box, you can apply an entire scheme to all of your system features or customize individual items. You can access the Display Properties dialog box by right-clicking on the desktop and selecting the Properties command from the shortcut menu that appears.

do it !

Change your system appearance using a scheme, and then customize an individual display setting.

1. Open the Display Properties dialog box. Click the Appearance tab to bring it to the front of the dialog box. The top half of the tab is a preview window that shows how system elements, such as the desktop, title bars, scroll bars, button text, and menu text will appear when you change them.

2. Click Windows Classic style in the Windows and buttons list.

3. Click Eggplant in the Color scheme list. Notice the changes that occur to different items in the preview window, shown in Figure 5-7.

4. Click [Apply] to put the Eggplant scheme into effect. The display changes should be reflected in a number of areas including the desktop, the taskbar, and the title bar of the dialog box.

5. Click [Advanced]. This will display the Advanced Appearance dialog box. In the Item list, Desktop should be set by default. If your Item list displays something other than Desktop, click the arrow [▼] and choose Desktop from the list.

6. Click the Color1 button [■ ▼]. A color palette will appear, as shown in Figure 5-8. Click the red square in the first column of the palette.

7. Click [OK] to close the Advanced Appearance dialog box.

8. Click [Apply] in the Display Properties dialog box.

9. Click [OK] to close the Display Properties dialog box. The desktop will change color if you do not already have wallpaper completely filling the desktop.

more

In addition to changing the styles of the windows and buttons and color scheme, you can change the size of the fonts using the Font size list box. The Font size list box is present under the Appearance tab of the Display Properties dialog box and provides three options: Normal, Large, and Extra Large Fonts. By, default, the Normal font size option is selected.

Figure 5-7 Preview of the Eggplant scheme

Title bar text and color for Eggplant scheme

Desktop color for the Eggplant scheme

Figure 5-8 Selecting a desktop color

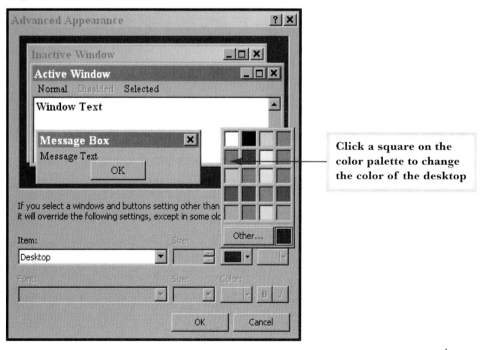

Click a square on the color palette to change the color of the desktop

Practice

Configure your system appearance scheme to the Windows XP style scheme.

<table>
<tr>
<td>

skill

</td>
<td>

Adding Wallpaper to the Desktop

</td>
</tr>
</table>

concept

The possibilities for changing the appearance of your desktop are not limited to the solid colors available on the Appearance tab. You can use the Desktop tab in the Display Properties dialog box to cover your desktop background with a picture which can be applied in different styles. Such pictures are known as Wallpapers.

do it !

Add wallpaper to your desktop and experiment with the style in which it is applied.

1. Open the Display Properties dialog box and click the Desktop tab to bring it to the front of the Display Properties dialog box.

2. The Background section of the tab contains a list box of preinstalled images that can be used as wallpaper. Scroll down the Background list box and click Rhododendron to select it. ◢ If you save an HTML document such as a Web page, you can use it as wallpaper just as you would use a regular image.

3. Once you select a wallpaper image, the Position list box will become active. Click the box to view the wallpaper display options. You can apply one of three display options to the image by clicking it: Center places the image at the center of the screen with its normal dimensions; Tile places multiple copies of the image across the screen so that the desktop is completely covered; Stretch enlarges the image so that it covers the entire background by itself.

4. Click Center in the Position list box. The preview changes to reflect the setting (see Figure 5-9).

5. Click [Apply]. Rhododendron is placed centrally on the desktop background.

6. Click [OK] to confirm the new wallpaper and close the dialog box.

more

You can customize your desktop settings using the Desktop Items dialog box (see Figure 5-10). Click [Customize Desktop...] on the Display tab of the Display Properties dialog box to open the Desktop Items dialog box. The Desktop Items dialog box contains Desktop icons and Desktop cleanup sections. The Desktop icons section enables you to put My Documents, My Computer, My Network Places, and Internet Explorer icons on the desktop. This section also provides an option to change the picture of the desktop icons. The Run Desktop Cleanup Wizard every 60 days check box in the Desktop cleanup section, if selected, removes the desktop icons that have not been used for past 60 days.

Figure 5-9 Setting up a Wallpaper

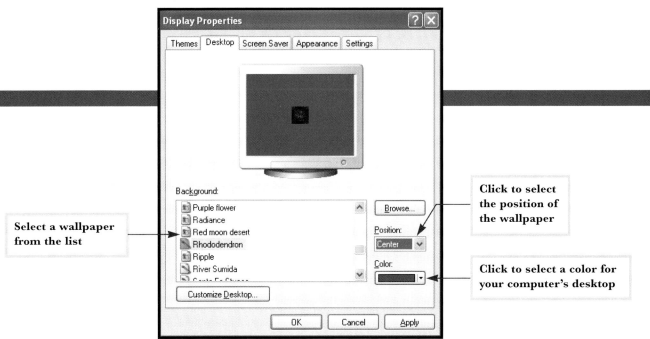

Select a wallpaper from the list

Click to select the position of the wallpaper

Click to select a color for your computer's desktop

Figure 5-10 Desktop Items dialog box

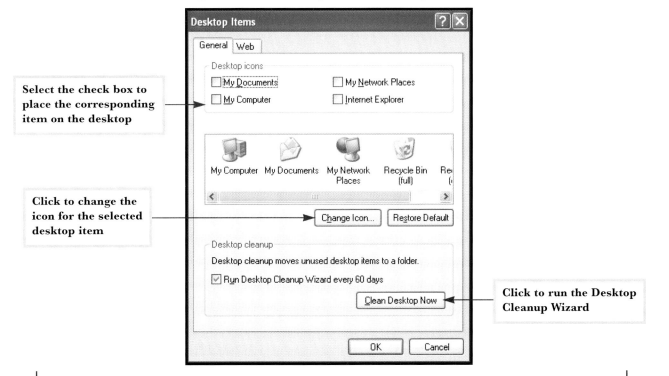

Select the check box to place the corresponding item on the desktop

Click to change the icon for the selected desktop item

Click to run the Desktop Cleanup Wizard

Practice

Apply a new wallpaper to your desktop background and apply the tile position to the selected picture.

skill | Working with Themes

concept

The appearance of your desktop is created using a set of icons, fonts, colors, sounds and other windows elements. All these settings together form a desktop theme, which gives a distinctive look to your desktop. In Windows XP, you can switch themes, create a new theme, and make changes in an existing theme. Whenever you make changes to an existing theme, you should save it with a different name. This is because after modifying a theme if you select a different theme without saving the changes with a different name, all the changes made to the theme are lost.

do it !

Modify a theme and save it as a new theme.

1. In the Control Panel window, click the Appearance and Themes option. The Appearance and Themes window will be displayed.

2. Click the Display option. The Display Properties dialog box will be displayed.

3. In the Theme section of the Display Properties dialog box, click the arrow to open the list and click My Current Theme.

4. Click the Desktop tab.

5. In the Background list, click Ascent.

6. Click the Screen Saver tab.

7. In the Screen saver section, click the arrow to open the list box and click Starfield.

8. Click the Appearance tab.

9. In the Color scheme list box, click Olive Green.

10. Click the Themes tab. The Theme list box will now display the selected theme name as My Current Theme (Modified) (see Figure 5-11).

11. Click ⌊ Apply ⌋. While applying the new theme, Windows XP displays the message Please Wait.

12. Click ⌊ Save As... ⌋. This will display the Save As dialog box (see Figure 5-12).

13. Type Starfield Theme in the File name text box.

14. Click ⌊ Save ⌋. This will display Starfield Theme in the Theme list box of the Display Properties dialog box.

15. Click ⌊ OK ⌋ to close the Display Properties dialog box.

16. Using the same procedure, revert the theme setting to the default theme, Windows XP.

more

In addition to creating a new theme, you can delete an existing theme. To delete a theme, in the Themes list box, click the theme you want to delete. Click ⌊ Delete ⌋ to delete the selected theme. You cannot delete the themes provided by Windows XP.

Figure 5-11 Display Properties dialog box

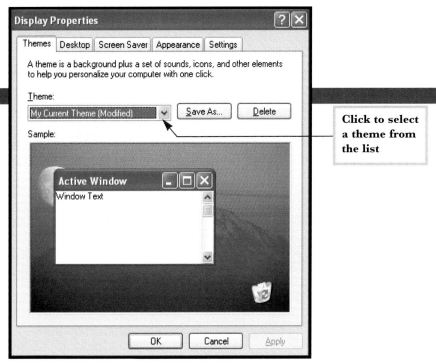

Click to select
a theme from
the list

Figure 5-12 Save As dialog box

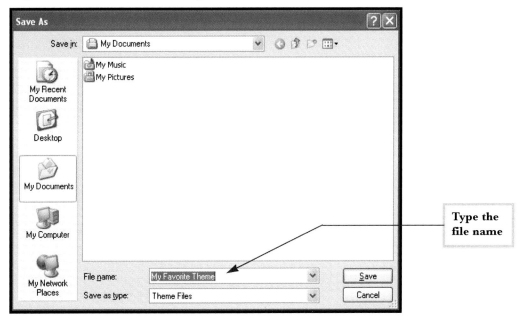

Type the
file name

Practice

Use the Starfield Theme you have created in this Skill to create a new theme.

skill | Changing the Size of Objects and Text

concept

There might be situations when you are not comfortable with the size of Windows objects displayed on your screen. In Windows XP, you can increase or decrease the size of the objects and text. You can change the size of objects by changing the DPI (dots per inch) settings of your machine. Changing the DPI setting for a selected monitor changes the size of all the screen elements you see.

do it !

Change your screen resolution by increasing the DPI setting of your machine.

1. Open the Display Properties dialog box.

2. Click the Settings tab.

3. Click [Advanced]. This will display the properties dialog box for your monitor (see Figure 5-13).

4. In the Display section, click the arrow to open the DPI setting list box.

5. Different monitors will show different options in the DPI setting list box. Click the DPI size larger than the current selected size. In this case, Large size (120 DPI) has been selected. This will display the Change DPI Setting message box (see Figure 5-14).

7. Click [OK] to close the message box.

8. Click [Apply] on the properties dialog box. If the required fonts are already installed on your machine, the General message box will be displayed to confirm that fonts are already installed. In case fonts are not installed on your machine, you will need to insert the required CD or to supply an alternate location of the required files.

9. Click [Close] on the Display Properties dialog box to close it.

10. Restart your computer when prompted.

more

The DPI setting list box also provides an option, Custom setting, to apply a DPI setting other than the ones shown in the list. Clicking the Custom setting option displays the Custom DPI Setting dialog box. In the Custom DPI Setting dialog box, you can either select one of the percentage options in the Scale to this percentage of normal size list box or drag the pointer on the ruler to specify a setting.

Figure 5-13 Properties dialog box

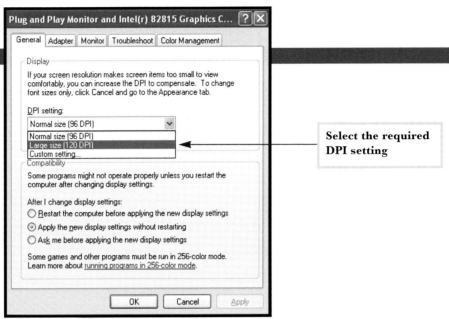

Select the required
DPI setting

Figure 5-14 Change DPI Setting message box

Practice

Return to the default DPI setting of your system.

skill | Adding Programs to the Start Menu

concept

The Start menu is divided into two sections: pinned item list and most frequently used programs. You can add programs, folders, and files to the pinned item list section of the Start menu. Adding items to the Start menu can save you time by giving you easy access to them regardless of your current activity.

do it !

Add the Calculator program to the top of the Start menu.

1. Click 🏁 start to open the Start menu and point to All Programs.

2. Again, point to the Accessories command and right-click the Calculator command.

3. Click the Pin to Start menu command on the shortcut menu (see Figure 5-15). This will add the Calculator program to the top of the Start menu (see Figure 5-16). 　　 You can add an item to the Start menu by dragging it to the Start menu folder in Windows Explorer or by dragging its icon directly to 🏁 start. You can access the Start menu folder by clicking the Documents and Settings in the Windows Explorer window folder and then clicking the user profile folder in Windows Explorer. When you drag a program icon to the Start button, the Start menu will open and you can then choose where to drop the icon.

more

You can also use the Taskbar and Start Menu Properties dialog box to add items to the Start menu. To display this dialog box, right-click 🏁 start and click the Properties command. On the Start Menu tab, click [Customize...] (for either Start Menu or Classic Start Menu) to display the Customize Start Menu dialog box (see Figure 5-17). Then, click the Advanced tab. The Start menu items section enables you to select the items you want to include in the Start menu. You can drag any item from Windows Explorer to the Start menu by selecting the Enable dragging and dropping check box, located in the Start menu items section of the Advanced tab. You can remove or add items, such as Favorites menu, Help and Support, My Network Places, and Run command by clicking the corresponding check box in the Start menu items section.

Figure 5-15 Adding the Calculator program to the Start menu

Click to add the
Calculator program
to the Start menu

**Figure 5-16 Calculator program in
the Start menu**

Calculator
program in the
Start menu

Figure 5-17 Customize Start Menu dialog box

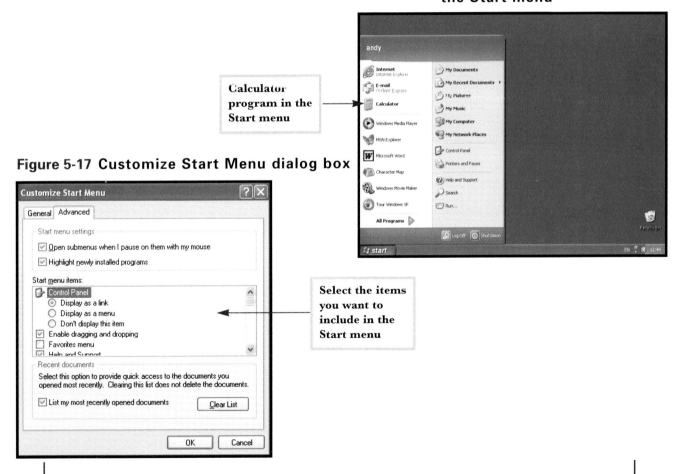

Select the items
you want to
include in the
Start menu

Practice

Add the Notepad program to the top of the Start menu.

skill Creating and Using Taskbar Toolbars

concept

You have already seen how the Standard Buttons toolbar makes executing commands and opening programs as simple as clicking a button. You may find that it would be useful to have other Windows XP features as accessible as those on the existing toolbars. To accomplish this, you can create your own custom toolbars and add them to the taskbar.

do it !

Create a taskbar toolbar for your desktop folder.

1. Right-click the blank space on the taskbar. On the shortcut menu point to Toolbars.

2. Click the New Toolbar command on the Toolbars submenu. The New Toolbar dialog box is displayed. The instructions at the top of the dialog box tell you to choose a folder or an Internet address. My Documents has already been selected and entered into the text box. Click Desktop in the list box to select it. Desktop is one of five built-in toolbars that you do not have to create yourself. The others are Address, Links, Language bar and Quick Launch. You can drag multiple toolbars to the same window to create a toolbar panel.

3. Click OK to close the dialog box and create the taskbar toolbar of desktop icons. All of the icons on the desktop can now be opened from their buttons on the taskbar. Since not all of the items fit, an arrow » is provided at the end of the toolbar. Click this arrow to slide the hidden items into view.

4. Right-click the taskbar to display a shortcut menu and ensure that the Lock the Taskbar option is not checked. Right-click the name of the new toolbar, Desktop. On the shortcut menu, you will see the Show Text command with a check mark next to it. Click Show Text to turn off the option. The buttons on the new toolbar now consist solely of icons. If icons on the Desktop toolbar are not visible, drag the small vertical line on the left of the Desktop toolbar towards the left. Your taskbar should resemble Figure 5-18. To view the Show Text option, the taskbar should be unlocked. To unlock the taskbar, right-click the taskbar and remove the checkmark beside the Lock the Taskbar command.

5. Click the My Computer button on the Desktop toolbar. The My Computer window will open. Click the Close button X to close the window.

6. Place the mouse pointer on the top of the Desktop toolbar. The pointer will change to ↕. Drag the Desktop toolbar towards the center of the desktop. The toolbar will appear as shown in Figure 5-19.

7. Drag the Desktop toolbar back to its previous location.

more

In addition to being able to create a toolbar for any folder on your hard drive, you can add a Web page to the taskbar as a toolbar. Open the New Toolbar dialog box and enter a URL into the text box instead of choosing a folder. When you create the toolbar, you will be able to view the Web page on your taskbar. If you decide to do this, it is a good idea to increase the size of the taskbar so you can view the contents of the page easily.

Figure 5-18 Taskbar with the Desktop toolbar

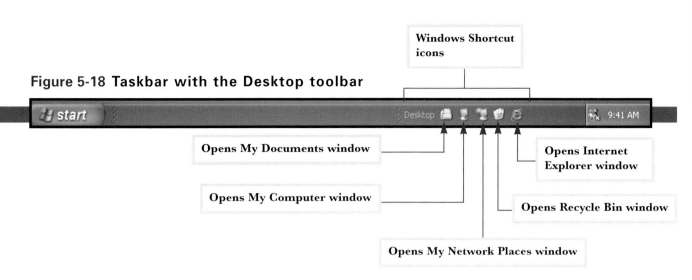

Windows Shortcut icons

Opens My Documents window

Opens My Computer window

Opens My Network Places window

Opens Internet Explorer window

Opens Recycle Bin window

Figure 5-19 Changing the size of the taskbar

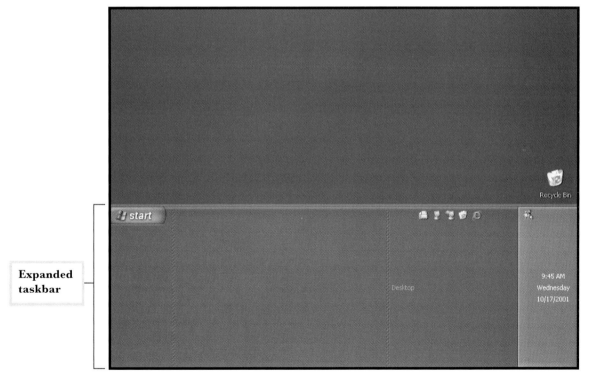

Expanded taskbar

Practice

Create a taskbar toolbar for My Computer. Hide the text on the toolbar so that it contains only icons. Use the toolbar to open a folder or drive on your computer. Then close the My Computer window.

skill | Adding Web Content to the Desktop

concept

In Windows XP, you can add a Web page to your desktop. By adding a Web page to your desktop, your desktop background no longer has to be a static picture or pattern. You can include Web pages, HTML documents stored on disk, and animated pictures in your desktop. Moreover, these items can be live, meaning that you can receive the latest updates to them, assuming you have an active connection to the Internet.

do it !

Add Yahoo.com to the Active Desktop.

1. Right-click the desktop and click Properties in the shortcut menu. This will open the Display Properties dialog box.

2. Click the Desktop tab to bring it to the front of the dialog box.

3. Click [Customize Desktop...]. This will display the Desktop Items dialog box.

4. Click the Web tab to bring it to the front of the dialog box. The Web pages box on the Web tab displays a list of Web items. You can select a Web page here to display it on your desktop. By default, the Web pages box contains one item, My Current Home Page (see Figure 5-20).

5. Click [New...]. This will open the New Desktop Item dialog box.

6. Type http://www.yahoo.com in the Location text box (see Figure 5-21).

7. Click [OK]. This will display the Add item to Active Desktop(TM) dialog box (see Figure 5-22).

(continued on WN 5.22)

Figure 5-20 Desktop Items dialog box

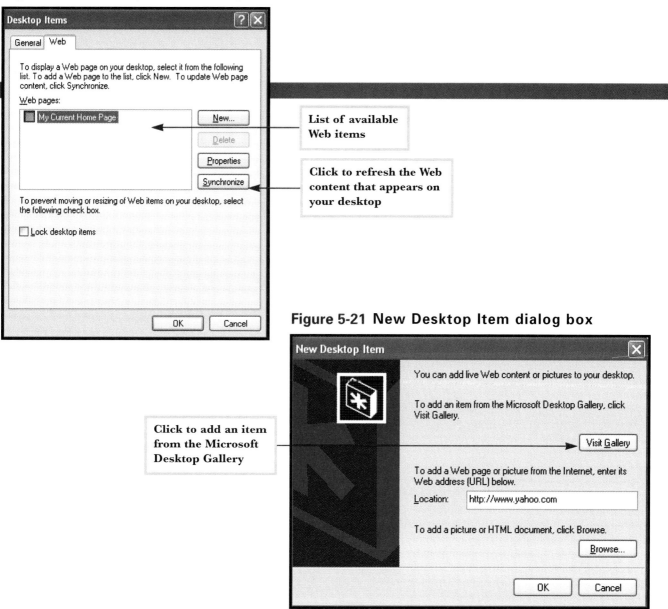

List of available
Web items

Click to refresh the Web
content that appears on
your desktop

Figure 5-21 New Desktop Item dialog box

Click to add an item
from the Microsoft
Desktop Gallery

Figure 5-22 Add Item to Active Desktop(TM) dialog box

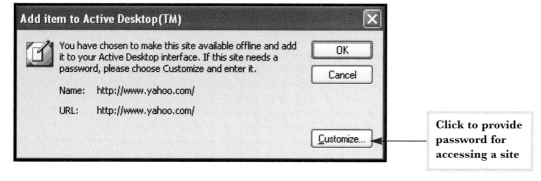

Click to provide
password for
accessing a site

skill Adding Web Content to the Desktop (continued)

do it !

8. Click [OK]. This will display the Synchronizing box. The site http://www.yahoo.com will be added to the list of Web items.

9. In the Web pages list, check the box next to http://www.yahoo.com, if it is not already checked.

10. Click [OK] to close the Desktop Items dialog box.

11. Click [Apply] and then click [OK] to close the Display Properties dialog box. The Yahoo home page will appear on your desktop's background complete with scroll bars, shown in Figure 5-23. The Web items added to the desktop are a part of your desktop's background. Therefore, they will not block access to your desktop icons, but will appear behind them.

12. Click the Close button X in the upper-right corner of the window. This deactivates the item, but does not remove it from the list of available items on the Web tab. Web items added to the desktop may be resized and repositioned just like regular windows.

more

When a Web item is selected on the Web tab of the Desktop Items dialog box, the Properties button will become available. Clicking the Properties button displays the Properties dialog box for the selected Web item. The Properties dialog box contains three tabs. The first tab, Web Document, displays a summary of important data related to the particular Web site (see Figure 5-24). The Schedule tab contains controls for programming how and when the updates will occur (see Figure 5-25). To update your Web items on the desktop manually, select the Synchronize command from the Tools menu of Windows Explorer or My Computer windows. This will display the Items to Synchronize dialog box. The Items to Synchronize dialog box displays a list of Web items from which you can select the item you want to synchronize. Using the Using the following schedule(s) option button, you can specify a schedule for updating the Web item. If you select the Only when I choose synchronize from Tools menu option button, you will have to synchronize the Web item manually. Finally, the Download tab allows you to control how you would like to be notified of updates to the Active Desktop item, and enables you to specify whether you want to download contents more than the top-level page of the Web site.

Figure 5-23 Desktop with the added Yahoo home page

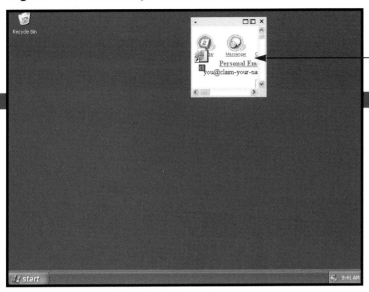

Inserted Yahoo
Web page on
the desktop

Figure 5-24 Web Document tab options

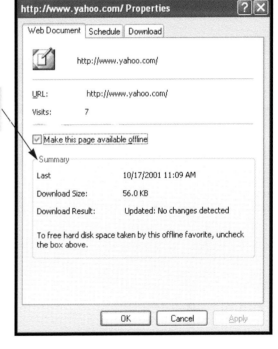

Summary of the
selected Web site

Figure 5-25 Schedule tab options

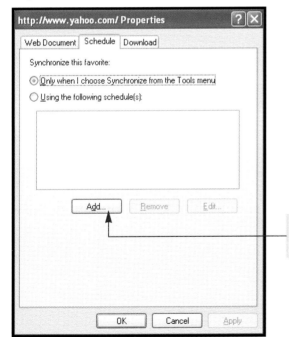

Click to set up a
new schedule

Practice

Add a Web item of your choice to your desktop. Make sure you know the Web page's URL before beginning. When you have finished, close the Web page added to the desktop.

shortcuts

Function	Button/Mouse	Menu	Keyboard
Add item to Start menu	Drag item to the Start button		
Open Display Properties dialog box		Right-click on the desktop, then click the Properties command	

A. Identify Key Features

Name the items indicated by callouts in Figure 5-26.

Figure 5-26 Customized features of Windows XP

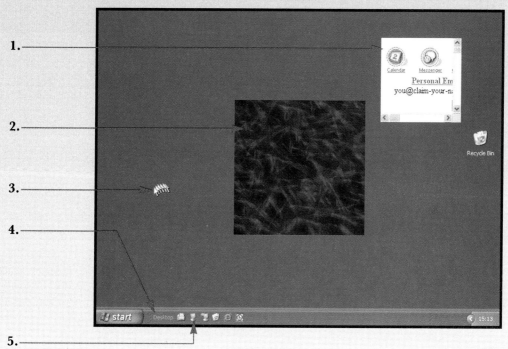

1.

2.

3.

4.

5.

B. Select the Best Answer

6. Determines how many idle minutes will pass before a screen saver is activated
    a. Background list box

7. Used to update Web items on the desktop
    b. Desktop

8. Windows XP's built-in toolbar
    c. New Toolbar command

9. Used to set wallpaper on the desktop
    d. Theme

10. Click this to create a custom toolbar on the taskbar
    e. Wait box

11. Collection of settings that determines the appearance of your desktop
    f. Synchronize command

quiz (continued)

C. Complete the Statement

12. You can customize many system settings by means of the:

a. Internet

b. Control Panel

c. Desktop

d. Internet Explorer Channel Bar

13. The controls for mouse pointer speed and pointer trails are located on the:

a. Pointer Options tab

b. Buttons tab

c. Motion tab

d. Mouse itself

14. When using a taskbar toolbar, you can do all of the following except:

a. Lock the taskbar

b. Show text on the toolbar buttons

c. Add wallpaper to the toolbar

d. Change the size of the toolbar

15. The Web items on the desktop you have inserted are listed on the:

a. Internet Explorer

b. Web tab of the Desktop Items dialog box

c. Desktop tab

d. Active Desktop submenu

16. Web items placed on the desktop:

a. Can be moved and resized

b. Can be moved but not resized

c. Can be resized but not moved

d. Will cover any icons or open windows on the desktop

17. To change the size of objects, you need to change the:

a. SMI settings

b. DPI settings

c. DIP settings

d. PID settings

18. All the following are the tabs of the Properties command except:

a. Schedule tab

b. Download tab

c. Web Document

d. Screen Saver

19. Custom setting option is accessed from the:

a. DPI setting list box

b. Background list box

c. Web items list box

d. Web tab of the Desktop Items dialog box

Build Your Skills

1. Use the Display Properties dialog box to customize your Windows XP display:

   a. Open the Display Properties dialog box.

   b. Add the screen saver Marquee.

   c. Set the Power wallpaper.

2. Create a new taskbar toolbar:

   a. Open the New Toolbar dialog box.

   b. Expand the (C:) drive icon and then the Program Files folder so that the Accessories folder is revealed.

   c. Select the Accessories folder and click OK to create an Accessories toolbar on the taskbar.

   d. Set the toolbar to show icons only.

3. Add a Web page to your desktop:

   a. Open the Display Properties dialog box.

   b. Open the Desktop items dialog box to the Web tab.

   c. Click the New button to insert the Web address http://www.altavista.com on your desktop.

   d. Once AltaVista's main search page is running on your desktop, resize the window so that you can view the page appropriately.

4. Create a new theme.

   a. Open the Display Properties dialog box.

   b. From the Theme list, select My Current Theme.

   c. Click the Desktop tab.

   d. In the Background list, click Peace.

   e. Click the Screen Saver tab.

   f. In the Screen saver section, click the arrow to open the list box and click Mystify.

   g. Save the new theme as Peace Theme.

interactivity (continued)

Problem Solving Exercises

1. Your boss at a New York investment banking firm has requested that you configure a new computer for him that uses the Windows XP operating system. You have been given a list of specifications for customizing the system:

    a. Set the system's clock to local time in Tokyo, Japan.

    b. Put Internet Explorer on the first level of the Start menu.

    c. Add an interesting, but professional, desktop background.

    d. Create a toolbar panel that consists of the Desktop toolbar, a toolbar for My Computer, and a toolbar for the Programs folder.

    e. Have two Web items related to financial news running on your desktop.

    f. Configure the mouse buttons for left-hand use, set double-click speed to slow, and pointer speed to medium.

2. Your boss has decided that he wants to learn how to customize Windows XP himself. Restore all of the items you changed in the previous problem to their original settings and close all new items you created.

3. The retirement community in which you volunteer has been trying to get its residents to learn how to use computers. Many of the residents are reluctant because they have difficulty seeing the display. Customize the display settings on your computer so that someone whose vision is impaired would have an easier time using it.

Windows and Multimedia Applications

skills

Personal computers are no longer the "glorified typewriters" that some people used to accuse them of being. Depending on your needs, they can serve in a number of capacities including as fully functioning publishing tools, communications devices, and entertainment systems.

Windows XP comes with several programs that enable you to work with text, pictures, sound, and video. As multimedia software has grown in popularity, sound capabilities have become increasingly important. With the proper equipment, Sound Recorder enables you to record and play back your own sound files. You can also use Windows Media Player to listen to your favorite audio CDs while you work.

WordPad is a simple word processing program that enables you to create your own text documents. You can store multiple copies of a file, edit a document using cut, copy, and paste commands, format your document to make it more visually appealing, and insert audio files into your WordPad document.

Paint is a drawing program that is useful for working with static images. With this application, you can create both simple and complex pictures. Paint offers a large color palette and a variety of drawing tools. It also includes a full range of manipulation commands that permit you to stretch, skew, and rotate images.

Lesson Goal:

In this lesson, you will learn to use Windows Media Player to listen to audio files and to copy tracks from a CD to the hard disk of your machine. You will also learn to use the WordPad application and to embed an audio file in the WordPad application. Additionally, you will learn to associate sounds with specific Windows events, watch video, use Paint to draw different shapes, and apply advanced Paint functions to the shapes.

skill | Exploring Windows Media Player

concept

Windows XP provides Windows Media Player that enables you to play and work on media files. Using Windows Media Player, you can organize the media files on your computer, listen to any radio station, play a CD, and view videos. Additionally, you can make the copies of your CDs using Windows Media Player.

The left panel of the Windows Media Player window (see Figure 6-1) provides you with the options with which you play a CD, skip the tracks you do not want to hear, and copy tracks from a CD. These options include:

◉ Now Playing: This option, when selected, displays the name of the artist, title of the track being played, and displays the audio in the form of different geometric shapes and colors. From the list of tracks, you can select a specific track or skip playing tracks that you do not want to listen to.

◉ Media Guide: This option enables you to find Windows Media files on the Internet. These media files are hosted and maintained by WindowsMedia.com. In the Media Guide, all the links to the latest movies, music, and video are present. These links are updated on a daily basis.

◉ Copy from CD: Using this option, you can copy tracks from a CD to your computer.

◉ Media Library: This option provides a collection of all the digital media content available on your computer. The media files include the links to content that you previously played.

◉ Radio Tuner: This option enables you to search and listen to the radio stations on the Internet. You can also create presets of your favorite radio stations to access them easily and quickly in the future.

◉ Copy to CD or Device: This option enables you to copy files from the Media Library to a CD.

◉ Skin Chooser: This option is used to change the appearance of the Windows Media Player.

do it!

Open Windows Media Player.

1. Click ⊞ start , point to All Programs, and then point to Accessories.

2. In the Accessories submenu, point to Entertainment.

3. In the Entertainment submenu, click Windows Media Player. This will display the Windows Media Player window (see Figure 6-1).

more

You can hide or unhide the Menu bar of Windows Media Player. To hide the Menu bar, click View on the Menu bar, point to Full Mode Options, and then click the Hide Menu Bar command. Similarly, you can unhide the Menu bar by selecting the Show Menu Bar command. If you want the Menu bar to be displayed only when you move mouse pointer over it, select the Auto Hide Menu Bar command from the Full Mode Options submenu.

Figure 6-1 Windows Media Player window

Menu bar

Windows Media
Player options

Practice

Open Windows Media Player and view the options displayed in the Windows Media Player window.

skill | Copying Tracks from a CD to Your System

concept

Using the Copy from CD option of the Windows Media Player window, you can copy tracks from CD to your system. By default, all the tracks are selected to be copied to your system. If you do not want to copy a particular track, you need to clear the check box next to the track. The tracks that you copy on your system are copied to the My Music folder by default and are listed in the Media Library. The My Music folder further contains the subfolders, which are labeled with the artist's name. This skill requires that you have a CD-ROM drive, a sound card installed in your computer, and an audio CD.

do it!

Copy tracks from a CD to your system.

1. Insert your CD in the CD-ROM drive.

2. Open the Windows Media Player window.

3. Click Copy from CD. This will display all the tracks of the CD in the Windows Media Player window (see Figure 6-2).

4. Click Copy Music . This will start copying the selected tracks to your system. As the tracks are copied from the CD, the Copy Status field on the Windows Media Player window displays the status of the process. You might get a notification that Windows Media Player is configured to protect content that is copied from a CD to your system from unauthorized use. Click OK to proceed copying tracks.

5. After copying the tracks, click the Close button X to close Windows Media Player.

more

You can change the location where the tracks are copied. To change the location, click Tools on the Menu bar and then click the Options command. This will display the Options dialog box. Click the Copy Music tab to view its options (see Figure 6-3). In the Copy music to this location section, click Change... . This will display the Browse for Folder dialog box. Select the location where you want to copy the tracks and click OK . This will close the Browse for Folder dialog box. Click Apply to save the changes, then click OK to close the Options dialog box.

Figure 6-2 Displaying tracks of a CD

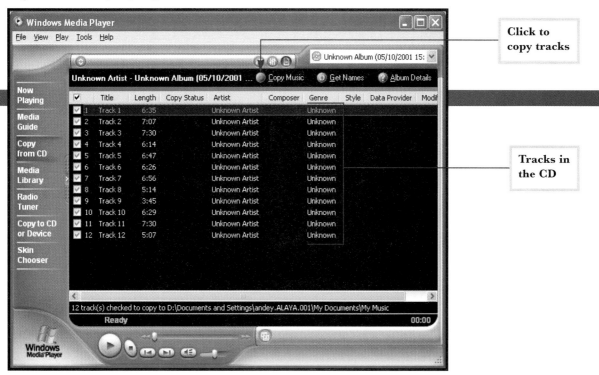

Click to
copy tracks

Tracks in
the CD

Figure 6-3 Copy Music tab

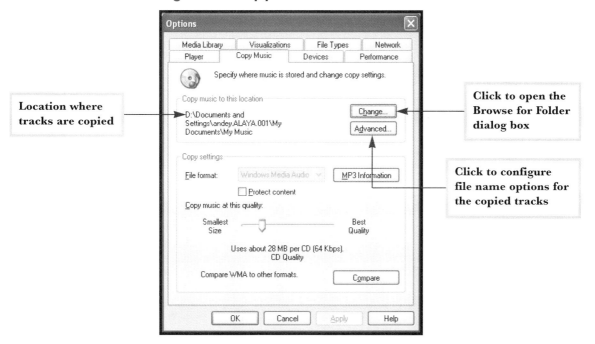

Location where
tracks are copied

Click to open the
Browse for Folder
dialog box

Click to configure
file name options for
the copied tracks

Practice

Insert an Audio CD in your CD-ROM drive and using Windows Media Player copy its tracks on to your system.

skill | Listening to Audio

concept

The Sound Recorder application is useful for both recording and playing sound files. Since recording sound requires that you have a microphone connected to your computer, this skill will focus on using Sound Recorder to listen to sound files. This skill requires that you have a CD-ROM drive, a sound card installed in your computer, an audio CD, and an output device such as speakers or headphones.

do it!

Use Sound Recorder to play a preinstalled sound file. Then, use Windows Media Player to play an audio CD.

1. Click **start**, point to All Programs, and then point to Accessories. On the Accessories menu, point to Entertainment, and then click Sound Recorder. The Sound Recorder window will be displayed.

2. Click File on the Menu bar, and then click Open. The Open dialog box will be displayed.

3. Click the arrow at the right edge of the Look in list box. Click the (C:) drive on the list, as shown in Figure 6-4, to display its contents.

4. In the contents window, locate the Windows folder and double-click it. You may need to use the horizontal scroll bar to bring the folder into view.

5. Locate the Media folder (scroll if necessary) and double-click it. Inside the Media folder you will see a list of files that end with the extension .wav. This extension identifies a file as a Windows Wave sound file, a particular sound format.

6. Press [T]. The first file that begins with T is selected.

7. Click Open. The Open dialog box will close and the file will be opened in the Sound Recorder window, shown in Figure 6-5.

8. Click the Play button to listen to the sound file.

9. Click the Close button to close the Sound Recorder.

10. To listen to an audio CD, start the Windows Media Player application. It is located on the same submenu as Sound Recorder (All Programs-Accessories-Entertainment).

11. Insert an audio CD into your computer's CD-ROM drive.

(continued on WN 6.8)

Figure 6-4 Open dialog box

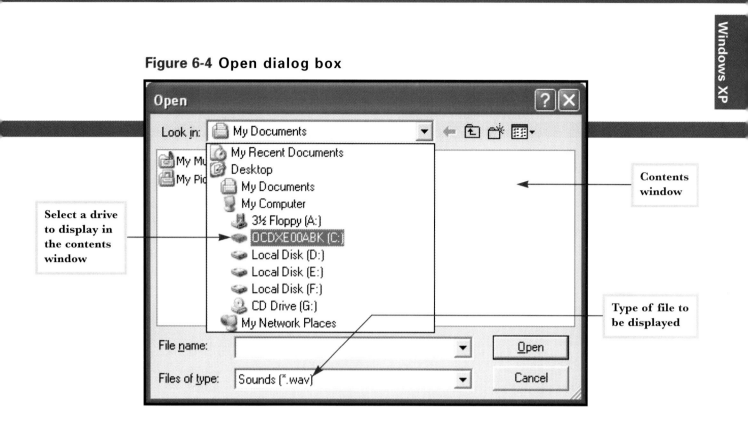

Contents window

Select a drive to display in the contents window

Type of file to be displayed

Figure 6-5 A sound file opened in Sound Recorder

Click to play the sound track

Time duration of the sound track

skill   Listening to Audio (continued)

do it!

12. In the Windows Media Player window, click the Play on the Menu bar to open the Play menu and then click the CD Audio command. The first track of the CD will start (see Figure 6-6).

13. Point to each of the buttons at the bottom of the Windows Media Player window with the mouse. As you do, a ScreenTip will appear with the button's function. The list of tracks on the right pane of the Windows Media Player window enables you to go directly to a particular track without having to use the Next button ▶️.

14. Double-click the track of your choice to play it.

15. When you are done listening, click Play on the Menu bar and then click Eject to remove the CD. ◀️ You can also use the keyboard shortcut [Ctrl]+[E] to remove the CD.

16. Click the Close button ☒ on the Windows Media Player window to close it.

more

You can use the shortcut menu of a track (right-click a track to open its shortcut menu) to change the name of the track of the CD currently loaded. Your computer will remember these settings so that each time you insert that particular CD, the names you changed will appear instead of the names that originally appeared, such as New Artist, New Title, and Track 01. You can also use the shortcut menu of a track to rearrange the order of the track in the play list or to disable the track.

Using Master Volume you can adjust the volume, balance, bass, and treble settings for audio files. To open the Master Volume window, click ⊞ start , point to All Programs, point to Accessories, point to Entertainment, and click the Volume Control command. This will display the Master Volume window (see Figure 6-7). The window provides separate controls for Master Volume, Wave, SW Synth, CD Audio, Line In, and PC Speaker. In addition to volume, you can adjust the left and right balance of each type of audio.

Figure 6-6 Playing an audio file using Windows Media Player

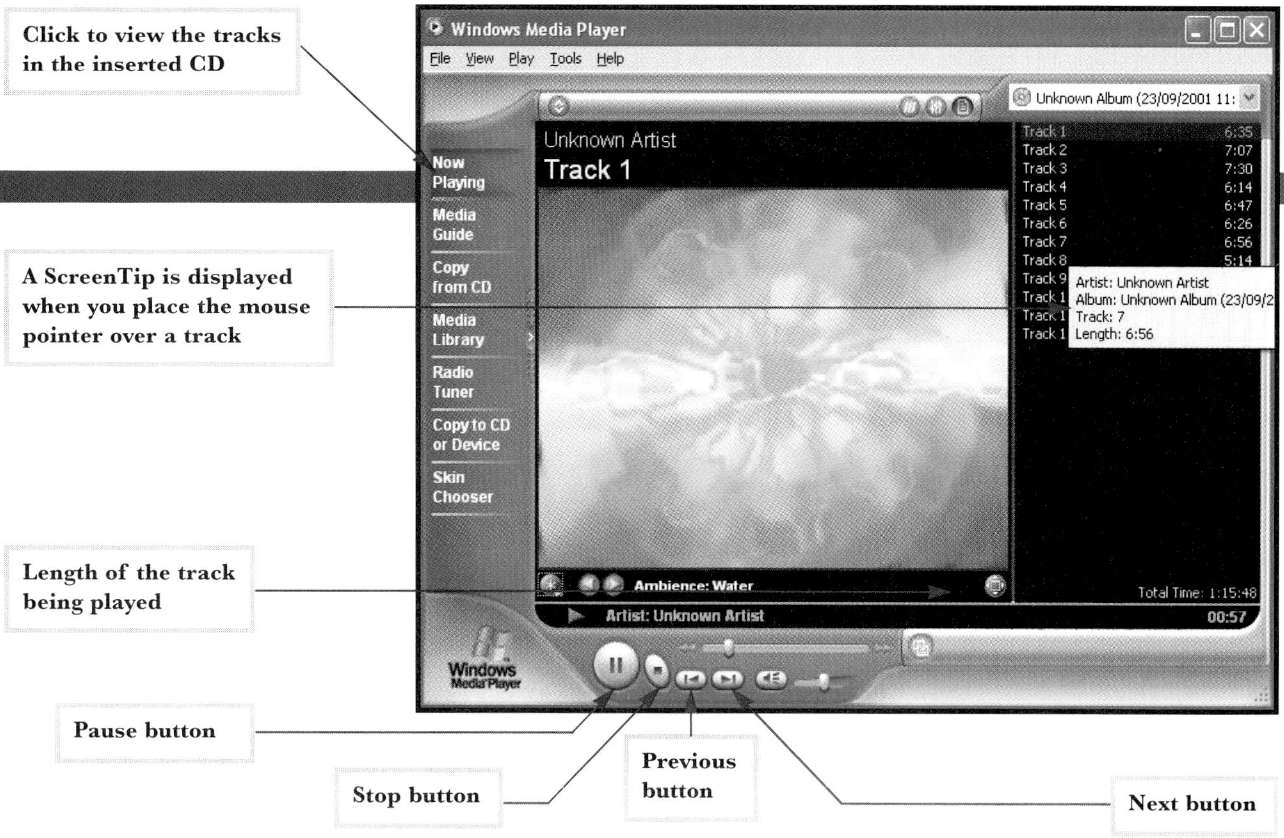

Click to view the tracks in the inserted CD

A ScreenTip is displayed when you place the mouse pointer over a track

Length of the track being played

Pause button

Stop button

Previous button

Next button

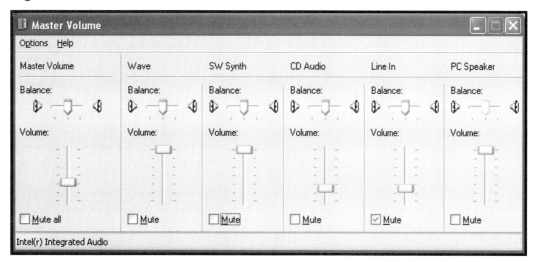

Figure 6-7 Master Volume window

Practice

Use Sound Recorder to listen to another wave file from the Media folder.

skill

Using WordPad

WordPad is Windows XP's built-in word processing program. With WordPad, you can produce simple or advanced text documents. If you have used a word processor before, you may already be familiar with some of the application's capabilities. If not, WordPad's inter-face makes taking advantage of its many features an easy task. You can create, edit, and for-mat text, save files, and print documents.

do it!

Use WordPad to create, edit, format, and save a text document.

1. Click ⧉start , point to All Programs, and then point to Accessories. On the Accessories menu, click WordPad.

2. When WordPad window is displayed, a blank document will appear in the document window. The application window also consists of a Title bar, Menu bar, Toolbar, Format bar, Ruler, and Status bar. See the opposite page for a table of WordPad's Toolbar buttons and their functions. The blinking insertion point at the top of the document window indi-cates that the program is ready to receive text. Use the keyboard to type the following text exactly as it appears on the page (maximize the WordPad window if necessary):

   WordPad will create multimedia documents?

3. Next, you will edit the text you entered. The insertion point should be just to the right of the question mark. Press [Backspace] to delete the character to the left of the insertion point, in this case the question mark. Type an exclamation point [!] where the question mark used to be.

4. Double-click the word will. The word becomes selected. When text is selected it can be edited, cut or copied and then pasted. Type the word can to overwrite the selected word. Your text should now read:

   WordPad can create multimedia documents!

5. Press [End] on the keyboard to move the insertion point to the end of the line.

6. Press [Enter] to move the insertion point to the next line. Then type the following text:

   Windows XP sounds like this:

7. Formatting your text allows you to change certain attributes of it such as size, font, color, style, and alignment. Before you format text, you must first select it.

8. Move the mouse pointer to the left of the word WordPad in your first line of text. The mouse pointer will appear as the standard pointer, but angled to the right instead of the left. The pointer is in an area known as the Selection bar, an unmarked column on the left edge of a document that enables you to select entire lines or entire paragraphs of text at once.

9. Click once in the Selection bar preceding the first line of text. The entire first line will become highlighted to indicate that it has been selected, as shown in Figure 6-8.

(continued on WN 6.12)

Table 6-1 WordPad Toolbar buttons

Button		Function
New		Creates a new, blank, WordPad document
Open		Opens a saved WordPad document
Save		Stores the active WordPad document with its current file name
Print		Prints one copy of the active WordPad document using the current printer settings
Print Preview		Shows how the active document will look when printed
Find		Searches for specified text in a document
Cut		Removes selected text and sends it to the Clipboard
Copy		Copies selected text and sends it to the Clipboard
Paste		Inserts the contents of the Clipboard at the insertion point
Undo		Reverses the last action performed
Date/Time		Opens the Date and Time dialog box

Figure 6-8 WordPad document

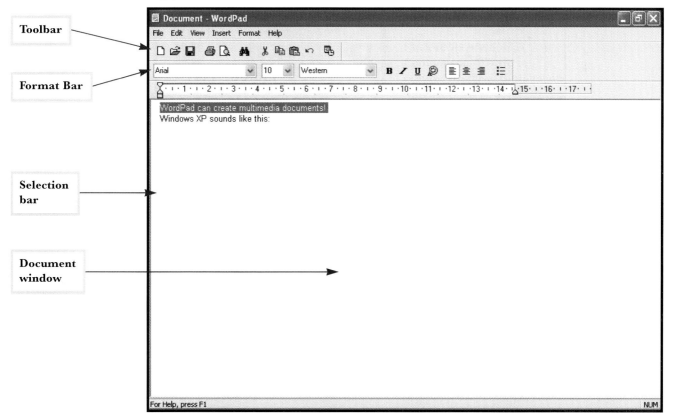

Toolbar

Format Bar

Selection bar

Document window

skill Using WordPad (continued)

do it!

10. Click the Font Size arrow ⌄ on Format Bar. A list of font sizes is displayed. Click the number 18 on the list. The selected text increases in size to 18 point. A point is a unit of measurement for text size equal to 1/72 of an inch.

11. Click the Bold button **B** on Format Bar. The selected text changes style from plain text to bold.

12. Place the mouse pointer in the Selection bar next to the first line. Drag downward until the second line of text is selected in addition to the first.

13. WordPad's default font is Arial. Click the Font arrow ⌄ on Format Bar to open a scrolling list of available fonts. Drag the scroll bar box to see the font Times New Roman. Click Times New Roman to change the font of your text.

14. Click the Center button ≣ on the Format Bar. The text, which had been left-aligned by default, is now centered on the page. Click to the right of the second line to deselect the text. Your formatted document should now resemble the document shown in Figure 6-9.

15. It is important to save your files so that you do not lose the work you have completed. To save a WordPad document, open the File menu and then click the Save command. The Save As dialog box, seen in Figure 6-10, will be displayed. Use the Save in list arrow to select the My Student Files folder you created on your hard drive in Lesson 2.
    The Save command enables you to overwrite the original document file with the current version. To save different versions of the same document in different locations, use the Save As command.

16. WordPad has given the file a default name Document in the File name text box. Double-click this name to select it. Then type the new name wndoit6-4.rtf.

17. Click Save to save the file to the selected location. Close the WordPad application.

more

Table 6-2 WordPad Format Bar buttons

Button	Function	Button	Function
Arial ⌄	Changes the font of the selected text	🎨	Changes the color of the selected text
10 ⌄	Changes the size of the selected text	≣	Aligns selected text to the left indent
B	Bolds the selected text	≣	Centers the selected text
I	Italicizes the selected text	≣	Aligns selected text to the right indent or margin
↶	Undoes the changes of the last action	≔	Adds bullets to the selected list

Figure 6-9 Formatted WordPad document

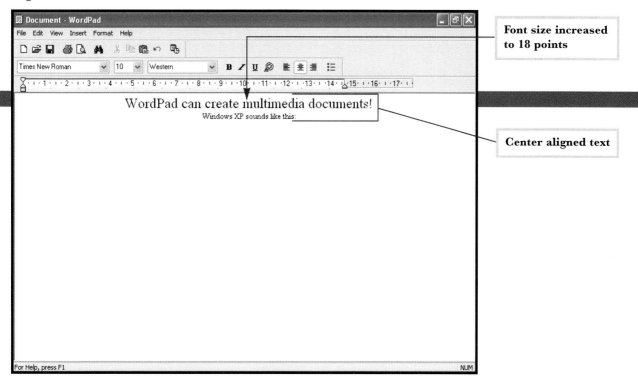

Font size increased to 18 points

Center aligned text

Figure 6-10 Save As dialog box

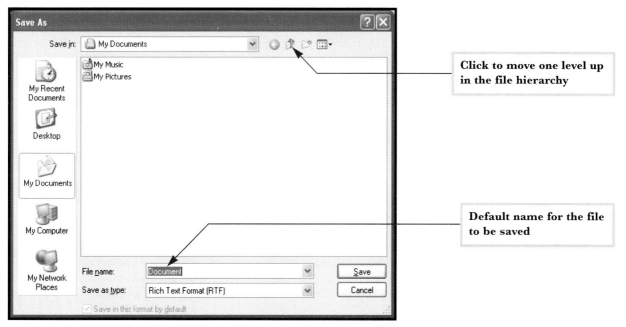

Click to move one level up in the file hierarchy

Default name for the file to be saved

Practice

Use WordPad to create a new document that will be an invitation to a dinner party. Enhance the invitation's appearance with WordPad's Format bar. When you are done, save the document in your My Student Files folder under the name wnprac6-4.rtf.

skill Embedding Sounds in a WordPad Document

concept

WordPad documents need not consist only of text. You can insert multimedia objects such as sounds, pictures, and movies into the body of your WordPad text document. As a result, you and anyone who views your document can have direct access to any files associated with it.

do it!

Embed a sound file in an existing WordPad document.

1. Open the WordPad application. Then, open the File menu and click the Open command. The Open dialog box, which is very similar to the Save As dialog box, will be displayed. Use the Look in list box to display the contents of your hard drive in the contents window. Then, double-click your My Student Files folder to open it. Select wndoit6-4.rtf, and click [Open]. The document you created in the last skill will appear in the WordPad window.

2. Click to the right of the second line of text to place the insertion point there.

3. Press [Enter] twice.

4. Click Insert on the Menu bar, and then click Object. The Insert Object dialog box is displayed.

5. In the Insert Object dialog box, you have the option of creating a new object or creating one from an already existing file. Click the Create from File option button.

6. The center of the dialog box will change to include the File text box and the Browse button (see Figure 6-11). Click [Browse...] to open the Browse dialog box.

7. Use the Browse dialog box to select the tada.wav audio file. The tada.wav file can be located at C:\Windows\Media. Then, click [Open]. The Browse dialog box will close and the path to the sound file will be displayed in the text box in the Insert Object dialog box. ◁▷ If you select the Link check box in the Insert Object dialog box, any changes made to the source file for an inserted object will be updated automatically the next time you open your document.

8. Click [OK] in the Insert Object dialog box to insert the sound file. The file will appear in the document as a sound icon, as shown in Figure 6-12. ◁▷ You can also insert pictures, video clips, and other objects.

9. Double-click the sound icon to play the audio file.

10. Save and close the WordPad file.

more

If you have a printer connected to your computer, you can print paper copies of your WordPad documents quite easily. If you select the Print command from the File menu, the Print dialog box will open, as shown in Figure 6-13. In the Select Printer section of the dialog box, you can select which printer will be used if you are connected to more than one, and adjust the printer's settings. In the Print Range section, you can specify to print all pages, current page, a range of pages, or just selected text. Using the Number of copies spin box, you determine how many copies of the document will be printed. The Collate check box enables you to specify whether multiple page documents will be collated. If you already know that the print settings are correct, click the Print button 🖨 on the Toolbar to bypass the Print dialog box and print your document immediately.

Figure 6-11 Insert Object dialog box

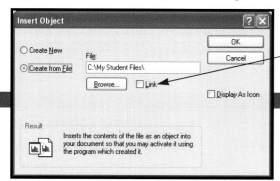

Select to establish a link between the inserted object and its source file

Figure 6-12 A WordPad document with the inserted sound file

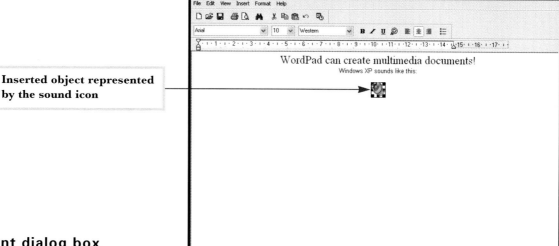

Inserted object represented by the sound icon

Figure 6-13 Print dialog box

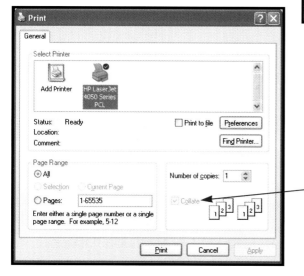

Activate this option to print one complete set of pages before starting the second set when printing more than one copy of a multiple-page document

Practice

Use the Save As command to save the current version of your WordPad document in My Student Files folder under the name wnprac6-4.rtf. Then insert another sound file from the Media folder. Save changes and close WordPad.

skill | Associating Sounds with Windows Events

concept

Associating sounds with Windows events serves several purposes. It enlivens your work experience by adding an entertaining element. More importantly, it gives you feedback regarding your activity and confirms that certain events have taken place. Finally, associated sounds can notify you of activities and problems occurring in programs that are concealed by other windows, or alert you when your attention is not focused on your computer.

do it!

Preview a sound that is already associated with a Windows event. Then, assign a sound to an event that does not currently have a sound associated with it.

1. Click [*start*], and then click Control Panel. This will display the Control Panel window.

2. In the Control Panel window, click Sound, Speech, and Audio Devices. This will display the Sound, Speech, and Audio Devices window.

3. Click the Sounds and Audio Devices link in the Sound, Speech, and Audio Devices window. This will display the Sounds and Audio Devices Properties dialog box.

4. Click the Sounds tab to bring it to the front of the Sounds and Audio Devices Properties dialog box (see Figure 6-14).

5. The Program events list of the Sounds and Audio Devices Properties dialog box shows a list of the windows and their program events that can have a sound associated with them. Events preceded by a sound icon 🔊 already have a sound associated with them. To preview an event sound, you must select the event in the list box. Click Exit Windows to select it, scrolling down if necessary.

6. Once an event is selected, the Sounds list box of the dialog box becomes active. The name of the associated sound, Windows XP Shutdown, appears in the Sounds list box. This is the sound you should hear every time you exit Windows, assuming you are using speakers or headphones. Click the Play button [▸] to hear the sound associated with Exit Windows.

7. Click Close program in the Program events list, an event that does not already have a sound associated with it, to select it in the Events list box. Notice that the Sounds list box, below the Program events list, displays (None).

8. Click the arrow at the right end of the Sounds list box. A list of pre-installed sounds will open.

9. Click the sound called tada.wav. A sound icon now appears next to Close program in the Program events list box, indicating that a sound has been assigned to it. 🔊 You can associate any Wave sound file stored on your computer with a Windows event. Click [Browse...] in the Sounds section of the Sounds and Audio Devices Properties dialog box, and then use the Browse dialog box to navigate to the desired sound file.

10. Click [Apply].

11. Click [OK] to close the Sounds and Audio Devices Properties dialog box.

more

Once you have set your event sounds exactly how you want them to be, you can save them as a scheme. That way, if you ever change your event sounds, you can restore them, or switch between schemes, without having to change each individual event sound. Assign the sounds of your choice to the events you want to include in the scheme, and then click [Save As...] in the Sound scheme section of the Sounds and Audio Devices Properties dialog box. The Save Scheme As dialog box will be displayed (see Figure 6-15) allowing you to enter a name for the scheme. Enter a name, click [OK], and your scheme will appear on the list in the Sound scheme section.

Figure 6-14 Sounds and Audio Devices Properties dialog box

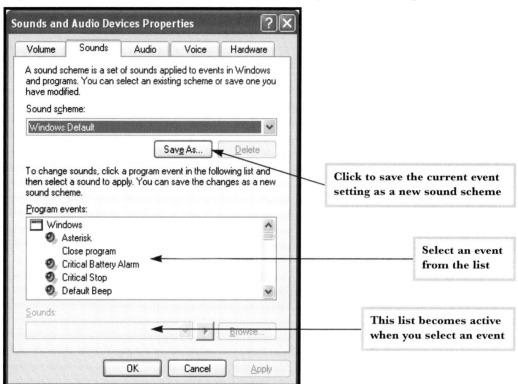

Click to save the current event setting as a new sound scheme

Select an event from the list

This list becomes active when you select an event

Figure 6-15 Save Scheme As dialog box

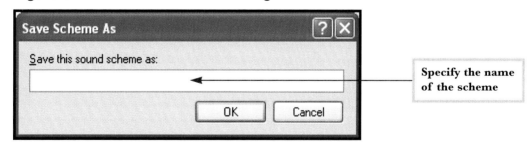

Specify the name of the scheme

Practice

Assign a sound to the Maximize program event.

skill   Watching Video

concept

Windows XP uses Windows Media Player as the default application for viewing video files. Windows Media Player is capable of handling a wide variety of file formats including MPEG audio and video, WAV audio, and AVI video.

do it!

Use Windows Media Player to watch a video clip.

1. Click ⏵ start, point to All Programs, and then point to Accessories. On the Accessories menu, point to Entertainment, and then click Windows Media Player. The Windows Media Player window is displayed.

2. Click File on the Menu bar, and then click Open. The Open dialog box will be displayed.

3. Click the arrow at the right edge of the Look in list box. Click the C: drive on the list to display its contents.

4. In the contents window, locate the Windows folder and double-click it.

5. In the Windows folder, click the Clock.avi file.

6. Click ⌷ Open . This will open the file in Windows Media Player window (see Figure 6-16). ◣ You can use Windows Media Player to view a video on the Web without saving the file on your own computer.

7. Click the Close button ☒ on the Windows Media Player window to close it.

more

In Windows Media Player, you can customize the video settings, such as brightness and contrast of the video. To specify these settings, click View on the Menu bar, point to Now Playing Tools, and then click Video Settings. This displays the slider bars for Brightness, Contrast, Hue, and Saturation below the video clip (see Figure 6-17). Using the slider bars you can increase or decrease each of these settings depending on your requirements.

Figure 6-16 A video file opened in Windows Media Player

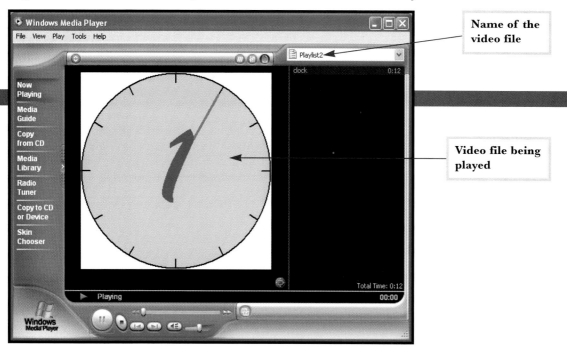

Name of the video file

Video file being played

Figure 6-17 Customizing the video settings

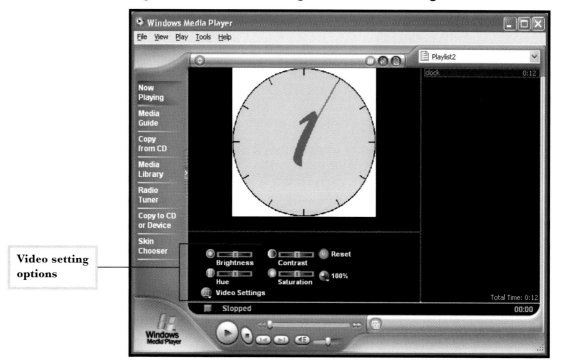

Video setting options

Practice

Open Windows Media Player and play any video clip.

skill | Using Paint to Draw Shapes

concept

The Paint application of Windows XP is useful for creating and editing images. Image files that you create with Paint are bitmap or BMP files. Images created in the Paint application can be sent as an attachment with an e-mail message, set as your desktop wallpaper, or can be saved as other image formats, such as jpeg.

do it!

Use Paint to create basic drawing shapes, fill them with color, and save the file.

1. Click **start**, point to All Programs, and then point to Accessories. On the Accessories menu, click Paint. Maximize the window by double-clicking its Title bar.

2. You should see two rows of buttons on the left side of the window, the Tool Box, and two rows of colored squares at the bottom, the Color Box (palette). If these items are not visible, activate them from their commands on the View menu.

3. If your canvas does not fill the entire work area, place the mouse pointer over the blue square at the bottom right corner of the canvas. Drag the blue square down, to the right until the border of the canvas reaches the bottom right corner of the work area. Release the mouse button. The canvas should now fill the available space.

4. Click the Rectangle tool button ▢ on Tool Box, and then move the pointer to the lower right part of the canvas. Once over the canvas, the pointer should appear as a cross ⊹ with a circle at its intersection, which acts like the crosshairs in an eyepiece. If you do not see this pointer, the tool is not active.

5. Shapes are drawn by dragging the crosshairs across the workspace. The initial click fixes the starting point of the shape you are drawing. You can continue to change the size of a shape as long as the mouse button is held down. Once you let go of the mouse button, the shape's size will be fixed. Drag the mouse pointer up, to the left to create a square, releasing the mouse button when the shape is approximately two inches by two inches (see Figure 6-18).

6. Click the Ellipse tool button ⬭ on Tool Box. This tool allows you to draw circles and ovals.

7. Move the mouse pointer towards the upper-left corner of the workspace. Then, drag down towards the right to draw a large circle.

(continued on WN 6.22)

Figure 6-18 Drawing with Paint

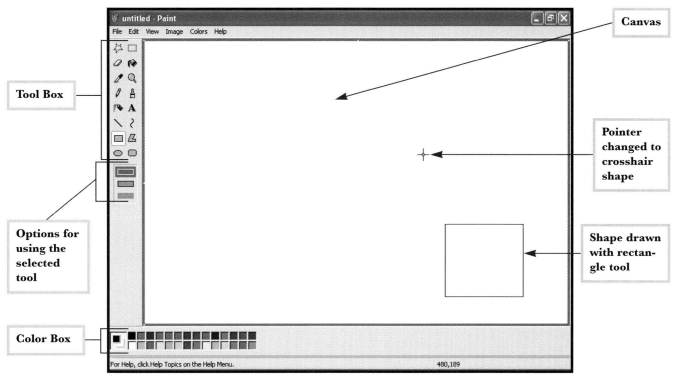

Canvas

Tool Box

Pointer changed to crosshair shape

Options for using the selected tool

Shape drawn with rectangle tool

Color Box

skill | Using Paint to Draw Shapes (continued)

do it!

8. Click the Fill With Color tool button 🎨 on Tool Box to fill color in the square shape. When you move the mouse pointer over the canvas it should change to the spilling paint jar icon as displayed on the button. This tool will fill any area defined by a border with a specified color.

9. Click the Blue square (third color from the right of the first row) in the Color Box.

10. Move the mouse pointer over the square you drew in step 4 and click to fill it with blue.

11. Click the Red square (third color from the left in the second row) in the Color Box and then fill the circle you drew with red by clicking within its border. Your work should now resemble Figure 6-19. ⬬ Double-clicking a color in the Color Box displays the Edit Colors dialog box in which you can edit the existing colors to create your own custom colors.

12. Open the File menu and click the Save command. Use the Save As dialog box to save the file in your My Student Files folder under the name PaintTest.bmp.

13. Click the Close button ❌ to close the file.

more

Table 6-3 Paint Tool Box buttons

Button	Function	Button	Function
Free-Form select	Selects an irregular shape	**Airbrush**	Draws freehand with a selected spray size
Select	Selects an area on the workspace	**Text**	Creates an insertion point for text
Eraser	Erases part of a drawing	**Line**	Draws a straight line
Fill With Color	Fills an area with a selected color	**Curve**	Draws a curved line.
Pick Color	Picks up a color from the picture for use with the Pencil, Brush, or Airbrush tools	**Rectangle**	Draws a rectangle or square
Magnifier	Zooms in and out on a part of the drawing	**Polygon**	Draws an irregular shape
Pencil	Draws freehand lines one pixel wide	**Ellipse**	Draws a circle or oval shape
Brush	Draws freehand with selected size and shape	**Rounded Rectangle**	Draws rounded rectangle or square

Figure 6-19 Drawn shapes filled with color

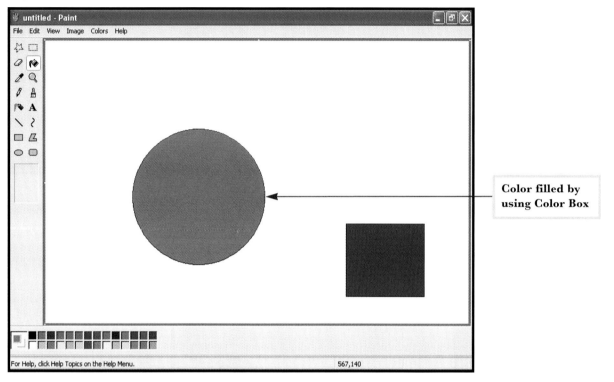

Color filled by using Color Box

Practice

Open a new Paint file and draw three shapes with the Rectangle tool and three with the Ellipse tool. Then fill each shape with a different color. Save the document as wnprac6-8.bmp.

skill | Using Advanced Paint Functions

concept

Just as you can edit a text document with a word processor, you can alter an image file with Paint. The Paint application has tools that allow you to move shapes that you have already drawn and add text to your drawings. Combining your shapes with text and other shapes will help you to design versatile, professional-looking images.

do it!

Move the picture and add a line of text to the picture.

1. Click ⟪start⟫, point to All Programs, and then point to Accessories. On the Accessories menu, click Paint. Use the Open dialog box to open the file PaintTest.bmp.

2. Click the Select tool button ⬚ on the Tool Box (make sure you do not click the Rectangle tool button ▢). Then move the mouse pointer over the canvas. Position the crosshairs on the upper-left corner of the square.

3. Drag the square, stopping just past its bottom right corner. When you release the mouse button, a dashed border will appear around the square, as shown in Figure 6-20. Everything inside this border is selected and can be edited. The eight small squares in each corner and at the midpoint of each side of the dashed box can be dragged to resize the selected area.

4. Move the mouse pointer over the selected area. The mouse pointer will change to a headed arrow movement pointer   . With this pointer you can move a selected area. Drag the square to the red circle. When the square is in position, release the mouse button.

5. Click a blank part of the workspace to deselect the square. Figure 6-21 shows the desired result.

(continued on WN 6.26)

Figure 6-20 Object selected with the Select tool

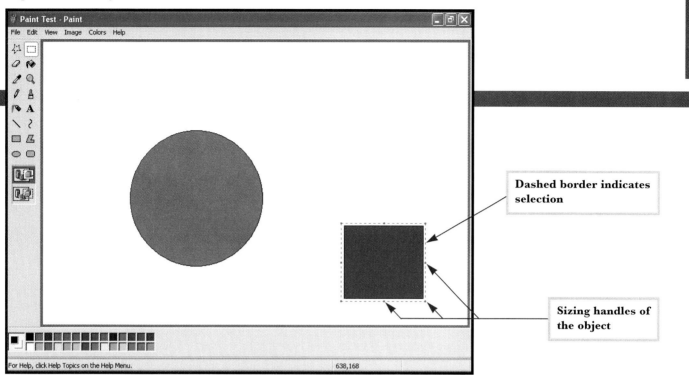

Dashed border indicates selection

Sizing handles of the object

Figure 6-21 Selected area moved to a new location

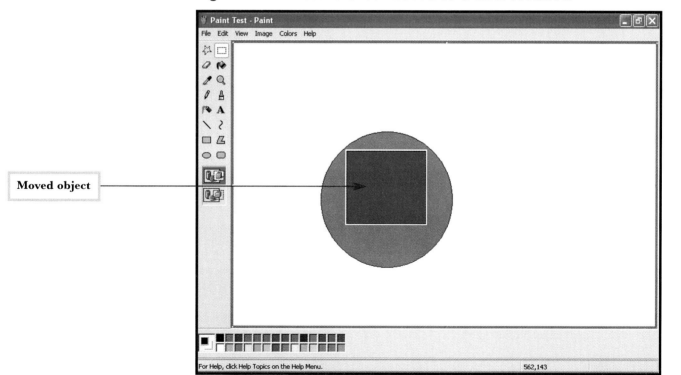

Moved object

skill | Using Advanced Paint Functions (continued)

do it!

6. To add text to a picture, you must open a text frame. Click the Text tool button **A**, and then click the small, blue square in the Color Box located in the lower-left corner of the window. The text you add to the document will be blue.

7. Move the mouse pointer to the left side of the circle, below the square, and drag diagonally down to the right to create a box that fills most of the bottom of the circle (see Figure 6-22).

8. As soon as you release the mouse button, the text frame will be set and become active, and the Text Toolbar is displayed, as shown in Figure 6-23.

9. Use Font, Font size, and Text styles on Text Toolbar to set the text to Times New Roman, 12 point, bold.

10. Click inside the text frame and then type My First Paint Picture. Then click outside the frame to insert the text into the picture. The Text Toolbar will close by itself. You can view important information about your paint file by choosing the Attributes command on the Image menu. The Attributes dialog box provides data such as the dimensions of your drawing and whether it uses black and white or color.

11. Save the changes you have made.

12. Close the Paint program.

more

Paint files are saved as files called bitmaps. Your desktop's background is also a bitmap. Therefore, any file you create using Paint can be used as a desktop background. The Paint application's File menu contains two Set As Background commands. With your Paint file open and all changes saved, choose Set As Background (Tiled) to cover the desktop with repetitions of the bitmap or Set As Background (Centered) to place the bitmap picture in the middle of the desktop. To remove your picture from the desktop background, open the Display Properties dialog box to the Desktop tab, and select (None) or another picture from the Background list box.

Figure 6-22 Creating a text frame

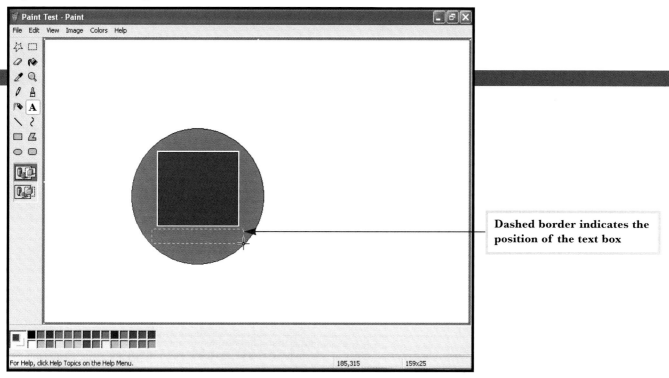

Dashed border indicates the
position of the text box

Figure 6-23 Text Toolbar

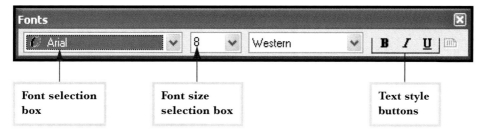

Font selection
box

Font size
selection box

Text style
buttons

 Practice

Open the paint file you created in the previous practice, wnprac6-8.bmp. Move the shapes you drew
so that they form a line running from the top left corner of the canvas to the bottom right corner. Save
the file as wnprac6-9.bmp.

shortcuts

Function	Button/Mouse	Menu	Keyboard
Open an existing file		Click File, then click Open	[Ctrl]+[O]
Open a new file		Click File, then click New	[Ctrl]+[N]
Save a file		Click File, then click Save	[Ctrl]+[S]
Print a document		Click File, then click Print	[Ctrl]+[P]
Cut selected text or object		Click Edit, then click Cut	[Ctrl]+[X]
Copy selected text or object to Clipboard		Click Edit, then click Copy	[Ctrl]+[C]
Paste item from Clipboard		Click Edit, then click Paste	[Ctrl]+[V]
Bold selected text		Click Format, then click Font	[Ctrl]+[B]
Italicize selected text		Click Format, then click Font	[Ctrl]+[I]
Undo last action		Click Edit, then click Undo	[Ctrl]+[U]

quiz

A. Identify Key Features

Name the items indicated by callouts in Figure 6-24.

Figure 6-24 Features of WordPad and Paint

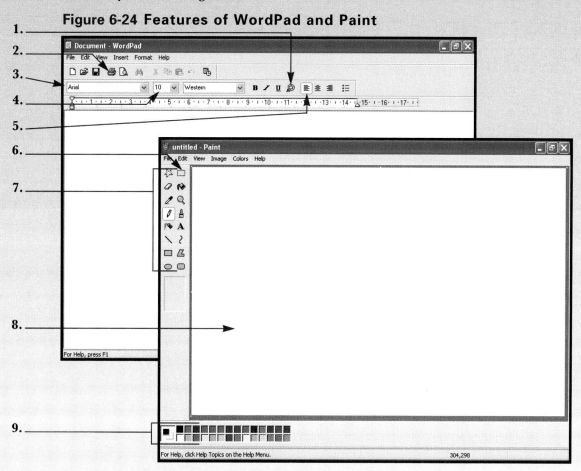

1.
2.
3.
4.
5.
6.
7.
8.
9.

B. Select the Best Answer

10. Application you can use to record and play sound files

11. Windows XP's built-in word processor

12. Program used for listening and viewing audio and video files, respectively

13. Application that is useful for creating and editing images

14. Allows you to adjust audio properties such as balance

15. Accessories subfolder in which you can find the Windows Media Player application

16. When typing in WordPad, press this to move the insertion point to the next line

17. Use this to place a sound file in a WordPad document

a. [Enter] key

b. Entertainment

c. Insert Object dialog box

d. Master Volume window

e. Paint

f. Sound Recorder

g. Windows Media Player

h. WordPad

quiz (continued)

C. Complete the Statement

18. In Paint, the four-way arrow pointer is used to:

a. Enter text

b. Resize a selected object

c. Move a selected object

d. Select an object

19. The two rows of buttons on the left side of the Paint window are known as the:

a. Tool Shed

b. Tool Box

c. Color Box

d. Palette

20. You can associate sounds with windows events in:

a. The Sounds and Audio Devices Properties dialog box

b. The Media folder

c. WordPad

d. Windows Media Player

21. To draw circles and ovals in Paint, use the:

a. Draw tool

b. Pencil tool

c. Curve tool

d. Ellipse tool

22. Image files you create with Paint are called:

a. MPEGs

b. Waves

c. AVIs

d. Bitmaps

23. By default, WordPad text is:

a. Centered

b. Left-aligned

c. Right-aligned

d. Italicized

24. In WordPad, to delete the character to the left of the insertion point, press:

a. [Delete]

b. [End]

c. The left mouse button

d. [Backspace]

25. Text you insert in a Paint picture must reside in a:

a. WordPad document

b. Picture frame

c. Text frame

d. Linked object

26. The row of buttons that allows you to change text characteristics in WordPad is called the:

a. Selection bar

b. Select tool

c. Format Bar

d. Status Bar

27. Before you format text in WordPad, you must:

a. Save the file

b. Select it

c. Insert a text frame

d. Preview it

interactivity

Build Your Skills

1. Create a WordPad document:

   a. Open WordPad.

   b. Enter the following text exactly as it appears on this page:

   Creating Web Pages

   Recent releases of the top word processing software packages such as Microsoft Word and WordPerfect have capabilities for creating HTML documents that can be used as Web pages on the World Wide Web. More sophisticated and powerful authoring tools for creating, editing, and publishing Web pages are also available, such as Microsoft FrontPage and Macromedia Dreamweaver. As a result, even newcomers to ciberspace can have a presence on the Web.

2. Edit the WordPad document you just created:

   a. Correct the spelling of the word cyberspace by replacing i with y.

   b. Change the word packages in the first sentence to the word applications.

   c. Use the Cut and Paste commands to move the last sentence so that it becomes the second sentence.

3. Format and save your WordPad document:

   a. Center the passage's title, Creating Web Pages, and change the font to 16 point Arial.

   b. Italicize the word cyberspace.

   c. Bold the words Microsoft Word, WordPerfect, Microsoft FrontPage, and Macromedia Dreamweaver.

   d. Save the document as wnskill6-1.rtf and close it.

4. Use Paint to create an image of a green highway EXIT sign:

   a. Open the Paint application. Select the Rounded Rectangle tool and draw a shape that is approximately two inches across by one inch high to create the outline of the sign.

   b. Click the light green square in the Color Box to select it as your foreground color. Then right-click the same square to select it as your background color also.

   c. Fill the shape with light green color.

   d. Select the Text tool and create a text frame that covers most of the middle of the rounded rectangle.

   e. Click the white color square to change the foreground color to white.

   f. Change the font to 28 point, Bold, Arial. Click in the text frame to activate it and type EXIT 22. Then click a blank part of the workspace to confirm the text frame.

   g. Save the file as wnskill6-2.bmp.

interactivity (continued)

Problem Solving Exercises

1. You have been hired by a new Internet software company called Webskill to do some freelance design work. Your project involves creating Webskill's logo. Once you come up with an idea, use Paint to draw the logo. Your idea can use simple shapes or complex designs, if you are so inclined. Your only restriction is that the logo must include the company name. When you are done with the designing of the logo, save the file and leave Paint open. Then open WordPad and write a proposal letter to the President of Webskill to introduce the logo. The letter itself must include a sample of the logo. To do this, you must share data between the two programs. Follow the procedure below:

> a. In Paint, use the Select tool to select your logo. Then select the Copy command from the Edit menu to send a copy of the selection to the Clipboard.

> b. Switch back to the proposal letter in WordPad. Place the insertion point at the location in the letter where you want the logo to appear by clicking there.

> c. Click the Paste button on Toolbar to embed the logo in the WordPad document. If you place the logo in the middle of the letter, the text that follows it may be affected. Edit your letter as necessary, and save the letter.

2. Your company, an advertising agency, has just hired several entry-level staff members. Most of them have limited experience using the Windows XP operating system. Management wants to be sure that the new employees learn the fundamentals of Windows, including its multimedia and data sharing capabilities. It is your job to produce a document in WordPad that details such procedures as how to associate sounds with Windows events, how to insert objects such as sounds in a WordPad document, and how to play sound files both independently and from within a document. The writing in your document should be informative and concise, and include examples.

Maintaining Your System

Even if you do not have a technical background, you can take measures to ensure that your computer continues to function properly and smoothly. Windows XP provides utility programs such as Disk Cleanup, Error-checking, and Disk Defragmenter that allow you to perform maintenance on your computer. You can run these programs individually or schedule all of them to run automatically. Either way, the efficiency with which your system operates will increase.

The Scheduled Task Wizard extends the idea of automating program execution to the other applications installed on your machine. It enables you to run a task or program on a regular schedule. For example, you can schedule your Web browser to open every morning at the same time, or run a particular maintenance task once every week.

You can also use Windows XP to alter the contents of your hard drive. By following a few simple instructions, you can add and remove programs as you see fit. The idea of installing software yourself may be intimidating at first, but the Add or Remove Programs utility in Control Panel should ease any anxiety. Removing programs helps you save storage space and eliminates the confusion that can be caused by having new and old versions of the same software installed on your computer.

skills

**≴ Viewing System
Information**

**≴ Managing Your
Computer
Performance**

≴ Scheduling Tasks

≴ Disk Cleanup

**≴ Checking a Hard Disk
for Errors**

≴ Disk Defragmenter

**≴ Backup or Restore
Wizard**

**≴ Files and Settings
Transfer Wizard**

**≴ Adding and Removing
Programs**

Lesson Goal:

In this lesson, you will learn to manage the performance of your computer, schedule tasks, and to use the disk cleanup tool to delete the unnecessary files on your hard disk. Additionally, you will learn to check your hard disk for errors, defragment a disk, backup your data, transfer files and settings from one computer to another, and to add and remove programs from your computer.

skill | Viewing System Information

concept

In Windows XP, you can view information related to your system configuration using the System Information tool. System Information is a system tool that enables you to view information of the local computer or of a computer to which your computer is connected. The system information includes the information related to the hardware, software, and the computer components.

The System Information category tree in the System Information window displays the following categories:

◉ System Summary: This category displays the general information, such as the operating system name, version, manufacturer, and the directory location, about your system.

◉ Hardware Resources: This category of the System Information window displays the information related to the resource assignments and the possible sharing conflicts among DMA, Forced Hardware, I/O, IRQ's, and Memory resources.

◉ Components: This category displays the information related to the system components, such as Multimedia, CD-ROM, Sound Devices, Display, Infrared, Input, Modem, Network, Ports, Storage, Printing, Problem Devices, and USB.

◉ Software Environment: This category contains the information related to the system configuration, system drivers, environment variables, and the current print job.

◉ Internet Settings: This category contains the information related to the explorer installed on your computer.

◉ Applications: This category contains the information related to the programs running on your computer.

do it!

View the system information related to the sound device of your computer.

1. Click ⊞ start , point to All Programs, point to Accessories, then point to System Tools and click System Information. This will display the System Information window (see Figure 7-1).

2. In the System Information category, click the plus symbol ⊞ beside Components to view the subcategories under the Components category.

3. Click the Sound Device subcategory. Information related to the sound device will be displayed in the details pane of the System Information window (see Figure 7-2).

4. Click the Close button ✖ to close the System Information window.

more

You can search for a specific category using the Find what text box in the System Information window. To search a specific category, type the category name in the Find what text box and click   Find . System Information tool will search each category starting from System Summary and displays the first search result. You can view the search results in other categories by clicking Find Next in the System Information window.

Figure 7-1 System Information window

System
Information
category tree

Information
about your
system

Details pane

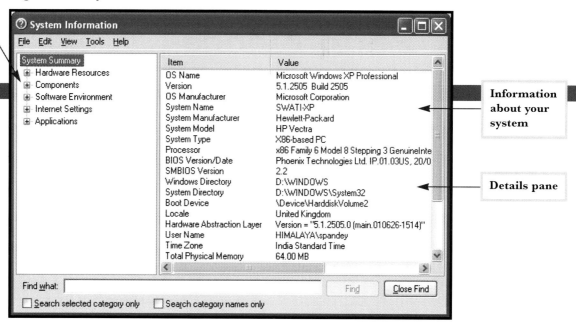

Figure 7-2 Sound Device subcategory details

Information
about the
sound device
installed on
your system

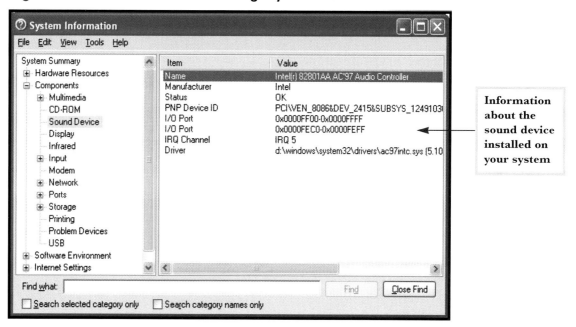

Practice

Open the System Information window and view the information related to the modem attached to your computer.

skill | Managing Your Computer Performance

concept

In Windows XP, you can improve the performance of the programs running on your system by changing the way in which the computer memory and processor time is used. You can set the properties of Windows to allocate more time to the programs that are currently running. With the result, the response time of the program running in foreground becomes fast.

do it!

Change the processor time allocated to the foreground and background programs.

1. Click **start** and click the Control Panel command. This will display the Control Panel window.

2. In the Control Panel window, click Performance and Maintenance. This will display the Performance and Maintenance window.

3. Click Systems. This will display the System Properties dialog box.

4. Click the Advanced tab to bring it to the front of the System Properties dialog box (see Figure 7-3).

5. In the Performance section, click [Settings]. This will display Performance Options dialog box (see Figure 7-4).

6. In the Performance Options dialog box, click the Advanced tab.

7. In the Process Scheduling section, you can either click the Programs option button or the Background services option button. Clicking the Programs option button assigns more processor resources to the foreground processes than the background processes and clicking the Background services option button assigns equal processor resources to all the programs.

8. After clicking the appropriate option button, click [OK] to close the Performance Options dialog box.

9. Click [OK] to close the System Properties dialog box.

more

Windows XP provides the options for settings the visual effects of your computer. Using the options under the Visual Effects tab of the Performance Options dialog box, you can customize the visual effects of your computer. For instance, you can animate windows when the windows are minimized or maximized, enable Web view in your folders, and display a list of hyperlinked tasks.

Figure 7-3 System Properties dialog box

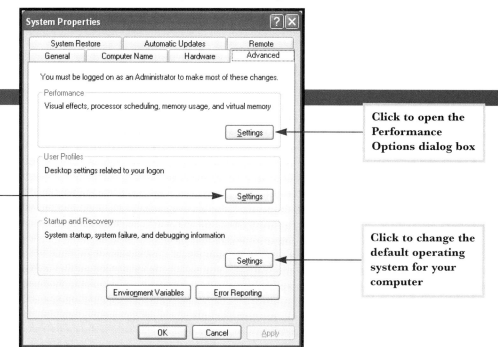

Click to open the Performance Options dialog box

Click to copy or delete a user profile

Click to change the default operating system for your computer

Figure 7-4 Performance Options dialog box

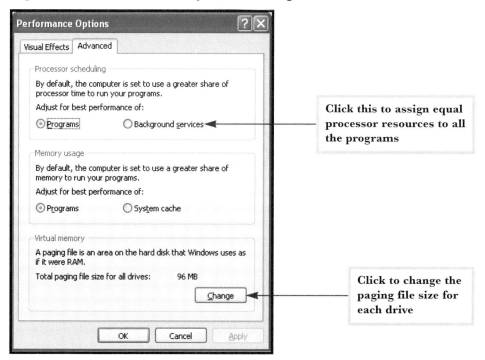

Click this to assign equal processor resources to all the programs

Click to change the paging file size for each drive

Practice

Using the Performance Options dialog box, change the processor time for the best performance of the background programs. Then revert back to the default setting of your system.

skill | Scheduling Tasks

concept

Windows XP allows you to automate a wide variety of tasks. By scheduling these tasks with the Scheduled Tasks window, you can run programs and utilities at a set time, such as every time you start your system, at a specific time during the day, weekly, or monthly.

do it!

Schedule Internet Explorer to run daily at 9:30 AM.

1. Click start and click the Control Panel command. This will display the Control Panel window.

2. In the Control Panel window, click the Performance and Maintenance link. This will display the Performance and Maintenance window.

3. Click Scheduled Tasks. This will display the Scheduled Tasks window. In the Scheduled Tasks window (see Figure 7-5), double-click Add Scheduled Task. The Scheduled Task Wizard wizard is displayed.

4. Read the introduction in the first screen, and then click Next > .

5. In the second screen of the wizard, you will see a list box displaying all the applications available for you to schedule. Scroll down the list until Internet Explorer is visible, and then click the application name to select it, as shown in Figure 7-6.

6. Click Next > .

7. In the third screen, you can name the task and choose when the task will be performed. Windows provides the suggested name Internet Explorer. Leave the name as it is displayed on the screen. Click the option button labeled Daily, and then click Next > .

8. The fourth screen provides three sections for determining the details of the scheduled task. The Start time box will show the current time with the hour selected. If the current hour is not 9, press 9 on the keyboard to replace it. Then click on the minute digits to select them and type 30. From AM/PM, select AM, if not selected by default.

9. In the Perform this task section, click the option button labeled Weekdays.

10. The Start date selection box will display the current date automatically. With the exception of the date, the dialog box should resemble Figure 7-7. Click Next > .

(continued on WN 7.8)

Figure 7-5 Scheduled Task window

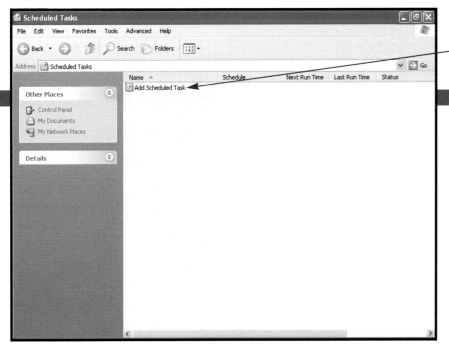

Double-click to open Scheduled Task Wizard

Figure 7-6 Selecting a task to be scheduled

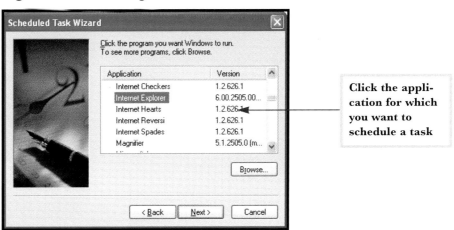

Click the application for which you want to schedule a task

Figure 7-7 Setting time, frequency, and start date

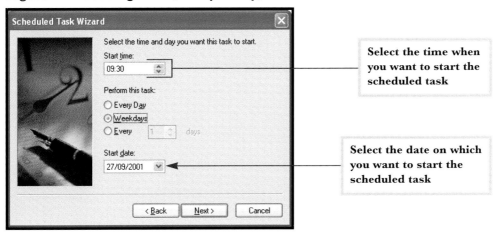

Select the time when you want to start the scheduled task

Select the date on which you want to start the scheduled task

skill Scheduling Tasks (continued)

do it!

11. In the fifth screen, you can specify the user name and the password of the user who has scheduled the task. Click [Next >].

12. The sixth screen is the last screen of the wizard and displays the details of the task being scheduled. Click [Finish]. This will close the Schedule Task Wizard wizard and the task you just created will appear in the Scheduled Tasks window. Internet Explorer will now run automatically at 9:30 AM every weekday, provided your computer is turned on.

13. Close the Scheduled Tasks window.

more

In the sixth screen of the Scheduled Task Wizard wizard, you will see a check box labeled Open advanced properties for this task when I click Finish. Selecting this check box causes a dialog box to appear as soon as you click [Finish]. The same dialog box will appear if you double-click a scheduled task in the Scheduled Tasks window. The dialog box includes three tabs that allow you to view and edit the properties of the task you have just scheduled or opened. The Task tab outlines the general properties of the job including the file path and name, what program it runs, and whether the task is enabled. The Schedule tab, as shown in Figure 7-8, summarizes the scheduling details you entered in the Wizard. It also provides you with the opportunity to adjust the schedule and create multiple schedules. On the Settings tab (see Figure 7-9), you can instruct Windows to delete a task when it has been completed and control the circumstances and conditions under which a task is permitted to run. If you no longer want a task to run, double-click it in the Scheduled Tasks window and then remove the check mark from the check box at the bottom of the Task tab. To delete a task permanently, simply drag it to the Recycle Bin.

Figure 7-8 Schedule tab

Summary of the
scheduled task

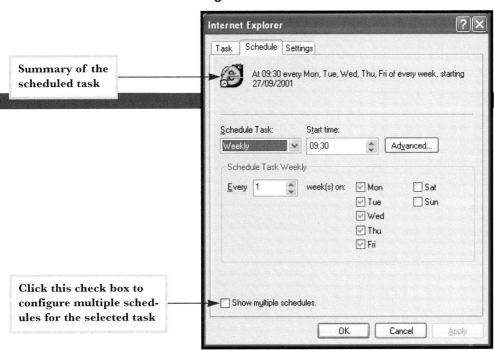

Click this check box to
configure multiple sched-
ules for the selected task

Figure 7-9 Settings tab

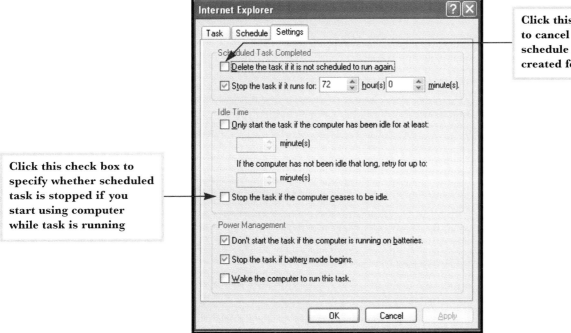

Click this check box
to cancel the task if a
schedule has not been
created for it

Click this check box to
specify whether scheduled
task is stopped if you
start using computer
while task is running

Practice

Schedule the Backup application to run every weekday at 1:45 PM beginning today. When you are
done, delete the Internet Explorer task you scheduled earlier in this skill.

skill | Disk Cleanup

concept

There might be situations when you run out of disk space on your system. These situations may arise due to the files that are not used by you or your system but are still lying on your hard drive. Using the Disk Cleanup program you can create free space on your hard drive. Disk Cleanup finds unnecessary data, such as temporary files and Internet cache files, and deletes it, creating more space for your important files.

do it!

Run the Disk Cleanup application manually to create free space on your hard drive.

1. Click **start**, point to All Programs, point to Accessories, point to System Tools, and click the Disk Cleanup command.

2. If you have more than one hard disk drive, a dialog box will be displayed asking you which disk drive you want to clean up. If your main hard disk (most likely C:) has not been selected automatically, click on the list arrow and select it from the list of drives.

3. Click `OK` to continue.

4. Disk Cleanup will begin the process of calculating how much space you will be able to clear on your hard drive. When it finishes, a dialog box will be displayed with two tabs. The Disk Cleanup tab options are displayed on the top (see Figure 7-10).

5. The top of the tab tells you exactly how much unnecessary data was found, in this case 406 KB. Below this, the data is broken down into categories so that you can see exactly how much space is being taken up by which types of files. For example, Disk Cleanup found 31 KB files in the Recycle Bin and 376 KB as System Restore files.

6. Preceding each category is a check box that allows you to determine which files will actually be removed by Disk Cleanup. Since only the second category is checked (and therefore suggested), the total amount of disk space gained is 376 KB out of 406 KB.

7. You will notice that a description of the selected file category, Recycle Bin, appears at the bottom of the tab. Select each of the remaining categories in turn and read their descriptions. These descriptions are very helpful in determining whether you should delete a particular type of file.

8. Leave only the second category checked and click `OK`. A confirmation dialog box will be displayed. Click `Yes`. Disk Cleanup deletes the unnecessary files.

more

The Disk Cleanup dialog box's More Options tab (see Figure 7-11) provides additional ways in which you can create free space on your hard drive. One way is to eliminate windows components that you do not use. Click `Clean up...` in the Windows components section of the tab to begin this process. You can also remove the programs that have been installed on your computer but do not get used. Click `Clean up...` in the Installed programs section of the tab for assistance in uninstalling such programs. The third section, System Restore, enables you to clean the system restore points. Click `Clean up...` in the System Restore section to clean all system restore points except the most recent ones.

Figure 7-10 Disk Cleanup tab

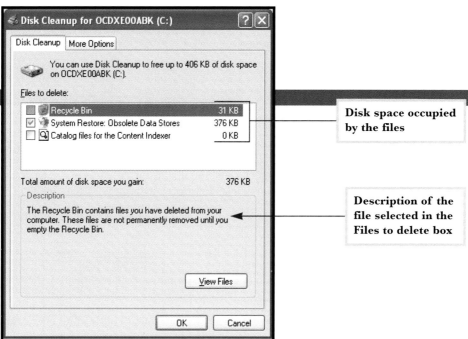

Disk space occupied by the files

Description of the file selected in the Files to delete box

Figure 7-11 More Options tab

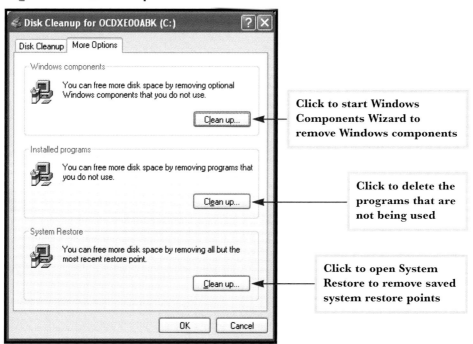

Click to start Windows Components Wizard to remove Windows components

Click to delete the programs that are not being used

Click to open System Restore to remove saved system restore points

Practice

If your computer has a second hard drive or backup disk, run Disk Cleanup on it.

skill | Checking a Hard Disk for Errors

concept

Windows XP's error-checking tool can be used to detect the errors in the hard disk of your system. The error-checking tool is used to find and correct errors that occur in the files on your hard drive and on the surface of the disk itself. Such errors, which can be in the form of physical damage or erroneous logic, can occur without your knowledge.

do it!

Check errors in your system's files for physical and logical errors.

1. Click [start], and then click My Computer. This will display the My Computer window.

2. In the My Computer window, click the drive that you want to check for errors.

3. Click File on the Menu bar and then click Properties. This will open the properties dialog box of the selected drive.

4. In the properties dialog box, click the Tools tab (see Figure 7-12).

5. In the Error-checking section of the dialog box, click [Check Now...]. This will display the Check Disk dialog box.

6. In the Check disk options section, leave the Automatically fix file system errors check box blank.

7. Select the Scan for and attempt recovery of bad sectors check box (see Figure 7-13).

8. Click [start] to begin the disk scanning procedure. The progress bar at the bottom of the dialog box will show the progress of the process.

9. When the process is completed results are displayed in the Checking Disk dialog box, as shown in Figure 7-14. If no errors are found, as in this case, click [OK] to close the Checking Disk dialog box.

10. Click [OK] in the properties dialog box to close it.

11. If error-checking finds errors on your hard disk, you will be asked if you want the errors to be fixed. If you are unsure, consult your instructor or Information Technology director before proceeding. You can also use the Chkdsk command in the command prompt to check and correct the hard disk for errors.

Figure 7-12 Properties dialog box of the selected drive

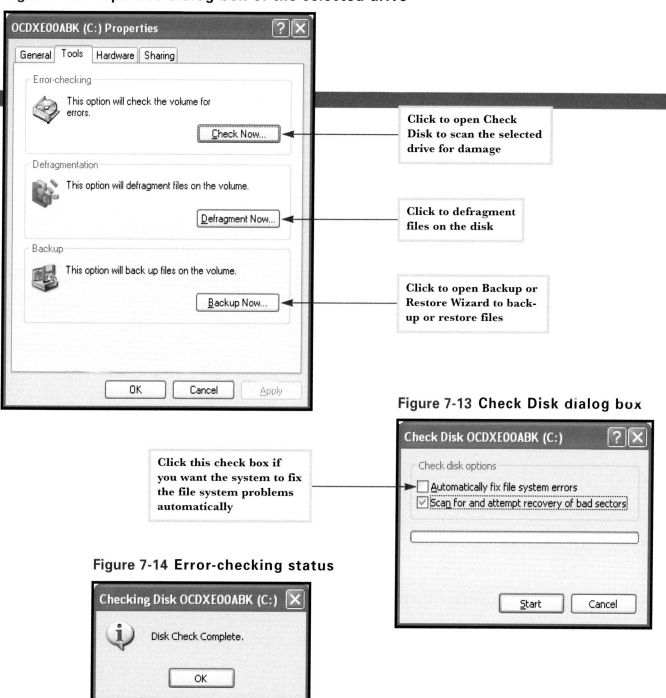

Click to open Check Disk to scan the selected drive for damage

Click to defragment files on the disk

Click to open Backup or Restore Wizard to back-up or restore files

Figure 7-13 Check Disk dialog box

Click this check box if you want the system to fix the file system problems automatically

Figure 7-14 Error-checking status

Practice

Insert a floppy disk into your 3½ inch floppy drive and check it for errors.

skill | Disk Defragmenter

concept

One of the most common complaints made by computer users is that their systems are running too slowly. Disk Defragmenter is one solution to this problem. A fragmented file is a file that is too large to be stored in one location on your hard disk, and is therefore split into pieces. When you want to use such a file, it takes your computer time to find the different pieces into which it has been divided. Disk Defragmenter remedies this problem by rearranging the disk's data so that pieces of the same file are stored next to each other and free space is consolidated. In addition, the program also creates a log of your most frequently used applications and groups them with their associated files at the beginning of the disk, thus optimizing the speed with which your system can process these items. You can run other applications at the same time as Disk Defragmenter. If the disk being defragmented is written to, however, the defragmentation process will be restarted. You may want to close certain programs so that Defragmenter can complete its work.

do it!

Run Disk Defragmenter to reorganize the data on your hard drive and optimize your computer's performance.

1. Click start , point to All Programs, point to Accessories, point to System Tools, and click the Disk Defragmenter command. This will display the Disk Defragmenter window.

2. The top section of the Disk Defragmenter windows displays the list of disk drives. Click your main hard disk and click Defragment . Clicking this button starts analyzing the selected drive and after few minutes the defragmentation process will begin (see Figure 7-15). While in progress, you can stop, pause, or view the details of the process. The process will take several minutes.

3. When it has finished, Disk Defragmenter will display a message that the defragmentation is complete for the selected drive (see Figure 7-16). Click Close .

4. Click the Close button X to close the Disk Defragmenter window.

more

You can view the details of the defragmentation process by clicking View Report in the Disk Defragmenter window or in the Disk Defragmenter dialog box. This will display the Defragmentation Report dialog box (see Figure 7-17). The Volume information section of the Defragmentation Report dialog box displays the details of the defragmented drive, volume, files, and folders. The Files that did not defragment section displays the details of the files that have not been defragmented. While it is not necessary to monitor the defragmentation process, it is a good idea to view its details at least once so that you can gain a better understanding of what it accomplishes.

Figure 7-15 Disk Defragmenter window

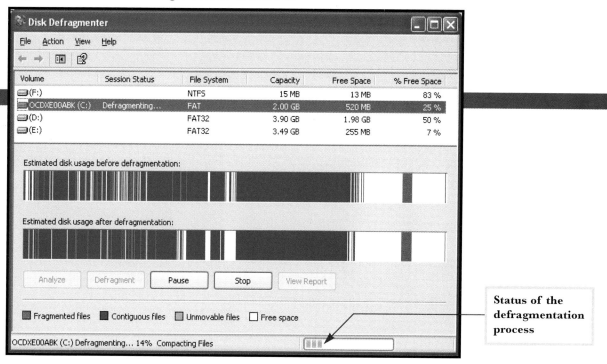

Figure 7-16 Disk Defragmenter dialog box

Status of the defragmentation process

Figure 7-17 Defragmentation Report dialog box

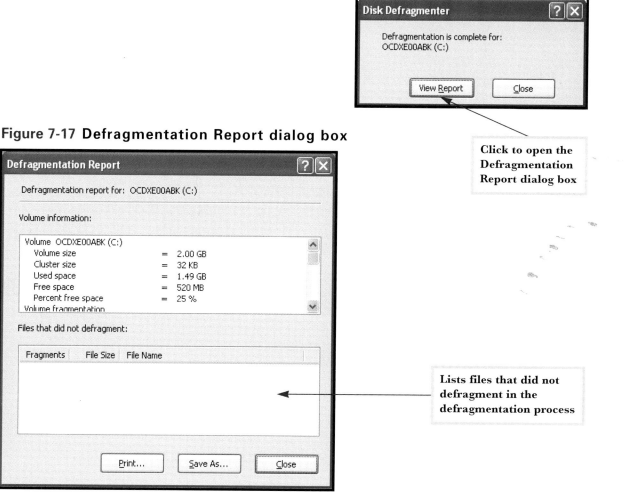

Click to open the Defragmentation Report dialog box

Lists files that did not defragment in the defragmentation process

skill   Backup or Restore Wizard

concept

There might be situations when you lose the data on your hard disk or are not able to access the data due to hard disk malfunction. To prevent data loss in such situations, you can backup your hard disk data. Windows XP provides the Backup or Restore Wizard using which you can backup your hard disk data and restore the data whenever required.

do it!

Use Backup or Restore Wizard to backup the data on your hard disk.

1. Click [start], point to All Programs, point to Accessories, then point to System Tools and click Backup. This will display the welcome screen of Backup or Restore Wizard.

2. Click [Next >]. This will display the Backup or Restore screen of the Backup or Restore Wizard. In this screen, Backup files and settings and Restore files and settings options buttons are displayed (see Figure 7-18).

3. By default, the Backup files and settings option button is selected. Click [Next >]. This will display What to Back Up screen. This screen enables you to select the items you want to back up. By default, My documents and settings option button is selected. You can select specific files from your hard disk by clicking the Let me choose what to back up option button.

4. Click [Next >]. This will display the Backup Type, Destination, and Name screen (see Figure 7-19). In this screen, you can specify the location where you want to backup your data. You can also specify name to your backup in the Type a name for this backup text box. Type Documents Backup.

5. By default, $3\frac{1}{2}$ Floppy (A:) is selected in the Choose a place to save your backup list box. Insert a floppy and click [Next >] to backup on the floppy disk. This will display the Completing the Backup or Restore Wizard screen. If the data is too large for one floppy, the system will prompt you to insert another floppy.

6. Click [Finish]. This will display the Backup Progress window, which shows the progress of the data backup process. Once the backup is complete, the Backup Progress dialog box will display the message that the backup is complete (see Figure 7-20).

7. Click [Close] to close the Backup Progress window.

more

Using the Backup or Restore Wizard wizard you can restore the data from the location where you stored it while making the backup. To restore the data, select the Restore files and settings option button in the Backup or Restore screen of Backup or Restore Wizard. The subsequent screens of the Backup or Restore Wizard wizard will guide you to restore the data.

Figure 7-18 Backup or Restore screen

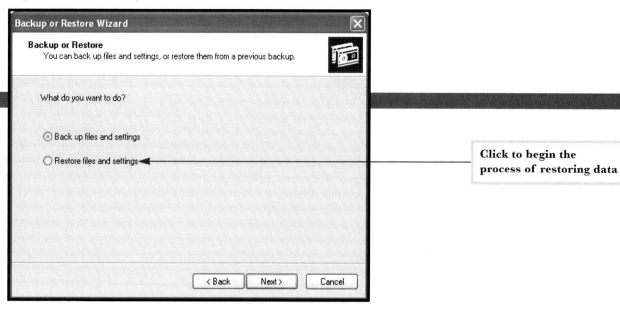

Click to begin the
process of restoring data

Figure 7-19 Backup Type, Destination, and Name screen

Specify the place
for your backup

Figure 7-20 Backup Process dialog box

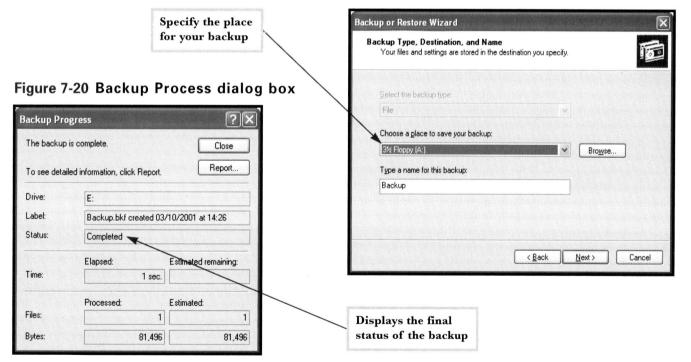

Displays the final
status of the backup

Practice

Use the Backup or Restore Wizard wizard to backup your important files.

skill | Files and Settings Transfer Wizard

concept

In Windows XP, you can move the settings and the data files from your old computer to the new computer, disk drive, or folder using the Files and Settings Transfer Wizard tool. Using Files and Settings Transfer Wizard, you can transfer the settings for the Internet Explorer and Outlook Express. You can also transfer the display settings, and dial-up connections.

do it!

Use Files and Settings Transfer Wizard to move settings from your local computer to a folder on your machine.

1. Click [*start*], point to All Programs, point to Accessories, then point to System Tools and click Files and Settings Transfer Wizard. This will display the welcome screen of the Files and Settings Transfer Wizard.

2. Click [Next >]. This will display the Which computer is this screen of Files and Settings Transfer Wizard. In this screen, New computer and Old computer options buttons are displayed.

3. Click the Old computer option button to transfer settings from your local computer to a new computer.

4. Click [Next >]. The Files and Settings Transfer Wizard prepares for the next step of the wizard and displays the Select a transfer method screen. This screen enables you to transfer your settings using direct cable, floppy drive, and other media, such as a disk drive or a folder on your computer.

5. Click the Other option button. This will activate the Folder or drive text box.

6. Click [Browse...]. This will display the Browse For Folder dialog box. Browse for the folder My Student Files, which you created on your hard drive in Lesson 2 and click [OK].

7. Click [Next >]. This will display the What do you want to transfer screen. By default, the Both files and settings option button is selected.

8. Click [Next >]. The Files and Settings Transfer Wizard starts collecting the files and folders. After collecting all files and folders, the Completing the Collection Phase screen is displayed.

9. Click [Finish]. This will close the Files and Settings Transfer Wizard.

more

To apply the settings on new computer, open the Files and Settings Transfer Wizard and in the Which computer is this screen, click the New computer option button. Then follow the instructions of the wizard. In the Select a transfer method screen, select the Other option button and browse the folder where you collected the files and settings. Again follow the instruction of the wizard to transfer the files and settings.

Figure 7-21 Which computer is this screen

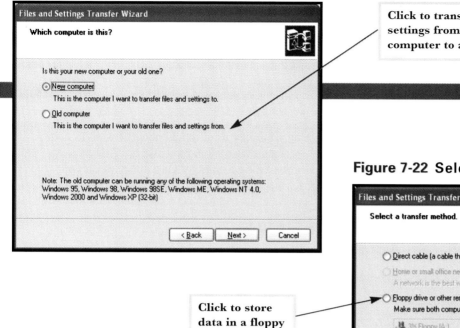

Click to transfer files and settings from an older computer to a newer one

Figure 7-22 Select a transfer method screen

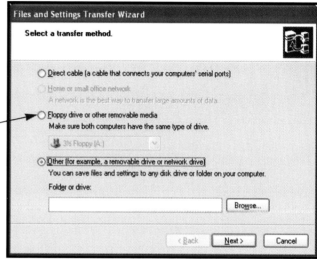

Click to store data in a floppy

Figure 7-23 Completing the Collection Phase screen

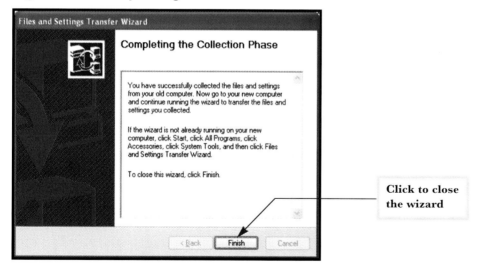

Click to close the wizard

Practice

Use Files and Settings Transfer Wizard to transfer files and settings from any other computer to your computer.

skill | Adding and Removing Programs

concept

As your computer skills continue to develop, you may want to add new software to your computer that will allow you to complete different tasks. You may also have the need to eliminate programs that you do not find useful and are simply taking up space on your hard drive.

do it!

Explore Windows XP's utility for adding and removing programs.

1. Open the Control Panel window. Then click the Add or Remove Programs link. The Add or Remove Programs dialog box is displayed.

2. To add a new program, click Add New Programs. The Add or Remove Programs dialog box will display CD or Floppy and Windows Update buttons (see Figure 7-24).

3. To install a program from a CD or Floppy click [CD or Floppy]. This will display the Install Program From Floppy Disk or CD ROM wizard. At this point you would need to insert a CD or floppy and follow the instructions of the Wizard until the installation procedure completes.

4. To remove or change a program, click Change or Remove Programs in the Add or Remove Programs dialog box.

5. Select the program you want to remove or change.

6. To change the selected program, click [Change] and to remove the selected program click [Remove]. The selected program will run its setup. Follow the instructions of the setup program to carry out the operation.

7. Click [Close] to close the Add or Remove Programs dialog box.

more

Not all programs behave the same way when you uninstall them. Some applications come with their own uninstall program that is activated when you click [Change] or [Remove]. In most cases, the procedure is still fairly simple and you will be guided through it. After you remove a program, you can always reinstall it from the original floppy disks or CD-ROM.

Figure 7-24 Add or Remove Programs dialog box

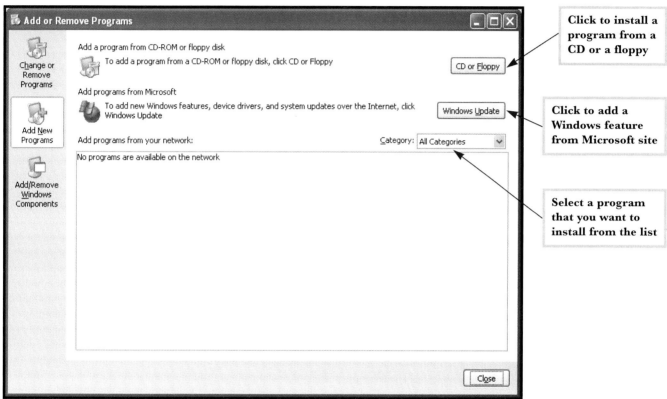

Click to install a program from a CD or a floppy

Click to add a Windows feature from Microsoft site

Select a program that you want to install from the list

Practice

(Optional)

Remove a noncritical program from your system and then reinstall it from its original location.

A. Select the Best Answer

1. Utility that removes unnecessary files from your computer

2. Displays the details of defragmentation

3. A category that displays the information related to the system configuration in the System Information window

4. Allows you to move the settings and data files from one computer to another

5. Allows you to run programs automatically at times you determine

6. Utility that reorganizes the data on your hard drive so that it can be accessed more efficiently

a. Defragmentation Report

b. Disk Cleanup

c. Disk Defragmenter

d. Files and Settings Transfer Wizard

e. Scheduled Tasks window

f. Software Environment

B. Complete the Statement

1. In the System Information window, information related to the programs running on your computer can be viewed under the:

   a. Components category

   b. Applications category

   c. Software Environment category

   d. Components category

2. The error-checking tool checks errors on:

   a. Files, folders, and the surface of the hard disk

   b. Only the surface of the hard disk

   c. Only the unused space on the hard disk

   d. The files and folders on your hard disk

3. To schedule a task, click Scheduled Tasks in the:

   a. Performance and Maintenance window

   b. System Information window

   c. System Properties dialog box

   d. Control Panel window

4. To add or remove software, double-click Add/Remove Programs in the:

   a. Files or Settings Transfer Wizard

   b. Control Panel window

   c. My Computer window

   d. Scheduled Tasks

5. To create free space on your hard disk, you click Disk Cleanup in the:

   a. My Computer window

   b. System Information window

   c. System Tools submenu

   d. Control Panel window

6. A file becomes fragmented when:

   a. It is used very frequently

   b. It is too large to be stored in one place

   c. Your computer cannot find it

   d. Your computer deems it unnecessary

interactivity

Build Your Skills

1. View System Summary of your system:

   a. Open the Start menu.

   b. Point to All Programs, point to Accessories, point to System Tools and then click System Information.

   c. Click System Summary.

2. Add new scheduled tasks:

   a. Open the Scheduled Tasks window.

   b. Schedule Outlook Express to run every weekday at 9:15 AM.

3. Check a disk for errors:

   a. Insert a floppy disk into your 3½ floppy (A:) drive.

   b. Open the Properties dialog box.

   c. Click the Tools tab.

   d. In the Error-checking section, click Check Now.

   e. Click Start.

   f. Close the Checking Disk window.

   g. Close the Properties window.

4. Defragment your hard disk:

   a. Open the Disk Defragmenter window.

   b. Select your main hard disk.

   c. Click the Defragment button.

   d. Close the Disk Defragmenter window.

interactivity (continued)

Problem Solving Exercises

1. You have a computer with a 10 gigabyte hard drive and still your machine has disk space shortage. In the past few projects you have extensively explored the Internet and have installed a number of programs. Use the Disk Cleanup utility of Windows XP to delete all unnecessary files from your computer's hard disk.

2. You are working as a director in an insurance company. You have a very busy schedule as most of the times you are busy in meetings. You want to backup your important data on regular basis. Using the Scheduled Task Wizard, schedule the backup process on your machine to run every day.

Sharing with My Network Places

Computer networks allow individual users to work together, communicate, and share resources. The World Wide Web is an example of a global network that nearly one hundred million people use each day. Much closer to home are the networking tools that come with Windows XP. Windows XP includes a utility called My Network Places that you can use to connect with other computer users in your office, school, or even your home. A computer network is a collection of digital devices that can communicate with each other using a shared language. The devices on a network can include computers, printers, scanners, fax machines, and modems. In most cases, computer networks use coaxial cables or twisted wire cables to connect the devices, much like a telephone or cable television system. The smallest class of computer network is a local area network, or LAN, that connects computers in a single office or building.

My Network Places allows you to view all of the devices connected to your network, share files and folders with other people on the network, and share network resources. If you are not connected to a network, you will not be able to complete the do it: steps in this Lesson. You also need to have administrative rights on the system on which you are working. However, you can read each Skill to become acquainted with network computing and My Network Places.

skills

≶ **Introduction to Networking**

≶ **Connecting to Other Computers**

≶ **Sharing Resources**

≶ **Mapping Network Drives**

≶ **Moving, Copying, and Deleting Shared Files**

≶ **Saving Files to Shared Directories**

≶ **Opening Network Files**

≶ **Finding Remote Files**

Lesson Goal:

In this lesson, you will learn about computer networking, connectivity among the computers in a network, resource sharing, and mapping network drives. Additionally, you will learn to move, copy, and delete the shared files and to save, open, and find files over the network.

skill | Introduction to Networking

concept

Windows XP is a powerful network operating system that allows people in an office or building to work together by sharing computer programs, files, folders, and resources like printers, modems, and scanners. You can designate a single computer in a network to be the server computer that stores network resources. The server can also store files centrally and control network resources, such as printers. A server must be powerful enough to run all of the shared software in an office without faltering or slowing. The other computers on the network are known as clients because they request software or files from the server.

This form of networking is called client–server computing, and is illustrated in Figure 8-1. Windows XP uses a type of networking known as peer to peer, which means that all computers on a network can act as both servers and clients (see Figure 8-2). Each computer has its own software loaded and uses the network to share resources and communicate with others. Many offices use a setup called a bus network in which computers can be added or removed from a single cable without disrupting the network. Client computers and other devices are connected to the network cable through a network interface card in each machine.

more

Network interface cards: Each of the devices on a computer network requires a network interface card. For desktop machines, you install a network card on the motherboard. Laptop computers use a small plug-in board called a PCMCIA card. Printers and scanners also require interface cards.

Mapping network drives: Windows XP allows you to establish a connection with a shared resource and maintain the connection permanently. By using this technique, you can access remote computers as easily as you can access your own hard drive.

File sharing: In a peer-to-peer network, you can grant others on the network permission to open files that you have designated for sharing. Moreover, you can work on files stored on the hard drives of other machines, and save files to other machines. To avoid conflicts, two users cannot open the same file at the same time. Files you do not designate as shared will not be available to others on the network.

Resource sharing: With network computing, a single printer or scanner can serve the needs of an entire office. This kind of resource sharing reduces expenses and simplifies maintenance of office networks.

Backup services: One of the most important aspects of network computing is its built-in security features. Often, one of the computers on a network is reserved for backing up files. During the day, users can work on these files. Then, in the evening, the network administrator makes a copy of all the files on tape or on a disk and stores the backup file in a safe location. This practice can prevent hours of important work from being lost.

Figure 8-1 Client–server computing

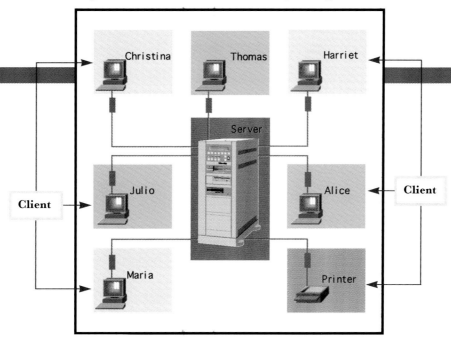

Figure 8-2 Peer-to-peer network

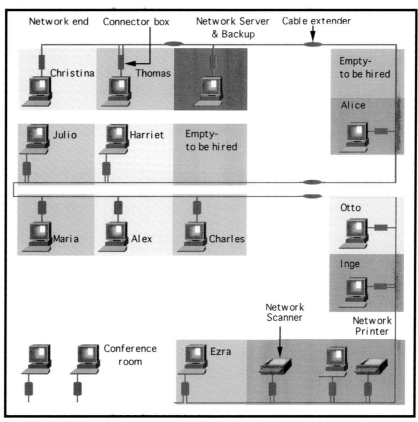

skill | Connecting to Other Computers

concept

Windows XP uses the networking technique called peer-to-peer networking where every computer on the network can act as a client and a server. Therefore, any computer on a Windows network can share files and printers as well as connect to the shared resources located on other computers on the network. Prior to accessing files and printers attached to other computers on your LAN, you must first connect to the network resource using My Network Places. My Network Places is used to organize network resources and give you access to them.

Windows networking is organized in a hierarchy. The network is subdivided into groups called workgroups. Workgroups consist of multiple computers that offer shared resources to the other members of the workgroup or the entire network.

do it!

Use My Network Places to view the contents of a shared folder on your network.

1. Click **start**, and then click My Network Places or double-click My Network Places on the desktop. This will display the My Network Places window.

2. Click the Entire Network link. This will display the Entire Network window. In the Entire Network window, double-click Microsoft Windows Network to display the Microsoft Windows Network window (see Figure 8-3). In this example, there is one workgroup, Workgroup. In case you do not have a workgroup in your network, in the Microsoft Windows Network window, double-click the domain name to display all the computers in the network.

3. Double-click Workgroup. All computers in the Workgroup workgroup are displayed (see Figure 8-4).

4. Double-click a computer icon 🖥 in the Workgroup window. A list of shared resources on that computer appears. In the example shown in Figure 8-5, the selected computer, Virgo, contains two shared folders. 🖴 Shared folders on your own computer are represented by a folder icon 📂 with an open hand along the bottom. If you view the same shared folder on another computer, the folder will be represented only by the folder icon.

5. Double-click the shared folder to open it and view its contents from the remote computer on your own system.

more

To find out your computer's name (as it appears in My Network Places), click **start**, click Control Panel, click Performance and Maintenance, and then click System. This will display the System Properties dialog box. Click the Computer Name tab. On the tab, you will see the identification features in the text fields containing your computer's name, domain name, workgroup name, and a description for your computer.

To change your computer's name, click Change... . This will display the Computer Name Changes dialog box. In the Computer Name text box, type a new name for your computer and click OK . You must restart the computer for the changes to take effect.

Figure 8-3 Microsoft Windows Network window

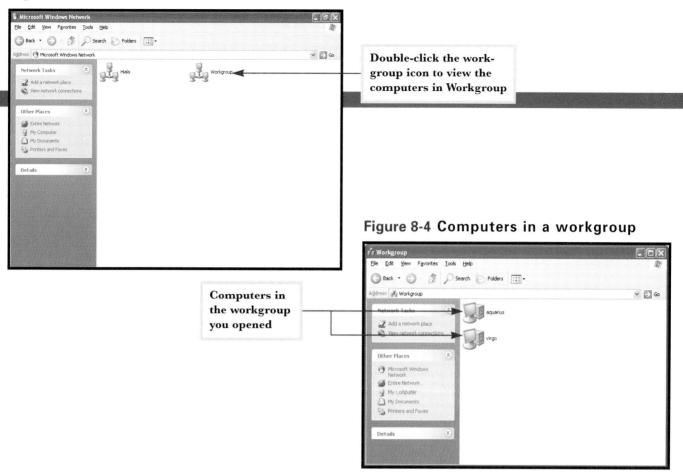

Double-click the work-group icon to view the computers in Workgroup

Figure 8-4 Computers in a workgroup

Computers in the workgroup you opened

Figure 8-5 Shared folders on a workgroup member

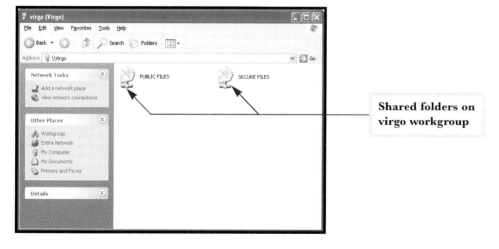

Shared folders on virgo workgroup

Practice

Using My Network Places, view the contents of a shared folder on your network.

skill Sharing Resources

concept

In a network, you can connect to resources located on other computers. In order for these resources to be available over a network, they must be designated as shared. You can share existing folders or create new ones for that purpose. In addition, you can allow varying types of access to the resources you make available to others.

do it!

Share a folder so that the other users on your network can access files on your computer.

1. Right-click the Windows desktop. A shortcut menu will be displayed.

2. Point to New and click the Folder command. A folder labeled New Folder will be created on the desktop.

3. Right-click the folder you just created. A shortcut menu is displayed.

4. Click the Sharing and Security command, as shown in Figure 8-6. A dialog box titled New Folder Properties is displayed. By default, the options under the Sharing tab are displayed.

5. Click the Share this folder option button.

6. Drag the mouse pointer over the default name, New Folder, in the Share name text box to select it. Then type Shared Files to replace the default name, as shown in Figure 8-7.

7. Click [Apply] and then click [OK] to close the dialog box.

8. Open My Network Places and view your computer's shared resources. The shared folder you created should appear when you double-click the icon for your computer.

more

Windows XP allows you to create rules, which govern who can read and write files on your computer. For example, you may want anybody to be able to read your shared files, but only allow certain people to modify them. These rules or permissions can be set on the Sharing tab of a folder's Properties dialog box. Different access permissions to a shared folder can be assigned to different users. To assign permissions to a specific user, click [Permissions] after clicking the Share this folder option button. This will display the Permissions for Shared Files dialog box. By default Everyone is displayed in the Group or user names list box and Full Control permission is assigned to Everyone in the Permissions list box. To add a user to the Group or user names, click [Add...]. This will display the Select Users or Groups dialog box (see Figure 8-8). Type the user names in the Enter the object names to select text box. Then click [OK]. This will add the user to the Group or user names list box in the Permissions for Shared Files dialog box. To assign various permissions to the added user, click the user name and select the appropriate permission check box in the Permissions list box.

Figure 8-6 The Sharing and Security command

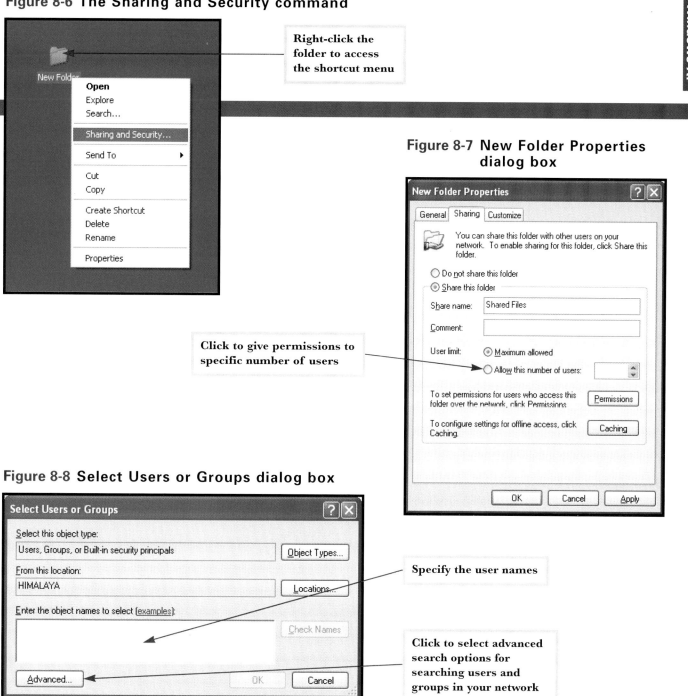

Right-click the
folder to access
the shortcut menu

Figure 8-7 New Folder Properties dialog box

Click to give permissions to
specific number of users

Figure 8-8 Select Users or Groups dialog box

Specify the user names

Click to select advanced
search options for
searching users and
groups in your network

Practice

Create a full access shared folder named wnprac8-3 on your desktop.

skill | Mapping Network Drives

concept

My Network Places allows you to access network resources quickly. However, there is an easier way to access frequently used network resources. Mapping a network resource such as a network drive allows you to access the specific shared folder as if it were a hard disk on your computer. Some older applications, that you want to run from the network, will run properly only if you execute them from a mapped drive.

do it!

Use My Network Places to map a network drive.

1. In the My Network Places window, click Entire Network. This will display the Entire Network window.

2. In the Entire Network window, double-click Microsoft Windows Network to display the Microsoft Windows Network window.

3. Double-click Workgroup.

4. Double-click a networked computer. In this example, we are connecting to a network directory on a computer called virgo. A list of shared folders opens.

5. Right-click a shared folder. In the example, the shared folder is called PUBLIC FILES. A shortcut menu is displayed, as shown in Figure 8-9.

6. Click the Map Network Drive command. A dialog box, shown in Figure 8-10, is displayed with a list box, which enables you to select the next available drive letter on your computer. In this example, it is drive H:.

7. Click the Reconnect at logon check box. Your computer will now connect to this shared resource whenever it is restarted. You can access files on mapped network drives from the DOS prompt just like you would access files on a hard disk or CD-ROM drive. At the DOS prompt, type the drive letter followed by a colon and press the [Enter] key.

8. Click Finish . This will display the contents of the mapped folder.

9. Open the My Computer window. Note that with your own local drives, there is now an additional drive in the window labeled Public files on 'virgo' (H:) (see Figure 8-11).

more

It may be necessary to disconnect a mapped drive. This may be required if the network administrator reorganizes the shared files or you no longer need to access files on the shared device as frequently as you once did. To disconnect a mapped network drive, open the My Computer window. Right-click the mapped network drive. Select the Disconnect command. The mapped drive will disappear and will not be restored when you restart your computer.

Figure 8-9 Mapping a network drive

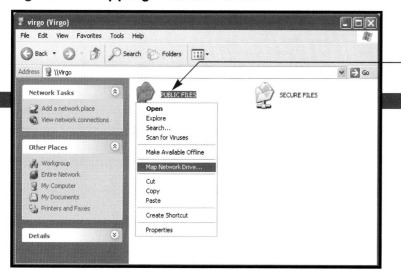

Right-click a shared folder to open a shortcut menu that will allow you to map the folder as a drive

Figure 8-10 Map Network Drive dialog box

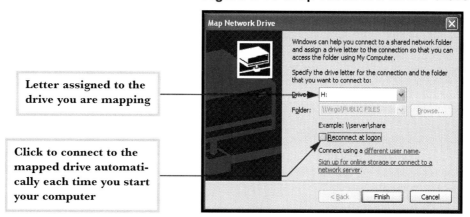

Letter assigned to the drive you are mapping

Click to connect to the mapped drive automatically each time you start your computer

Figure 8-11 Mapped drive in the My Computer window

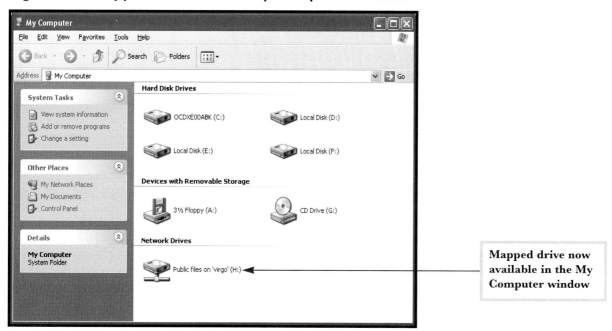

Mapped drive now available in the My Computer window

skill

Moving, Copying, and Deleting Shared Files

concept

You may wish to exchange files between your computer and another computer on the network. Often, network users will utilize a particular server to make backup copies of their files. You may also find it necessary to use disk space on a different computer if you do not have sufficient space available on yours. Moving a file over the network stores it physically on a different computer and removes the source file from the original machine. Copying a file duplicates the file and leaves the source file intact.

do it!

Move a file from your desktop to a shared directory on the network. Then copy the file from the shared directory back to your desktop.

1. Right-click the Windows desktop. On the shortcut menu that appears, point to the New command. The New submenu will open. Click the Text Document command. Windows will create a blank text document called New Text Document.txt on the desktop.

2. Open the Workgroup window and double-click a computer in the workgroup. In this example, the computer named virgo is chosen.

3. The selected computer will display the shared directories. In this case, the PUBLIC FILES directory is selected.

4. Right-click the New Text Document.txt file and drag it into the shared directory while holding down the right mouse button. If the window is maximized or obscures the file you created, click 🗗 and/or move the window to another part of the screen before dragging. When you release the mouse button in the destination window, a shortcut menu will open.

5. Click the Move Here command, as shown in Figure 8-12. When the move is complete, you will see the New Text Document.txt file in the shared directory. The file will no longer appear on your desktop.

6. Drag the file back to the Windows desktop using the left mouse button. When the operation is complete, the file will appear in both the folder and the desktop. When you drag a file or a folder on a local machine, the file or folder is moved to the specified location. However, when you perform the same action between a local machine and a network drive, the file or folder is copied and not moved.

7. Drag the copy of New Text Document.txt in the shared folder to the Recycle Bin. The Confirm File Delete message box appears. Click [Yes]. The file is deleted immediately. It does not remain in the Recycle Bin. When you delete a file from a shared directory, it cannot be recovered.

Windows XP

more

You can use the Cut, Copy and Paste commands to copy and move files between network drives just like you would manipulate text, graphics, or other files locally. You can access these commands from the shortcut menu that appears when you right-click a file. To move a file, select it and then choose the Cut command from the shortcut menu. Then use Windows Explorer to select the network drive to which you want to move the file. Finally, choose the Paste command to complete the move. To copy a file, follow the same procedure, but use the Copy command instead of the Cut command. This will leave the file in its original location while adding a copy to the network location you specified. You also can use the keyboard shortcuts [Ctrl]+[X] to cut, [Ctrl]+[C] to copy, and [Ctrl]+[V] to paste.

You can move a file without using any menus by holding down the [Shift] key when you release the left mouse button after dragging. Instead of copying the file, Windows will move it.

Figure 8-12 Moving a file over a network

Menu appears when you right-click and drag a file to its destination folder

Select whether you want to move, copy, or create a shortcut to the file

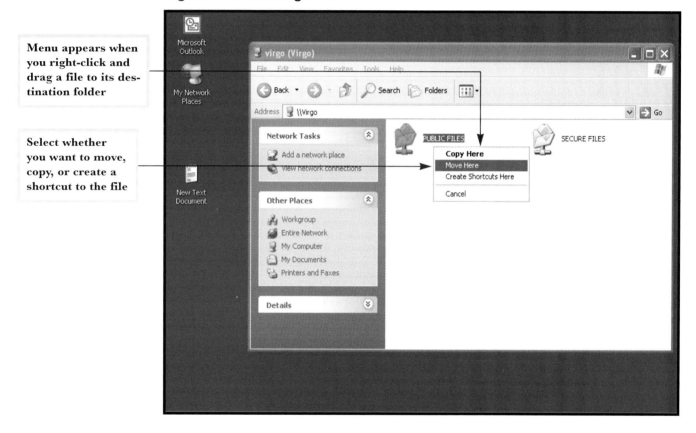

Practice

Create a text file named wnprac8-5.txt on your desktop and move it to a shared folder on your network. Once the move is complete, delete the file from the shared folder.

skill | Saving Files to Shared Directories

concept

Windows XP compatible programs allow you to save files directly across the network without using My Network Places or mapped drives. Saving the file directly reduces the amount of time spent in opening and closing windows, and copying and moving files. Furthermore, having only one version of the file reduces confusion if multiple people are working on the document. If a central server is used, one person's version of the document may overwrite another's, deleting that person's work. Windows prevents more than one person from using a file at the same time, ensuring that there is only one active version.

do it!

Create a WordPad document and save it in a shared folder on the network.

1. Click **start**, point to All Programs, point to Accessories, and then click WordPad. This will display the WordPad window.

2. In the WordPad window, type Do It! 8-6: Saving Files to Shared Directories.

3. Open the File menu and click the Save As command. The Save As dialog box is displayed.

4. Click the Save in arrow near the top of the dialog box. A list of all the drives available to you opens.

5. Move the mouse pointer over My Network Places (see Figure 8-13) and click once.

6. Double-click Entire Network and then double-click Microsoft Windows Network.

7. Double-click Workgroup. All the computers in the Workgroup workgroup are displayed.

8. Click the name of the computer on which you want to save the file. Then click [Open] (see Figure 8-14). The shared folders on that computer will appear in the contents window

9. Click the shared folder in which you would like to save the file (see Figure 8-15). Then click [Open] to open the folder.

10. Click the default file name, Document, in the File name text box to select the name of the file (you are not selecting the file itself, just its name).

11. Type wndoit8-6 to replace the default file name with your own file name.

12. Click [Save] to save the file in the folder you selected on the network computer. By default, the file will be saved with .rtf extension. You can change the extension of the file by selecting a different format from the Save as type list.

more

If you have to save files frequently to a specific folder in a shared volume, you can avoid navigating through the My Network Places by using a shortcut to the folder. When saving the file, double-click the shortcut in the Save As dialog box to go directly to the shortcut location, regardless of whether the shortcut points to a folder that is on your local computer or is on a shared directory elsewhere on the network.

Figure 8-13 The Save As dialog box

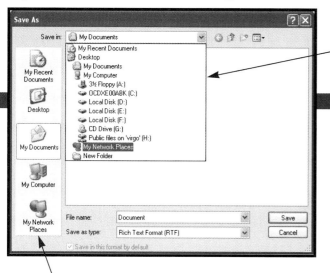

Use the Save in list box to select a drive, folder, or location, such as My Network Places for saving a file

Shortcut to My Network Places

Figure 8-14 Selecting a computer in a workgroup

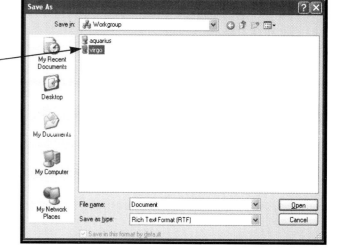

Click a computer in your workgroup to select it

Figure 8-15 Selecting a shared folder

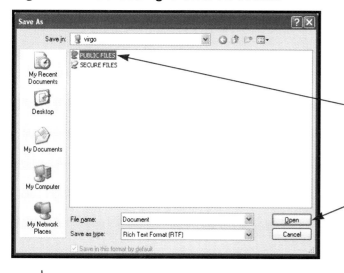

Click a shared folder to select it

Click to open the shared folder

Practice

Create a Paint file and save it to a shared directory on your network as wnprac8-6.bmp.

skill   Opening Network Files

concept

On occasion, you may need to access a file someone else is working on to make your own contributions to it. Members of your organization can save their files to a shared location, allowing you to access them from your own computer over the network. If you have experience opening your own local files, you will find that opening a network file is quite similar. In order for this Skill to be completed, a WordPad file must be placed in a shared network directory. Ask your instructor or network administrator for assistance in this matter.

do it!

Open a WordPad file from a shared directory on another computer that is connected to your network.

1. Open the WordPad application.

2. Open the File menu and click the Open command. The Open dialog box will be displayed.

3. Click the Look in arrow. A list box will open.

4. Click My Network Places on the list, as shown in Figure 8-16. Navigate to the Workgroup workgroup.

5. Double-click the computer that contains the file you would like to open. A list of the computer's shared resources will be displayed in the contents window.

6. Double-click the shared directory that contains the file you would like to open.

7. Click the file you would like to open, as in Figure 8-17. Then click ⬚ Open ⬚. The dialog box closes and the file appears in the WordPad window. You can now work on the file just as if it were stored on your own computer. You can save changes made to a file only if you have the Full Control permission.

8. Close the file.

more

You can also open a file saved in a shared directory on another computer, using Windows Explorer. For this, open the Windows Explorer window and navigate to the computer where the file you want to open is located. Double-click the file to open it.

Figure 8-16 Open dialog box

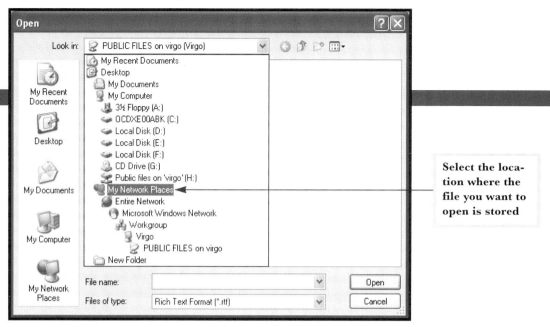

Select the location where the file you want to open is stored

Figure 8-17 Opening a network file

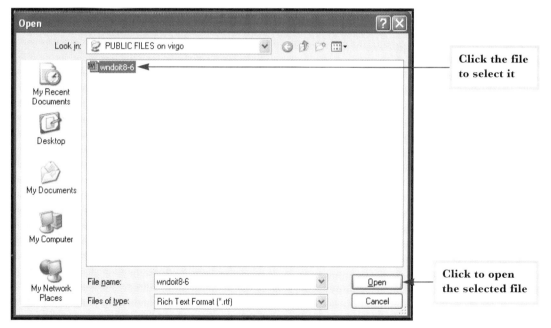

Click the file to select it

Click to open the selected file

Practice

Open the Paint file wnprac8-6.bmp that you saved to a shared directory on your network, in the previous skill.

skill | Finding Remote Files

concept

File hierarchies can become very complicated. Sometimes, you will know the name of a file and what computer it is stored on, but not know where it is within the file hierarchy. The Windows Search command allows you to locate files in a networked directory quickly just as though they were on your local computer. This Skill requires that a file be placed on a network drive that you can access.

do it!

Use the Search command to search for a file that is stored on another computer.

1. Click ⏴**start** to open the Start menu.

2. Click the Search command. This will display the Search Results window (see Figure 8-18).

3. Click the All files and folders command on the Search Companion pane of the Search Results window. This will display search options in the Search Companion window.

4. Click the Look in arrow ⌄ to open the list and then click Browse. This will display the Browse for Folder dialog box, listing the various drives and folders that are available to you.

5. In Choose directory to search section, click the plus symbol ⊞ to the left of My Network Places to expand it.

6. Click ⊞ to the left of Workgroup.

7. Click ⊞ to the left of the computer you want to search. In this case computer selected is Virgo. A list of shared folders will be revealed.

8. Click the folder you want to search. In the example, PUBLIC FILES has been selected (see Figure 8-19).

9. Click ⟨ OK ⟩. The dialog box closes and the name of the computer you selected appears in the Look in list box of the Search Companion pane.

10. Type wndoit8-6 in the All or the part of the file name text box. ⬤▬ You can use wild-card characters to look for all files of a particular type. For example, enter *.doc to search for all Word documents.

11. Click ⟨ Search ⟩. Result of the search is displayed in the right pane of the Search Results window (see Figure 8-20).

more

Some networks contain dozens of workgroups and hundreds of computers. This may make finding a specific computer difficult. The Search Companion pane of the Search Results window contains the options, Computers or people. When you click this option, two more options are displayed in Search Companion. Click A computer on the network option. The Computer name text box is displayed. Enter the name of the computer you want to search and then click ⟨ Search ⟩. The result of the search is displayed in the right pane of the Search Result window.

Figure 8-18 Search Results window

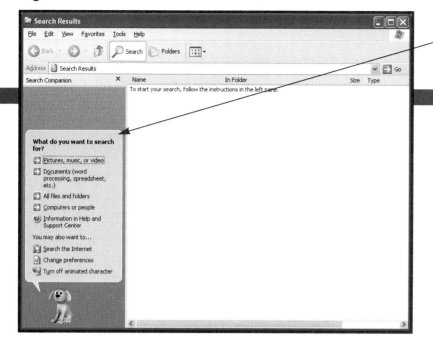

Search Companion pane

Figure 8-19 Browse For Folder dialog box

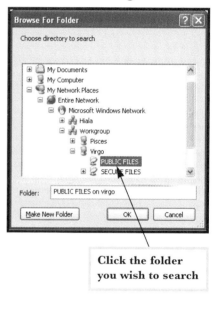

Click the folder you wish to search

Figure 8-20 Displaying the search result

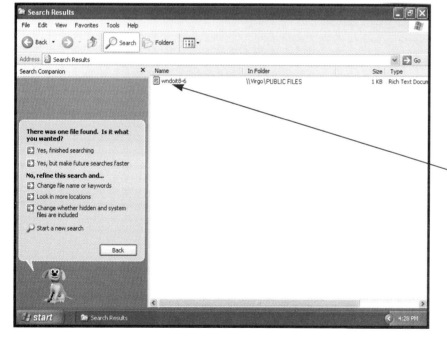

Searched for file

Practice

Search for the Paint file wnprac8-6.bmp, which you created and saved earlier in this lesson.

shortcuts

Function	Button/Mouse	Menu	Keyboard
Open Search Result window	Search	Click View, then point to Explorer Bar, click Search	[Alt]+[V], [E], [S]
Cut a selected file		Click Edit, then click Cut	[Ctrl]+[X]
Copy a selected file		Click Edit, then click Copy	[Ctrl]+[C]
Paste a cut or copied file		Click Edit, then click Paste	[Ctrl]+[V]

A. Identify Key Features

Name the items indicated by callouts in Figure 8-21.

Figure 8-21 Important networking icons

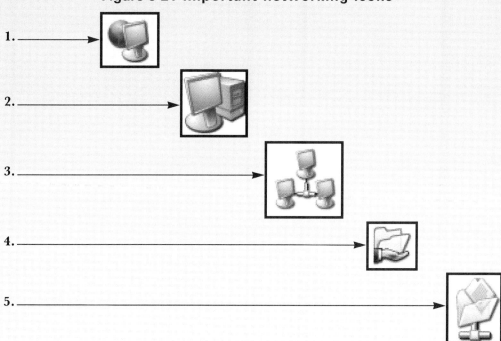

1. _____

2. _____

3. _____

4. _____

5. _____

B. Select the Best Answer

6. Gives you access to all of the computers with shared resources on your network   a. Mapped drive

7. Allows you to regulate who can access your files   b. My Network Places

8. Allows you to access a shared resource as if it were a drive on your computer   c. Open dialog box

9. Permits you to save a file on another computer   d. Reconnect at logon check box

10. Enables your computer to connect to a shared folder upon restart   e. Save As dialog box

11. Permits you to access a file that resides on another computer   f. Search command

12. Allows you to locate a particular file in the network   g. Sharing tab

quiz (continued)

C. Complete the Statement

13. A folder icon that includes a hand at the bottom of it indicates:

  a. A folder that someone else has shared over the network

  b. A folder that you do not have permission to open

  c. A shared folder on your own machine

  d. A drive that you have mapped

14. To copy a file from a shared directory to your desktop:

  a. Drag it with the left mouse button

  b. Double-click its icon

  c. Right-click the desktop

  d. Drag it holding down the [Shift] key

15. A shared file on a central server can be opened by:

  a. One person at a time

  b. Two people simultaneously

  c. Only the person working at that server

  d. The entire network simultaneously

16. To search for a network file from the Search Companion pane, click the:

  a. Named: text box

  b. Search button

  c. OK button

  d. Browse button in the Look in: list box

17. A file that is stored in a remote shared directory cannot be:

  a. Deleted

  b. Copied

  c. Opened

  d. Recovered once it is deleted across the network

18. To open the System Properties dialog box, you click Performance and Maintenance in the:

  a. My Computer window

  b. Control Panel window

  c. My Network Places window

  d. My Documents window

19. A subdivision of a network is called a:

  a. Workgroup

  b. Neighborhood

  c. Map

  d. Shared resource

20. A networked computer has all of the following general identification features with the exception of a:

  a. Computer name

  b. Workgroup

  c. Computer description

  d. Password

interactivity

Build Your Skills

1. Use My Network Places to examine your network:

   a. Open the My Network Places window.

   b. Click Entire Network.

   c. Double-click Microsoft Windows Network.

   d. View the workgroups in your network.

   e. Close the My Network Places window.

2. View your computer's network properties and change its description:

   a. Open the Control Panel window.

   b. Click Performance and Maintenance.

   c. Click System.

   d. In the System Properties dialog box, click the Computer Name tab.

   e. Type a new description in the Computer description text box.

   f. Click the OK button. Note: changes you make to your computer's identity will not become valid until you restart your computer.

3. Create a shared folder on your hard drive:

   a. Open Windows Explorer.

   b. Create a new folder on your hard drive named wnskill8-1 shared.

   c. Right-click the folder you just created.

   d. Select the Sharing and Security command on the shortcut menu.

   e. Share the folder as wnskill8-1 sharing.

4. Use My Network Places to map a network drive:

   a. Open My Network Places.

   b. Double-click a computer in your workgroup that has shared folders.

   c. Right-click the shared folder you want to map.

   d. Click the Map Network Drive command.

   e. Activate the Reconnect at logon check box.

   f. Click OK.

interactivity (continued)

Build Your Skills (continued)

5. Move a file from your hard drive to another drive on your network:

   a. Open WordPad and create a word processing file that says: Build Your Skills.

   b. Save the file to your desktop as wnskill8-1.txt. Close WordPad.

   c. Move wnskill8-2.txt from your desktop to the shared folder you mapped in question 4.

6. Open and edit a file located on another computer; then copy the file to your desktop:

   a. Open WordPad.

   b. Use the Open command to open wnskill8-1.txt from the shared folder to which you moved it.

   c. Add the text Copying a Shared File to the document.

   d. Use the Save command to save the changes you have made.

   e. Close WordPad.

   f. Use My Network Places to place a copy of wnskill8-1.txt back on your desktop.

Problem Solving Exercises

1. Your company has just purchased a new computer for you with a 10 gigabyte hard drive. Since you now have far more storage space than you need, you have been asked to allow your co-workers to use your hard drive for storing backup copies of their important files. Create a full access shared folder on your desktop called Backup. Then, using WordPad, create a text document named Read Me.txt that explains the purpose of the shared folder you created. Save the document in the Backup folder, and then place a copy of Read Me.txt in your My Documents folder.

2. You will be hosting an important business dinner at your home next weekend. Your boss has asked you to provide a simple map with directions so that no one has difficulty finding the location. Create the map and directions using the Paint application. Then, save the file to your desktop. Your boss has offered to create a shared directory into which you can place the map so others can access it (ask a classmate, co-worker, or your instructor to create this folder). Since this is a folder you may use frequently in the future, map the folder as a drive on your computer. Then copy your Paint file from your desktop into the shared folder on the drive you mapped.

glossary

Accessories

Programs built into Windows that are useful for everyday tasks.

Active Desktop

Gives you the ability to integrate live Web content and animated pictures into your desktop.

Active window

The window you are currently using. When a window is active, its title bar changes color to differentiate it from other open windows and its program button is depressed.

ActiveMovie Control

Windows program that is capable of playing a variety of audio and video file formats.

Add or Remove Programs

A Windows' utility in the Control Panel that enables you to install or delete computer programs in a few easy steps.

Address Bar

Used for entering a Web address manually; can also be used to view a local folder or drive.

Address Book

Component of Outlook Express that enables you to store contact information such as home and business addresses, phone numbers, e-mail addresses, etc.

Appearance tab

In the Display Properties dialog box, lets you customize the appearance of individual system items or apply an appearance scheme.

Attach button

Permits you to e-mail a computer file.

Back button

Allows you to return to the Web page or system window you viewed previously.

Background tab

In the Display Properties dialog box, used to apply wallpaper to your desktop.

Bitmap (bmp)

Basic image file format used by Windows.

Blind copy

An e-mail in which the recipient cannot see the e-mail addresses of all the people to whom you have copied the mail; see also "carbon copy."

Browsing

Examining Web pages in the manner of your choice.

Bus network

A computer network in which computers can be added or removed from a single cable without disrupting the network.

Carbon copy

An e-mail for which the recipient can see the e-mail addresses of all people to whom you have copied the mail; see also "blind copy."

CD Player

Windows application that lets you play audio CDs.

Check box

A small square box that enables you to turn a dialog box option on or off by clicking it.

Classic Style

A folder option that requires a double-click to open an icon and a single-click to select it.

Click

To press and release a mouse button in one motion; usually refers to the left mouse button.

Client–Server

A computing model in which computers known as clients request and receive data from a central computer with high storage capacity called a server.

Clipboard

A temporary storage area for cut or copied text or graphics. You can paste the contents of the Clipboard into any Windows program, such as WordPad or Microsoft Word. The Clipboard holds the information until it is replaced with another piece of text, or until the computer is shut down.

Close

To quit an application and remove its window from the desktop. The Close button appears in the upper-right corner of a window, on the title bar.

Command

Directive that carries out an application feature or provides options for carrying out a feature.

Command button

In a dialog box, a button that carries out an action. A command button usually has a label that describes its action, such as OK, Cancel, or Help. If the label is followed by an ellipsis, clicking the button displays another dialog box.

Control menu

Contains commands related to resizing, moving, and closing a window.

Control Panel

A utility used for changing computer settings. You can access the various control panels through the Start menu, My Computer, or Windows Explorer.

Copy

To place a duplicate of a file or portion thereof on the Clipboard to be pasted in another location.

Cursor

The blinking vertical line in a document window that indicates where text will appear when you type. Also referred to as the insertion point.

Cut

To remove a file, or a portion of a file, and place it on the Clipboard.

Cut and paste

To remove information from one place and insert it in another using the Clipboard as the temporary storage area.

d

Date/Time Properties dialog box

Allows you to set your system clock and calendar.

Deleted Items folder

Outlook Express folder that functions much like the Windows Recycle Bin.

Desktop

The on-screen area, created using the metaphor of a desk, that provides workspace for your computing tasks.

Desktop theme

The appearance of your on-screen area created by a set of icons, fonts, colors, sounds, and/or other elements that give a distinctive look to your desktop.

Dialog box

A box that explains the available command options for you to review or change before executing the command.

Disk Cleanup

Windows utility that removes unnecessary files from your computer, creating more free space.

Disk Defragmenter

Windows utility that rearranges the data on your hard disk so that pieces of the same file are stored next to each other and free space is consolidated; defragmenting thereby makes it possible to access files more efficiently.

Document window

The window within the application window in which a file is viewed and edited. When the document window is maximized, it shares a border and title bar with the application window.

Double-click

To press and release the mouse button twice rapidly; usually refers to the left mouse button.

Drafts folder

In Outlook Express, allows you to store messages that you have not finished composing.

Drag

To hold down the mouse button while moving the mouse.

Edit

To add, delete, or modify elements of a file.

E-mail

A method of sending electronic messages from one computer to another over the Internet.

Entire Network icon

Gives you access to the other workgroups that are a part of your network.

Error-checking tool

Used to find and correct errors that occur on files on your hard drive and on the surface of the disk itself.

f

Favorite

A shortcut to a local, network, or Internet address that you have saved so that you can access the location easily.

Favorites Explorer Bar

Makes your Favorites menu part of the browser window so that it is always available.

Favorites menu

Allows you to store shortcuts to your favorite Web pages and other files for easy access.

File

A document that has been created and saved under a unique file name.

File hierarchy

A logical order for folders and files that resembles how you would organize files and folders in a filing cabinet. Your file hierarchy displays where your folders and files are stored on your computer.

File management

The skill of organizing files and folders.

Files and Settings Transfer Wizard

A step-by-step utility for moving the settings, data files, display settings, and/or dial-up connections of your old computer to a new computer, disk drive, or folder; especially useful for transferring settings of programs like Internet Explorer, Outlook Express, etc.

Find command

Allows you to search for local or network files, other computers on your network, Internet addresses, and more.

Folders

Subdivisions of a disk that work like a filing system to help you organize files.

Folders Explorer Bar

Default left panel of Windows Explorer; shows all of the drives and folders available on your computer.

Footer

Text that appears at the bottom of a printed document.

Format

The way information appears on a page. To format means to change the appearance of data without changing its content.

Format Bar

Toolbar that allows you to format text in a WordPad document.

Formatting Toolbar

Allows you to change the characteristics of the text in an e-mail message and insert objects.

Forward button

Allows you to revisit a Web page or system window from which you have browsed back.

Forward command

Used to pass a message you have received to another e-mail address without having to retype or copy the message.

Frame

An independent component of a Web page.

Full

A file-sharing setting that allows others to read and edit your shared files.

Graphical user interface (GUI)

An environment made up of meaningful symbols, icons, words, and windows that control the basic operation of a computer and the programs it runs.

Header

The summary information for an e-mail or newsgroup message. Also, the text that appears along the top of a printed page.

Help button

A button in a Help window that opens a dialog box or a program to provide an answer to your question.

Highlight

When an item is shaded to indicate that it has been selected.

History Explorer Bar

Displays links for all of the Web pages you have visited recently.

Home page

The page to which your browser opens upon launch or clicking the Home button; also can refer to the main page of a particular Web site.

Horizontal scroll bar

Changes your view laterally when all of the information in a file does not fit in the window.

Hypermedia

Text, pictures, and other objects that are linked to files on the Web and will access those files when clicked. Also known as hyperlinks.

HyperText Markup Language (HTML)

Platform-independent computer language used to write Web pages.

Icon

Pictorial representation of programs, files, and other screen elements.

Inbox

Holds the e-mail messages you have received in Outlook Express.

Inbox Assistant

Creates filters that route incoming messages to a specific folder based on criteria you supply.

Internet

A worldwide computer network made up of numerous smaller networks.

Internet Connection Wizard

Runs you through the process of setting up an Internet account.

Internet Explorer

Windows' Web-browsing application.

k

Keyboard shortcut

A keyboard equivalent of a menu command (e.g., [Ctrl]+[X] for Cut).

l

LAN (Local Area Network)

The smallest class of a computer network, connecting computers in a single office, department, building, etc.

Landscape orientation

Page setup in which the left-to-right length is greater than the top-to-bottom length.

Launch

To start a program so you can work with it.

Links toolbar

Makes Favorites available as buttons in your browser window.

List box

A drop-down list of items. To choose an item, click the list box drop-down arrow, then click the desired item from the list.

Lurk

To read the messages on a newsgroup without participating in the discussion; a recommended action if you are new to the newsgroup, but as a long-term activity is considered improper Internet etiquette.

Maintenance Wizard

Automates Windows maintenance utility programs.

Map Network Drive

Command that connects your computer to a remote shared folder as if it were a local drive.

Maximize

To enlarge a window to its maximum size. Maximizing an application window causes it to fill the screen; maximizing a document window causes it to fill the application window.

Menu

A list of related commands in an application.

Menu bar

Lists the names of menus containing application commands. Click a menu name on the Menu bar to display its list of commands.

Minimize

To shrink a window to its minimum size. Minimizing an application window reduces it to a button on the Windows taskbar.

Mouse

A palm-sized, hand-operated input device that you roll on your desk to position the mouse pointer and click to select items and execute commands.

Mouse buttons

The two buttons on the mouse, called the left and right mouse buttons, that you use to make selections and issue commands.

Mouse pointer

The usually arrow-shaped cursor on the screen that you control by guiding the mouse on your desk. You use the mouse pointer to select items, drag objects, choose commands, and start or exit programs. The appearance of the mouse pointer can change depending on the task being executed.

Multitasking

The ability to run several programs on your computer at once and easily switch among them.

My Computer

A tool used to view the files and folders that are available on your computer and how they are arranged. The default icon, a PC, appears on the desktop.

My Network Places

Enables you to view and access the computers that make up your network.

n

Netiquette

A slang expression for "Internet etiquette"; legal and appropriate behavior expected of users on the Internet to make the Internet an effectively functioning tool for exchange of facts and opinions.

Network

Two or more computers, printers, scanners, fax machines, and/or other digital devices linked together to allow for the sharing and exchanging of data; see also "LAN."

Network Neighborhood

Allows you to view and access the computers that make up your network.

New Toolbar command

Allows you to create a custom toolbar that can be placed on the taskbar or in its own window.

Newsgroup

An electronic bulletin board on the Internet used to post messages on a specific topic.

o

Operating system

Controls the basic operation of your computer and the programs you run on it. Windows 2000 is an operating system.

Organize Favorites command

Allows you to rename your Favorites and restructure your Favorites hierarchy.

Outbox

Stores e-mail messages you have composed in Outlook Express until you send them.

Outlook Express

E-mail software that comes with Windows.

p

Paint

Windows' built-in drawing program.

Pattern

Used to fill in the area of the desktop that is not covered by wallpaper.

Peer-to-peer network

A network in which all computers on it can act as both servers and clients.

Personalized menus

Feature that permits the Start and Menu bar menus to adapt to your usage by temporarily hiding the commands you use infrequently so the others are more accessible.

Point

To place the mouse pointer over an item on the desktop.

Pop-up menu

The menu that appears when you right-click certain places in the Windows environment.

Portrait orientation

Traditional document setup in which the top-to-bottom length is greater than the left-to-right length.

Post

To send a message to a newsgroup.

Program

A software application that performs specific tasks, such as Microsoft Word or WordPad.

Program button

The button that appears on the taskbar to indicate that an application is open. The active program is represented by an indented button.

Properties

The characteristics of a specific element (such as the mouse, keyboard, or desktop display) that you can change. Properties also can refer to characteristics of a file such as its name, type, size, and location.

r

Radio button

A small circular button in a dialog box that allows you to switch between options.

Read-Only

A file-sharing setting that prevents others from editing your shared files.

Recycle Bin

An icon on the desktop that represents a temporary storage area for deleted files. Files will remain in the Recycle Bin until you empty it, at which time they are permanently removed from your computer.

Reply to All

Allows you to send a direct response to an e-mail message that is also received by each recipient of the original message.

Reply to Author

Allows you to send a direct response to an e-mail message.

Restore

To return a window to its previous size before it was resized (either maximized or minimized). A Restore button usually appears in the upper-right corner of a window, on the title bar.

Right-click

To click the right mouse button; often necessary to access specialized menus and shortcuts. (The designated right and left mouse buttons may be reversed with the Mouse control panel to accommodate user preferences.)

Run

To open an application.

S

ScanDisk

Windows utility that finds and corrects errors on your hard disk.

Scheduled Task Wizard

A Windows' feature that extends the idea of automatic program execution by enabling you to run a task or program on a regular schedule (e.g., opening your Web browser at the same time daily or running a maintenance program weekly).

Screen saver

A moving or changing image that covers your screen when you are not working; installed on a computer to prevent fixed images from becoming permanently embedded into your display.

ScreenTip

A yellow help box that Windows provides to explain a particular feature.

Scroll bar

A graphical device for moving vertically and horizontally through a document with the mouse. Scroll bars are located along the right and bottom edges of the document window.

Scroll bar box

A small gray box located inside a scroll bar that indicates your current position relative to the rest of the document window. You can advance a scroll bar box by dragging it, clicking the scroll bar on either side of it, or clicking the scroll bar arrows.

Search command

Allows you to search for local or network files, other computers on your network, Internet addresses, and more.

Search engine

A Web site that generates Web links based on criteria you provide.

Search Explorer Bar

Permits you to keep an Internet search in the browser window and visit links at the same time. Also allows you to search local and network drives for files and folders.

Select

Highlighting an item to indicate that it is the active object on the screen. Usually done in order to perform some operation on the item.

Selection bar

The unmarked column on the left side of the WordPad document window or similar word processing program that allows you to select entire lines or paragraphs of text at once.

Sent Items folder

Folder that automatically stores a copy of each e-mail message you send in Outlook Express.

Set as Wallpaper

Command that allows you to use an image as desktop wallpaper.

Shared folder

A folder that is accessible over a network to computers other than the one on which it is stored.

Shortcut

A link that takes you directly to a particular file, folder, or program without having to pass through each item in its file hierarchy.

Shut down

The process you go through to turn off your computer when you finish working. After you complete this action, it is safe to turn off your computer.

Sound Recorder

Windows application that lets you record and play audio; requires a CD-ROM drive, sound card, audio CD, and output device such as speakers or headphones.

Start button

A button on the taskbar that accesses a special menu that you use to start programs, find files, access Windows Help, and more.

Stationery

A picture used to enhance the appearance of an e-mail message.

Surfing

A synonym for browsing.

System Tray

The box at the right edge of the taskbar that houses your system clock and various utility icons.

t

Task Scheduler

Allows you to automate Windows tasks.

Taskbar

A bar, usually located at the bottom of the screen, that contains the Start button, shows which programs are running by displaying their program buttons, and shows the current time.

Taskbar and Start menu command

Allows you to control the behavior and content of the taskbar and the Start menu.

Thumbnails View

Allows you to view previews of all image files in a folder rather than file icons.

Title bar

The horizontal bar at the top of a window that displays the name of the document or application that appears in the window.

Toolbar

A graphical bar containing buttons that act as shortcuts for common commands.

Triple-click

In some programs, performing this action is an easy way to select an entire line or block of text.

u

Uniform Resource Locator (URL)

The address of a file on the Internet.

Usenet

Short for "User Network," a network of computer servers connected to the Internet that holds thousands of newsgroups.

v

Vertical scroll bar

Moves your view up and down through a window, allowing you to view portions of a document that are not currently visible.

w

Wait box

Determines how many idle minutes Windows will wait before initializing a screen saver.

Wallpaper

A picture you apply to your desktop.

Wave (wav)

A Windows sound file.

Web

A subset of the Internet that allows users to publish documents on special computers called servers so that others (clients) can access them.

Web browser

A computer application that allows you to view documents on the World Wide Web.

Web Style

A folder option that allows you to select an icon by pointing to it and open an icon with a single click.

Web tab

In the Display Properties dialog box, used to control Active Desktop content.

Window

A rectangular area on the screen in which you view and work on files.

Windows Explorer

A tool that allows you to view the hierarchy of folders on your computer and all the subfolders and files in a selected folder. Windows Explorer is very useful for moving and copying files among folders.

Windows Media Player

Windows' audio and video player, capable of playing a variety of sound and movie formats, including MPEG audio and video, WAV audio, and AVI video.

WordPad

Windows' built-in word processing program.

Workgroup

A group of computers that is a subdivision of a network.

index